# The Cult of Emptiness

Buddhism Series

# THE CULT OF EMPTINESS

*The Western Discovery of Buddhist Thought*

*and the Invention of Oriental Philosophy*

Urs App

UNIVERSITYMEDIA
2012

Printed on acid-free and lignin-free paper

Library of Congress Cataloging-in-Publication Data
App, Urs, 1949–
    The Cult of Emptiness: The Western Discovery of Buddhist
    Thought and the Invention of Oriental Philosophy. / Urs App.
    p.  cm.  — (UniversityMedia, Buddhism Series)
    Includes bibliographical references and index
    ISBN 978–3–906000–09–1 (acid-free paper)
    1. Philosophy—History—16th century—17th century.
    2. Buddhism—Zen—Philosophy—History.
    3. Europe—Intellectual life—16th century—17th century.
    4. Japan—China—India—Philosophy—Religion.
    5. Orientalism—Europe—History—16th century—17th century.
I. Title.

ISBN 978-3-906000-09-1 (hardcover)

To my friends

Steven Antinoff & Naomi Maeda

# Contents

# Preface

Whereas the discovery by Europeans of the continents of our earth has been the subject of countless studies and its protagonists (such as Columbus) are universally known, research on the European discovery of our globe's "spiritual continents"— its religions and philosophies—is still in its infancy. The Christian West's discovery of Asia's largest religion and fount of philosophies, Buddhism, is a case in point: though it triggered one of the most significant and influential spiritual and cultural encounters in world history, even the most basic questions remain unanswered. What did Europeans first learn about Buddhist thought? When and where did this discovery take place and who was involved in it? What did Westerners learn about Buddhist and related philosophies of Asia, how did they understand or misunderstand them, and what were the repercussions of such discoveries in Europe?

While trying to find answers to such questions I kept coming across references to a single "Oriental philosophy." I vividly remember my first encounter with this strange creature. In the process of tracing Schopenhauer's Oriental sources in the Schopenhauer Archive in Frankfurt in the mid-1990s, I was struck by a note the young philosopher had scribbled into his copy of a Latin translation of the Upanishads—India's seminal philosophical texts—that had been published in 1801 under the title of *Oupnek'hat*:

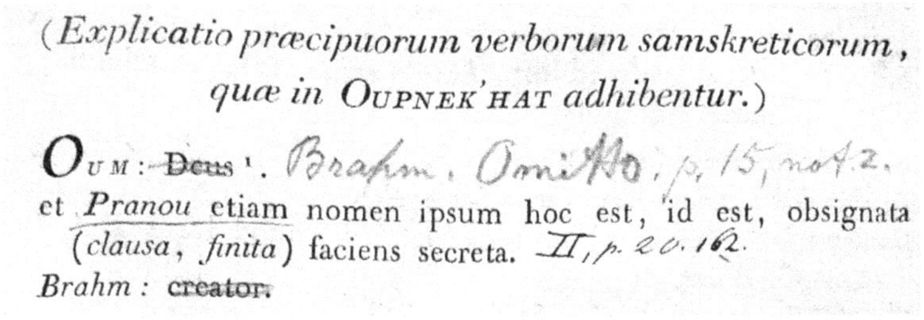

*(Explicatio prœcipuorum verborum samskreticorum, quœ in OUPNEK'HAT adhibentur.)*

O~UM~:~~Deus~~ ¹. *Brahm. Omitto, p, 15, not.2.*
et *Pranou* etiam nomen ipsum hoc est, id est, obsignata
(*clausa, finita*) faciens secreta. *II, p. 20.162.*
*Brahm :* ~~creator~~.

FIG. 1: SCHOPENHAUER'S NOTES IN ANQUETIL-DUPERRON'S OUPNEK'HAT
(ANQUETIL 1801, VOL. 1,:7)

The line that startled me begins with the sacred Indian word OUM
that translator Anquetil-Duperron equated with God (*Deus*). That
Schopenhauer would replace Anquetil's "Deus" by "Brahm" was to
be expected; but what in the world had "Omitto" to do with the
Indian Upanishads, some of which are older than Buddhism? Having specialized in Chinese and Japanese religions, I gathered that
"Omitto" refers to the Buddha of Infinite Light Amitābha who is
known in Japan as *Amida* and in China as *Amituo*. The note indicated by Schopenhauer's handwritten cross-reference ("p. 15, not.
2") confirmed this. But Anquetil's footnote to "Deus," which attempted to explain why OUM is the equivalent of God, led to even
more confusion since it furnished an explanation linking *Omitto* to
the Egyptian god *Phta*. What was going on here? How did China's
*Omitto* Buddha end up in the first European Upanishad translation
as the equivalent of the sacred word OUM, the Hindu Brahman, the
Judeo-Christian God, and the Egyptian god Phta? Both my consternation and my interest grew when I read in Anquetil's long introduction that the *Books of Solomon*, the ancient Chinese *Jings* (classics),
the sacred Indian *Vedas*, and the Persian *Zend Avesta* all transmit
"the same dogma" (1801:viii) and that this doctrine "made its way,
under the name of *doctrina orientalis*, from India to Persia, and from

Persia to the Greeks and Romans" (p. cviii). In support of this thesis, Anquetil cited numerous European historians of philosophy asserting the existence of an extremely ancient "Oriental philosophy."

Since I had spent half of my life in Asia and studied a few Asian languages and philosophies, I knew very well that there is no single "Oriental philosophy" in existence, just as there is no single "Oriental language" or "Oriental cooking." This had to be a Western invention. I also knew from my research on the European discovery of Asian religions that a similar invention—the idea of a single "Oriental religion"—played a crucial role in the pre-modern European perception of Asia and the genesis of modern orientalism.[1] So: how and by whom was this "Oriental philosophy" invented, what is its connection with Buddhism and other Asian as well as European religions and thought systems, and what role did this invention play in the European encounter with Asia?

As I followed traces of this strange creature from the nineteenth century back in time, I kept encountering characterizations of a common "inner" doctrine of this philosophy that had an unmistakable scent of Zen Buddhism. Thanks in large measure to my friends Steven Antinoff and Naomi Maeda I had in my twenties begun to study this particular form of Buddhism (called *Zen* in Japan, *Son* in Korea, *Chan* in China, and *Thien* in Vietnam) and subsequently spent a good part of my academic career exploring various facets of it. Since this happens to be the form of Buddhism popular with elites in Japan, China, and Vietnam when European missionaries first explored Asian religions and philosophies during the sixteenth and seventeenth centuries, such knowledge was a crucial asset for the journey to the roots of Anquetil's "doctrina orientalis." This book deals with the seeding stage from mid-sixteenth century Japan to the turn of the eighteenth century when this flower of imagination took root in the main hotbeds of pre-Enlightenment Europe, Holland and France. Perhaps more importantly, this book presents

1 Urs App, *The Birth of Orientalism*. University of Pennsylvania Press, 2010.

3

a completely new vision of Europe's discovery of Buddhism and for the first time describes the protagonists and most influential sources of the early phase of this momentous encounter between East and West.

In my youth I had been fascinated by tales about famous explorers of our globe. The voyage of discovery that led to this book was as long, adventurous, and full of surprises as the exploits of the heroes of my childhood. I was fortunate to be accompanied by my wife Monica Esposito whose love, curiosity, learning, and sense of humor were a constant source of inspiration and joy. My thanks must also go to my Capucin teachers at the Collegium St. Antonius in Appenzell (Switzerland) whose lessons in Latin, Greek, and scholastic philosophy bore such strange and exotic fruit, and to a long line of teachers of Japanese, classical Chinese, and other languages as well as a large and colorful collection of Zen masters, philosophers, university professors, historians, librarians, and living as well as deceased relatives and friends. I am especially indebted to my mentors in philology, the late Profs. Seizan Yanagida and Yoshitaka Iriya, to Prof. Richard DeMartino, to my generous brother Pius App, and to those who most helped me cope with the sudden passing of my wife as the redaction of this book was in its final stages: Drs. Adriana and Valerio Pozza-Esposito, my son Alexander Huwyler, Rev. Taizan Egami and his family, Mark Thomas, Dr. Christian Wittern, A. J. Dickinson, Dr. Alexander and Ursula Ilg, Dr. Filippo and Paola Panzuto, my little granddaughter Leila, and Momo.

Inline references consisting only of page numbers always refer to the last full reference. Unless a translator is indicated, all quotations from sources with non-English titles were translated into English by me. The letters "v" or "r" after page numbers signify *recto* (front of page) and *verso* (back). I made an effort to faithfully reproduce spellings of historical sources, for example the "u" and "v" of Latin and old Italian, or old English and French orthography ("perswade," "premiére," "vuide") that might seem erroneous to modern readers.

Unless otherwise indicated, all tables and illustrations are by me or reproduce materials from my private library. Chinese characters written in "short" forms in the original texts are reproduced as such. The mixture of "short" and "long" forms is thus not due to oversight. In order to facilitate study, I decided to structure the index at the end of this volume by themes as well as by alphabet. This entailed some problematic decisions, for example the separation of general "Buddhist" from specific "Zen" doctrines and texts; but I trust that the advantages outweigh the shortcomings for those willing to *read* the index and to explore key themes such as "esoteric / exoteric doctrines" (pp. 270-1) or "first principle" (pp. 272-3). References to book titles are listed under the author's name. Thus Kircher's *China illustrata* is not listed under C but under "Kircher" along with other works by Kircher used in this study. Buddhist sutras are listed under "Buddhist texts," Zen terms like *honbun* under "Zen doctrinal elements" (pp. 292-4), issues related to the invention of the Buddha's deathbed confession under "Buddha's deathbed confession" (pp. 260-1), and so on. Given the volume of the index, cross-references were reduced to a minimum.

The calligraphy on the cover (*mu* 無; "no," "nothing," or "nothingness") is by the Japanese Zen master Hakuin Ekaku 白隠慧鶴 (1686–1769). Centuries before they began to study Buddhist texts from India in the Sanskrit and Pali languages, Europeans encountered this "nothingness" in Japan. Indeed, Zen's *mu* played a central role in Europe's discovery of Buddhism and in the deeply connected invention of an "oriental philosophy" which I describe in this book. Hakuin's wonderful work of art on the cover and Shin'ichi Hisamatsu's calligraphies in the body of this book belong to the Hisamatsu Shin'ichi Kinenkan in Gifu city, Japan, whose director I wish to thank for his permission to use my photographs.

Zortea (Italy), October 21, 2011

# List of Figures

# List of Tables

# PART I

*Sixteenth Century*

# Chapter One

# Translation Hazards

I t is entirely fitting that the story of the Western discovery of Buddhism and the invention of a single "Oriental philosophy" should begin with a fiasco involving the Arlecchino mechanism. Arlecchino is a main character of the Italian *commedia dell'arte* who thinks that the whole world is exactly like his family and acts accordingly. The comic as well as tragic potential of such projection of the familiar on the realm of the unknown is apparent in the case of Texas governor Miriam "Ma" Ferguson who barred the teaching of foreign languages about eighty years ago, saying, "If English was good enough for Jesus Christ, it's good enough for us" (Kristof 2004).

Our initial cast consists of a group of Jesuit mission pioneers and ANJIRŌ (often also called Yajirō, born c. 1511[2]), a murderer who had fled Japan and was among the first Japanese to reach India. Anjirō met FRANCIS XAVIER (1506–1552), one of the seven founders of the Jesuit order, in Malacca near Singapore in December of 1547 and subsequently embraced Christianity with a vengeance. Sent to Goa on the West Indian coast in 1548, he joined a number of Jesuit novices who had just arrived from the opposite side of the world. They included two young men from Spain (Cosme de Torres and Juan Fernández) and two from Portugal (Balthasar Gago and Luís Fróis). They lived with Anjirō for almost a year in Goa's St. Paul College, and all were destined to play roles in the invention of Oriental philosophy.

---

2  Much information about this man is collected in the recent biography by Kishino (2001).

Francis Xavier decided to employ Anjirō as translator in his Japan mission but soon had to realize that this "man of great faith and piety" is "a common man ... unfamiliar with Japanese literary sources, which, just as our books that are written in Latin, employ a practically alien language" (DocJ 1:86). Nevertheless, Francis Xavier wanted him "to be instructed in the Christian faith and to translate the entire Christian doctrine into the Japanese language" (p. 29). He had hardly an idea of the problems this involved. Anjirō proved to be a good student, was soon baptized, and confirmed in a letter to Ignatius of Loyola his faith "in God, creator of all things, and in Jesus Christ who was crucified to redeem us" (p. 43). It was probably Cosme de Torres who interviewed Anjirō about the religion of his native Japan and furnished the information to Father Nicolò LANCILLOTTO (d.1558) who included it in the first-ever report about Japanese religion to reach Europe (pp. 45-6). This report of 1548 was packed with surprises.

Anjirō told the missionaries about the life of "Sciacca" (Jap. Shaka, i.e. Shakyamuni Buddha) who only three months after his birth had taken three steps, pointed to heaven and earth, and said: "I alone am in heaven and on earth" (p. 52).[3] When the king of the remote land, Sciacca's father, ordered him to marry a relative, Sciacca fled to the mountains where he lived in penitence for seven years. Then he began to preach a new religion and gained as many as 8,000 disciples (p. 53). Anjirō informed the Jesuits that before Sciacca's mission many gods had been worshipped in his country. However, Sciacca taught them that there is "only one God, creator of all things" (p. 53). He had his followers "destroy all idols of that land" and gave them a picture of God featuring a man with three heads (p. 53). I break off Anjirō's fanciful biography of Buddha at this point because it is already clear that Anjirō portrayed him as a kind of apostle of

3 The traditional legend has the Buddha take seven steps in each direction immediately after birth, point to heaven and to earth, and proclaim: "In heaven and on earth I alone am to be honored."

Christianity. Anjirō's picture of Japanese religion followed a similar line and featured a full-blown cult of saints, belief in a future life, paradise, hell, purgatory, devils, and guardian angels (p. 57). Anjirō asserted that the priests of his country pray the *Ave Maria* at the same times and in identical manner as Christians (pp. 57-8) and that they also have prayers that sound like the *Pater noster*. Like Latin prayers in church they are recited in a language only understood by the literate (p. 58). In Japanese sanctuaries, Anjirō asserted, people worship statues of saints decorated like those in Europe, including that of a woman who, exactly like the Virgin Mary, carries "her son in her arms" (p. 60).

Anjirō's Arlecchino-style projection—"your religion is just like ours at home"—was was probably matched by Lancillotto's; at any rate Lancillotto thought the Japanese must have received their religion "from some Christian heretic who founded this sect" (p. 68). The French polymath Guillaume POSTEL (1510–1581) who got hold of a copy of Lancillotto's report was so impressed by Anjirō's data that he immediately sat down to write the West's first book featuring Japan and its amazing religion: *Les merveilles du monde* (1552). In true Arlecchino fashion, Postel identified the Buddha's father as Joseph and his mother as the virgin Mary (Postel 1552:20r-v), and he came to the conclusion that the story of Xaca (Shakyamuni) is "nothing other than a dark cloud extracted from Evangelical history" (p. 22r).

After their arrival in Japan on August 15 of 1549, the Jesuits were the consternated beneficiaries of another Arlecchino effect. While in India, Anjirō had told the missionaries that the founder of Japanese religion hailed from Cengicco (*Tenjiku* 天竺), a country he was unable to locate on a map. Lancillotto thought that it must lie in the large area to the north and west of China then known as "Scythia" (DocJ 1:51). However, unbeknownst to both Anjirō and the missionaries, *Tenjiku* actually refers to the Indian subcontinent. On old Japanese world maps *Tenjiku* has the shape of India and, since the existence of Europe was still ignored, is located near the Western extremity of the world. After their arrival in Japan, the Jesuits were quickly identified as *Tenjikujin* 天竺人: "men from *Tenjiku*," the motherland of Buddhism. In India the Brahmins had expressed nothing but repulsion and disdain toward the "outcast" European missionaries. In Japan, by contrast, the Jesuits found to their astonishment that priests and monks were extremely interested in news from *Tenjiku* and in the missionaries' teachings. Some members of the Buddhist clergy allowed them to preach at their temple gates and even invited them to stay in their monasteries. Helped by their trusty interpreter Anjirō, the missionaries explained to throngs of curious Japanese that all inhabitants of their faraway homeland *Tenjiku* believed in "Dainichi." Schurhammer, the biographer of St. Francis Xavier, reports (1982:4.225) that the founder of the Jesuit Japan mission used to roam the streets of Yamaguchi city shouting "Dainichi wo ogami are!" ("Pray to Dainichi!"), thus imploring everybody to worship Vairocana Buddha, the great Sun Buddha who is particularly venerated in Anjirō's Shingon sect of Japanese Buddhism. The Jesuit descriptions of the horrors of hell (Jap. *jigoku* 地獄) and the delights of the Pure Land (Jap. *jōdo* 淨土) sounded all too familiar to their Japanese audience. The Japanese were impressed by the scientific knowledge of the men from *Tenjiku* that gave a ring of truth even to some of their more outlandish claims such as that Dainichi had created the world in six days, had impregnated a virgin, and had a human son who was brutally executed but subsequently rose from the dead and ascended to the Pure Land.

Anjirō's Arlecchino-style translation of Christianity into Buddhism thus bore doubly strange fruit. On one hand it seduced the Jesuits into urging the Japanese to have absolute faith in the Buddhadharma of Dainichi, and on the other it caused the Japanese to regard the missionaries as fervent Buddhist reformers. The letters and mission records of the Jesuits contain overwhelming evidence both for the Jesuits' use of Buddhist vocabulary—most fatally *Dainichi*

for God and *buppō* (佛法, Buddha dharma) for religion—and for
the fact that the Japanese regarded them as representatives of Indian
Buddhism.

FIG. 2: THE DAIDŌJI DEED ( CARTAS EVORA, 1598: 61 *RECTO* & *VERSO*).

One of the striking proofs for this is the oldest Chinese-character document to be published in Europe, the 1551 deed by the Duke of Yamaguchi confirming the donation of an abandoned Buddhist temple to the Jesuit missionaries[4] (see Fig. 2). I translate the essential part of this document as follows:

| English translation of the original Japanese text (actual content of the Duke's deed) | English translation of the Portuguese "translation" as published (how Jesuit missionaries presented the deed) |
|---|---|
| The bonzes who have come here from the Western regions may, for the purpose of promulgating the Buddhist law, establish their monastic community at the Buddhist temple of the Great Way. | [The Duke] accords the great Dai, Way of Heaven, to the fathers of the occident who have come to preach the law that produces Saints in conformity with their wish until the end of the world. |

TABLE 1: DAIDŌJI DEED TRANSLATED FROM JAPANESE AND PORTUGUESE

The left column, which reproduces what the Japanese text actually says, shows the Arlecchino mechanism on the Japanese side: the Jesuits appear as representatives of Buddhism who inherit a Buddhist temple in order to promote the Buddhist religion. The right column, by contrast, exhibits Arlecchino at work on the European side. Here, the Great Way of Buddhism is transformed into the "Way of Heaven," the Buddha dharma into the "law that produces saints," and the "Buddhist bonzes" appear as "fathers of the occident." Advertised by posters of this edict and by word of mouth, the Jesuits' Yamaguchi temple was soon inundated by curious visitors. The priests and laymen from various Buddhist denominations who wanted to question

4  See Schurhammer 1928:26–7 and App 1997b:236. For the original text, transcription, and commentary along with the Latin, Portuguese, and English translations of the entire document see App 1997a:232–9.

the long-nosed Buddhists from *Tenjiku* about their doctrines were so numerous that the Jesuits had trouble finding the time to read mass. The Shingon priests were especially pleased to learn that the cosmic Ur-Buddha Dainichi, their principal object of worship, was so exclusively and fervently venerated in the motherland of Buddhism. After Anjirō had deserted the Jesuits and returned to the less holy but more profitable trade of naval piracy, Francis Xavier grew increasingly suspicious about his former interpreter's terminology and began to fear a total fiasco as he realized how wrong he had been in assuming that the Japanese knew the Christian creator God (Schurhammer 1928:35–6). After two years of preaching the law of Dainichi,[5] Francis Xavier suddenly began to call God "Dios" instead of "Dainichi" and ordered Cosme DE TORRES (c. 1510–70) to interview priests of various Japanese sects to plumb the depth of the "Sprachproblem" (language problem), as his biographer Schurhammer chose to call it. The only possible interpreter for such interviews was Juan FERNÁNDEZ (1526–76) who—partly thanks to Anjirō and despite the lack of instructional materials—had managed to pick up some spoken Japanese during his first two years in the country.

While the first two-year phase of the Jesuit Japan mission was very much colored by Anjirō's unwitting Arlecchino approach—Christianity translated into Buddhist terms—a new, even more fascinating, and far more influential enterprise began with the Torres / Fernández interviews in the fall of 1551: the translation of Buddhism into Christian terms. This process necessitated the study of Japanese religions and played, as we will see, a seminal role in the European invention of Oriental philosophy. It is hardly surprising that this pro-

5 In 1562, when the missionary d'Almeida visited a flock of Christians who a decade earlier had been converted by Francis Xavier, he used the word "Dios" for God. Suddenly he was interrupted by the question "Is the Dios of which you talk the same as Dainichi?" The questioner explained: "Father Magister Francis preached to us that Dainichi is God and that we must pray to him!" (Schurhammer 1928:27)

cess was also shaped by Arlecchino-style projection of the familiar on the unfamiliar. This makes it doubly important to investigate the beginning of this venture in some detail. What happened in the earliest phase of Buddhism's translation into Western terms?

As I will show in this book and its sequel, a core portion of the content of "Oriental philosophy" as presented in the seventeenth, eighteenth, and early nineteenth centuries originated in sixteenth-century Japan. Fossils allowing the reconstruction of the genesis of this European invention include such sources as the Jesuit reports about Japanese religions of 1551 and 1556. But the role of Rosetta stone in my archaeology of this invention is played by a marvelous discovery in the year 1902 in the city of Evora, Portugal. Its museum housed a painted Japanese folding screen that had made its way from Japan to Portugal in the late sixteenth century. In the following centuries some of its paper lining became visible. Just like European book binders who often used recycled printed paper from unsold stock to strengthen the covers and spine of books, makers of Japanese folding screens tended to reinforce the paintings on the wooden frame by lining them with recycled paper. In this case dozens of pages featuring handwriting in brush and Japanese ink were used. The examination of these fragments by twentieth-century Japanese historians showed that almost half of the sixty-eight items are related to Aı Gozaemon Ryōsa, a top government official who before and after his Christian baptism (1583) served as counselor and secretary to Japan's ruler Toyotomi Hideyoshi (Gonoi 2000:85-91,104). The other half consists of documents and letters from the Jesuit Japan mission. In 1963 the majority of extant fragments was for the first time published in a Japanese book that also contained essays by Japanese specialists about the content and significance of this extraordinary find (Ebisawa 1963). Having studied these materials in the mid-1990s, I later came across a second book about the Evora screen. Published in Portuguese and Japanese, it contained research essays as well as relatively good photographic reproductions of all text fragments (Itō 2000).

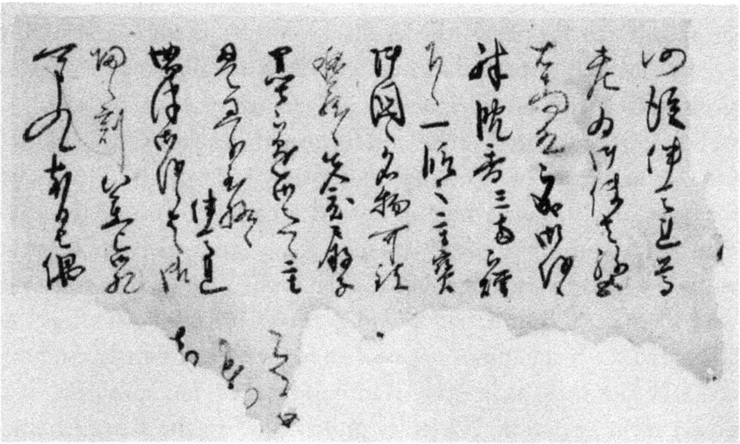

FIG. 3: LETTER FRAGMENT FOUND IN THE EVORA SCREEN (ITŌ 2000:219)

The true significance of this discovery for the history of the European discovery of Oriental thought only began to dawn on me in the course of my work on *The Birth of Orientalism*. Whereas mission reports tend to only communicate what the Jesuits understood or thought they understood from their conversations with Japanese informers, the Evora screen fragments echo one of the earliest known reports by Japanese informants about Japanese religions and contain some of its original terminology. This makes them an extremely precious source that allows partial reconstruction of information delivered by Japanese experts. But the value of the famous Rosetta stone that led to Champollion's deciphering of Egyptian hieroglyphs derived from the fact that it featured both a text and its translations. The reason why I call the Evora screen fragments the "Rosetta stone of Oriental philosophy" is that we have an almost contemporary

Latin version for the parts that interest us most. Thus we can not only infer, based on the Japanese Evora screen fragments, the thrust of information supplied by the Japanese informers along with some of their sources but also how this original information was understood and transformed by the Jesuits. I will show in the course of this book that this interpretation, first published in Valignano's 1586 *Catechismus Christianae fidei*, deeply influenced other missionaries as well as European intellectuals and furnished crucial building blocks for the invention of "Oriental philosophy." While the history of ideas teems with cases where an invention cannot be traced to a specific source and where guesswork must play a large role, our "Rosetta stone"—the Japanese fragments hidden in the Evora screen together with their Latin counterpart in Valignano's *Catechismus*—offers the chance to study the initial stages of an intercultural translation process. We can thus, as it were, examine the seed and sprouting of a flower of imagination, "Oriental philosophy," in the sixteenth and seventeenth century. The bloom of this flower in the eighteenth and its eventual fading in the nineteenth centuries are a large topic that must be explored separately.

Uebersicht der Geschichte der Philosphie.

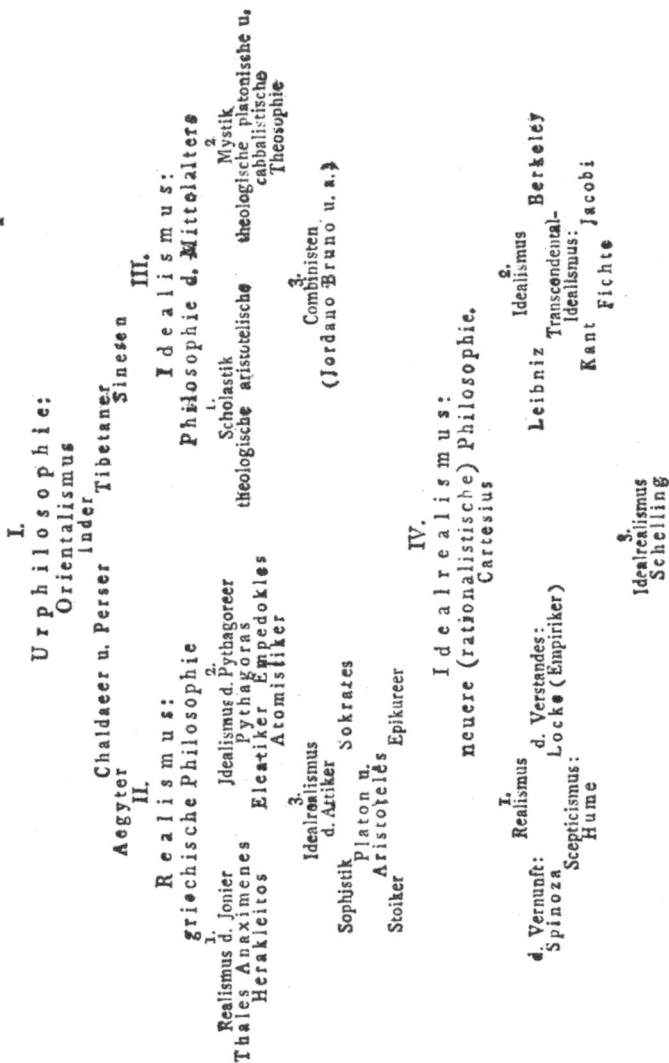

I.
Urphilosophie:
Orientalismus
Inder
Aegyter   Chaldaeer u. Perser   Tibetaner   Sinesen

II.
Realismus:
griechische Philosophie

III.
Idealismus:
Philosophie d. Mittelalters

1.
Realismus d. Jonier
Thales Anaximenes
Herakleitos

2.
Idealismus d. Pythagoreer
Pythagoras
Eleatiker Empedokles
Atomistiker

3.
Idealrealismus
d. Attiker
Sophistik   Platon u. Sokrates
Aristoteles
Stoiker   Epikureer

1.
Scholastik
theologische aristotelische

2.
Mystik
theologische platonische u.
cabbalistische
Theosophie

3.
Combinisten
(Jordano Bruno u. a.)

IV.
Idealrealismus:
neuere (rationalistische) Philosophie.
Cartesius

1.
Realismus d. Verstandes:
d. Vernunft:   Locke (Empiriker)
Spinoza
Scepticismus:
Hume

2.
Idealismus
Leibniz   Idealismus   Berkeley
Transcendental-
Idealismus:
Kant Fichte Jacobi

3.
Idealrealismus
Schelling

FIG. 4: AST'S SYNOPSIS OF THE HISTORY OF PHILOSOPHY (1807:492) WITH
AN ORIENTAL UR-PHILOSOPHY OF INDIAN ORIGIN THAT SPREAD TO
THE EAST (TIBET, CHINA) AND WEST (PERSIA, EGYPT, GREECE)

# Chapter Two

## THE ZEN SHOCK

In order to understand the earliest phase of the European discovery of Buddhist thought and the invention of "Oriental philosophy" we first need to examine early reports by Jesuits about Japanese Buddhism that only exist in Portuguese, Spanish, Italian, or Latin versions. Like the Evora screen fragments, they are based on information furnished by Japanese informants; but unlike with our "Rosetta" texts from Evora, no Japanese notes or translations are known to exist. All we have at our disposal are reports showing how the missionaries understood what was said. This forces us to make more or less informed guesses about the Japanese terminology and the intended meaning of the Japanese informants. The first two of these early reports reached Francis Xavier in the fall of 1551 just prior to his departure from Japan. Both reports were based on discussions and debates at the Temple of the Great Way (Daidōji) where Cosme de Torres and Juan Fernández were allowed, as the Duke of Yamaguchi put it, "to promulgate the Buddhist law" (see Table 1).

Cosme de TORRES (c. 1510–1570), the author of the first report, was born in Valencia, became a priest, and settled on the island of Mallorca as a professor of grammar before leaving Spain in 1538 for Mexico.[6] After an ill-fated expedition to the Philippines he met Francis Xavier and accompanied him to Goa where he joined the Jesuit society in 1548. There Torres instructed and interviewed Anjirō, and one year later he joined Francis Xavier, Juan Fernández, and Anjirō

6 This paragraph with biographical information relies on Schurhammer 1929:11-19.

23

on the journey to Japan. In 1552, after Francis Xavier's departure, Torres became superior of the Jesuit Japan mission, a post he kept until his death in 1570. Since Father de Torres was not as familiar with the Japanese language as his fellow Spaniard Juan FERNÁNDEZ (1526–1576), it fell to Fernández to converse with Japanese priests and laymen and to redact notes in transliterated Japanese.

Brother Fernández from Cordoba had joined the Jesuits at a young age and was sent to India together with Luís FRÓIS (1532–97), a Marrano from Portugal. On the ship to Goa, Fernández and Fróis were joined by Balthasar GAGO (d. 1583) from Portugal who had joined the Society of Jesus at age 20. These Spanish (de Torres and Fernández) and Portuguese (Gago and Fróis) missionaries happen to be the four men who, after the fiasco with Anjirō (whom they all knew very well), were most centrally involved in the "translation" of information about Japanese religions that interests us in this and the following chapters.

For months the Buddhist temple of the missionaries in Yamaguchi was besieged by Buddhists who tried to learn about contemporary Indian Buddhism. On September 29 of 1551 Torres reported:

> Those [missionaries] who come to these regions must be very learned in order to be able to respond to the very lofty and difficult questions they pose from morning until night. They are so very persistent that since the day when Master Francisco came to this town, which is five months ago, there never was a day without priests and laymen asking us all sorts of questions from early in the morning almost through the night. (DocJ 1:217)

Japan missionaries not only had to be very learned, prudent, patient, and humble, Torres explained to his fellow Jesuits, but also "very experienced in meditation because the majority of these priests and laymen pass almost their entire life in this exercise in order to know how and from where man comes into being and into what he is transformed when he dies" (p. 229). Torres wrote that these

24

men belong to the Zen sect and specified that some members of this sect who are "great meditators" assert that "there is no soul and that when man dies, everything dies, because what came from nothing returns to nothing" (p. 214). These letters by Torres from late September of 1551 are the first Western documents to mention Zen by name and to bring up themes such as "nothingness," "no soul," and "no yonder"—themes that were, as we will see, bound for a brilliant career in the West.

One month later, on October 20 of 1551, Torres's interpreter Juan Fernández sent a much more detailed second report to Francis Xavier. It was based on his notes in Japanese taken during debates with Japanese Buddhists. Though these notes are lost, the Spanish report based on them permits some educated guesses about the translation process. The questions of interest in our context were mostly posed by the missionaries and seem on the surface quite straightforward. First, the missionaries asked the Japanese what they do to become saints ("qué hazían para se hazer sanctos"; p. 242). We know that in their translation of the Yamaguchi deed (see Table 1), the Jesuits rendered the term *buppō* 佛法 (Buddha dharma) as "the law that produces saints." We can deduce from this that they took the Japanese word *butsu* or *hotoke* 佛 (Buddha) to mean "saint." Whereas the missionaries thought they asked about the way to become a saint in the Christian sense, the Japanese heard a question about the way to become an enlightened buddha. Their answer contains the phrase "what is made from nothing returns to nothing," a phrase that is found several times in these early reports and later formed part of Buddha's "deathbed confession" story (see Chapter 10). The Jesuits tried to counter this pernicious notion by explaining to the Japanese that there is a principle that gave rise to all things ("hum principio, el qual dio principio a todas las cosas," p. 242). They were doubtlessly thinking of the creator God and must have been dismayed by the trajectory of the Japanese response:

25

They admitted that this is so, saying that it is a principle from which all things come: men, animals, and plants, and that all created things have this principle in them ... This principle, they say, is neither good nor evil, involves neither glory [paradise] nor punishment [hell], and neither dies nor lives, so that it is a non-being.[7]

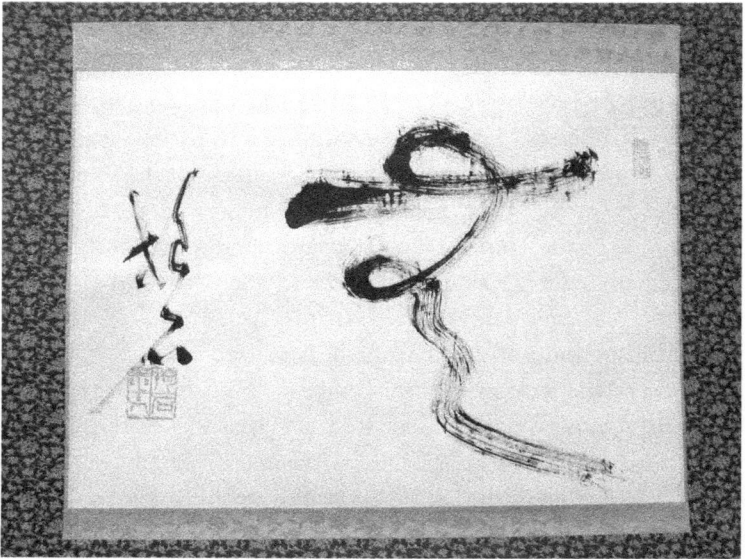

FIG. 5: SHIN'ICHI HISAMATSU: MU 無 (NOTHINGNESS)

This "non-being" or "nothingness" may have been the *mu* 無 that is so central in Japanese Zen and is often understood in the sense of Mahāyāna "emptiness" (Skt. *śūnyatā*, Jap. *kū* 空). The *Heart Sutra*, a

---

7 "El qual ellos concedieron que havía, diziendo que este es hun principio del qual proceden todas las cosas, hombres, bestias, plantas, y cada cosa criada tiene en sí aquel principio ... El qual principio dizen que no es ni bueno ni malo, ni tiene gloria ni pena, ni muere ni bibe, de manera que es hun no ser." (DocJ 1:243)

text that even many Japanese laypersons know by heart, explains for example:

> All dharmas are marked with emptiness ... in emptiness there is no form nor feeling, nor perception, nor impulse, nor consciousness ... There is no decay and death, no extinction of decay and death. There is no suffering, no origination, no stopping, no path. There is no cognition, no attainment and no non-attainment. (tr. Edward Conze)

Of course the missionaries knew nothing about Mahāyāna philosophy, and to them this "first principle" that is a "non-being" and does not distinguish between good and evil sounded barbaric. This is how the "nothingness" and "emptiness" of Mahāyāna Buddhism made its entrance into European literature. It is the first sign of a gulf that played a crucial role in the invention of "Oriental philosophy": the gulf between the missionaries' first principle, which for them of course was their creator God, and the *mu* 無 and *kū* 空 (nothingness and emptiness) of the Japanese Zen adepts. Even at this earliest stage the specter of nihilism and atheism raised its head. Fernández reported:

> They said that neither God nor saints exist because all things by nature are without beginning in the world and without someone who makes them begin. (DocJ 1:248)

The Japanese thus appeared to believe in the eternity of the world and to reject the notions of a creator God as well as sainthood. We do not know how the Jesuits formulated their question in Japanese; but it is possible that a Zen master, asked about *hotoke* (buddhas), decided to shock the missionaries by quoting Bodhidharma's "nothing holy" or Linji (Rinzai)'s "kill the Buddha, kill the patriarchs." But this is mere speculation. Whatever the informants uttered, the written report confronted its European readers with the awful thought that tonsured, rosary-wielding Japanese clerics could actually be atheists who believe in the eternity of matter and have not the slightest notion of a creation out of nothing. This impression was reinforced by what the Jesuits learned about the founder figure Shaka or Xaca (Shakyamuni Buddha). Their reports show Shaka no longer as a wayward apostle of Christianity, as Anjirō had portrayed him, but rather as a blasphemous impostor who already as a seven-year-old boy pointed toward heaven and earth while uttering that he alone was in heaven and on earth (p. 256). When speaking about "former saints" like Amida, Shaka claimed that one could be saved by praying to them, and he wrote many books in this vein. But at age forty-nine he abruptly changed idea, declaring that he had hitherto been ignorant and that this ignorance was the reason why he had written so much (p. 257). Through meditation he had suddenly realized that salvation could not be obtained via sacred scriptures, worship, or prayers but solely through meditation (p. 257).

Fernández's account diverges significantly from traditional Buddhist legends. These differences are of particular interest to us since they furnish data about the translation process. Some are probably due to Fernández's insufficient understanding of Japanese,[8] but others may reflect the ideology of Zen interlocutors. For half a millennium the Buddhist sects of China had been quarreling about who possesses the Buddha's ultimate teaching and which scripture contains it when the Zen movement arose in seventh- and eighth-century China. In some of China's Buddhist monasteries, monks with a particular interest in meditation began to form groups and to promulgate particular reformist doctrines. As this movement gradually gained profile, it felt compelled to differentiate itself more clearly from traditional Buddhist movements and dreamed up an elaborate lineage

8   The traditional account has the Buddha take seven steps and make his declaration immediately after birth, and the number forty-nine often indicates the number of years that the Buddha taught (enlightenment at age thirty, death at age seventy-nine).

scheme that sought to establish a direct "mind-to-mind" transmission originating from the Buddha. Bodhidharma, Zen's legendary first Chinese patriarch, functioned as a crucial link between India (where he supposedly was the twenty-eighth patriarch after Buddha) and China. He thus fulfilled the important role of transmitter. As the sectarian identity of this reform movement was gradually established there was a growing need to give more definition to its doctrinal identity. This resulted in a quatrain whose elements were in place by the ninth century. The informers of Torres and Fernández clearly had it in mind when explaining to the missionaries that texts, prayers, and worship are worthless and only meditation counts:

[It is] a special transmission outside of scriptural teachings
That does not establish words and letters.
It points directly at man's mind:
Seeing one's nature signifies becoming a buddha.[9]

What is of particular interest in Fernández's account is that this purported difference between Zen and other Buddhist sects acquired an unheard-of biographical dimension: before age forty-nine the Buddha supposedly wrote many books containing the doctrines of non-Zen sects. At that point, however, he suddenly realized while meditating that all of his writings and teachings had been regrettable expressions of ignorance. So he stopped writing, and from that point onward he exclusively taught Zen doctrine which emphasizes meditation and awakening to one's true nature (DocJ 1:257).

Of course we cannot know precisely what the Zen monks told Fernández and Torres, but the missionaries' account of the Buddha's life clearly involves some misunderstandings. East Asian Buddhist sects including Zen usually believe that the Buddha was enlightened at age thirty, taught for forty-nine years, and died at the age of seventy-nine. Some claim that particular texts of the huge and extremely varied corpus of Buddhist scriptures stem from some special period of the Buddha's life, for example the period immediately after

9  Cf. App 1994:12.

his enlightenment (the *Avataṃsaka Sutra* or the *Forty-two Sections Sutra*) or the day of his death (the *Nirvāṇa Sutra* or the *Bequeathed Teachings Sutra*). Most Buddhist sects regard one or several scriptures as the Buddha's highest or ultimate teaching; for instance, the Pure Land denomination sees the three *Pure Land Sutras* as most fundamental, and the Tendai and Nichiren denominations the *Lotus Sutra*. Fernández's account is thus an interesting invention that projects sectarian rivalry on the Buddha's life story. The abrupt and complete reversal of ideas and teachings at age forty-nine and the Buddha's rejection of all former teachings and scriptures as ignorant (p. 257) appear to have been the fruit of Torres's or Fernández's (mis)understanding of explanations about Zen ideology. The result was a story that not even a Zen fanatic would have dared to invent. Shakyamuni's stunning change of mind was immediately denounced as a lie by interpreter Fernández and his superior Torres:

> We asked them: if this was really the case, then why did Shaka, in that hour of his forty-ninth year, say that he was ignorant when he wrote those books, and that only those who meditate will be saved? It was therefore a lie; and had he been a true saint without beginning and end, then he could not possibly have lied because there is no lie in the creator and savior of the world. And since he lied in this instance, it is all the more obvious that what he said at age seven was also a lie, namely, that he alone is in heaven and on earth; and also that those who worship him and practice what he formerly taught cannot be saved. All of it was lies. (p. 257)

One more theme in Fernández's report must be mentioned because it also had a great future: the idea that man's soul is not God's creature but rather part of God himself. When the Jesuits asserted that the soul cannot see God as long as it is bound to a filthy body, the Zen interlocutors wholeheartedly agreed, albeit with a startling rationale:

They agreed, saying that the souls of men are gods because they have no body, and that for this reason they are neither born nor do they perish. (p. 247)

It is likely that Fernández's "the souls of men are gods" was another Arlecchino-style interpretation because no representative of Zen would say anything like it. My guess is that the Japanese visitors quoted the Zen saying "your very mind is Buddha" (Jap. *sokushin sokubutsu* 即心即佛) and attempted to explain that One Mind (Jap. *isshin* 一心) or Buddha-nature (Jap. *busshō* 佛性) is free from birth and death (Jap. *fushō fumetsu* 不生不滅). As this example shows, the translation of Zen doctrine into Christian terms was no simple task.

We can note the following points of interest in these first Jesuit reports of 1551:

1. *The Arlecchino effect:* The beginning of the translation by missionaries of Buddhism into European / Christian terms already shows both its enormous risks and potential. It is far more than just a "language problem" or a case of problematic missionary accommodation, as Schurhammer (1928) claimed.

2. *The influence of Zen:* Many of the visitors in Yamaguchi as well as the Duke, who had given them permission to promulgate Buddhism, were Zen adepts. At the time and in the regions frequented by the missionaries Zen was dominant among the ruling classes.

3. *Creation and nothingness:* A recurring theme of early reports is the need to distinguish an eternal creator God from his creatures. This is why the world must not be eternal and cannot simply return to nothing.

4. *Atheistic religion:* The spectacle of shave-pated, extremely devoted, contemplative monks equipped with rosaries and other accoutrements of piety who openly deny the existence of God ("neither God nor saints exist") must have been a shock to Europeans used to classifying the world's religions in four categories: Christianity, Judaism, Islam, and paganism. The surprise about this strange phenomenon rippled through European literature for centuries.

5. *Soul*: Equally shocking were assertions to the effect that for man everything ends with death, that there is no soul (Jap. *mushin* 無心, no-mind), or that man's soul is God (Jap. *sokushin sokubutsu* 即心即佛, your very mind is Buddha).

6. *The Buddha's lie*: The Fernández report of 1551 contains a unique biographical invention. It asserts that at age forty-nine Buddha suddenly rejected all of his earlier writings and doctrines and subsequently exclusively taught meditation—a change of opinion that the Jesuits denounced as a lie.

# Chapter Three

## THE BUDDHA'S PROGRESS

After Francis Xavier's departure from Japan in late 1551, the personnel of the tiny Japan mission was slightly boosted in 1552 through the arrival of three Jesuits including the Portuguese Balthasar GAGO (d. 1583) who became the understudy of Juan Fernández (DocJ 1:554-5). When Gago arrived in Funai in February of 1553 he at first stayed with a follower of Zen (Bourdon 1993:259). Though he had some success with the sick and the possessed, the progress of his mission was severely compromised by the dominance of Zen among the aristocracy (pp. 260-1). Some Zen adepts denied just about everything the Jesuits happened to affirm while others claimed that the Jesuits' teaching of *Deos* is identical with their doctrine (Schurhammer 1928:47). Such issues, exacerbated by festering problems of terminology and understanding, made it increasingly important for the missionaries to gain solid and detailed information about Japan's religions.

It is in such dire straits that a certain "Paulo KYŌZEN" (d. 1557) enters the picture. This highly praised man became the Jesuits' most important informant about Japanese religions between his baptism in 1554 and his death in 1557. Paulo was "a great expert in the [Japanese] language and well informed about the gods and sects of Japan" and also "arranged the language of the books so that [the Japanese] understood what Juan Fernández wrote" (DocJ 2:569). According to Duarte da Sylva, this native was "particularly knowledgeable about the doctrine of the Zen sect which is most powerful in this land. They hold that there is nothing after this life."[10] Paulo's real name was Chōzen. Before his conversion he had been a high-ranking Tendai priest,[11] and his knowledge of Buddhism and its founder triggered the first real breakthrough in Western knowledge about this religion. The most important outcome of his tutoring is a document originally written in 1556 in Spanish that subsequently was translated into Portuguese and Italian (pp. 652–4). In Spanish it is called *Sumario de los errores* (Summary of Errors), and though Balthasar Gago may have had a hand in it, its probable authors are the two Jesuits most familiar with Japan's language and religions, Torres and Fernández.[12] Of these two missionaries, Fernández was most versed in Japanese and thus likely to have translated what the apostate Tendai priest Paulo explained. Though the *Sumario* may have been redacted by Torres or Gago, Paulo Chōzen and Fernández probably played the central roles in its genesis.

This *Sumario* of 1556, aspects of which will be analyzed in this and the next chapter, is extremely important in several respects: 1. It is the first Western document in which Shinto and Buddhism are identified as Japan's main religions. 2. It contains the earliest information about East Asian religions gained from a knowledgeable native informant. 3. It is the first Western text to identify *buppō* (佛法,

---

10 "Chama-se Paulo, mui sabido na ley dos genxos, que hé a que mais força tem nesta terra. Têm que nam há nada depois desta vida." (Letter by Duarte da Sylva of Sept. 10, 1555; DocJ 1:523).

11 My thanks to Naomi Maeda who helped me identify this "Paulo" as the Tendai monk Chōzen 長禪 who before his conversion to Christianity lived in a monastery on Mt. Tōnomine.

12 See DocJ 2:652-4 for speculation about the authorship and information about different versions of this important document. It is possible that Gago translated the original Spanish *Sumario de los errores* into Portuguese. Though manuscripts in several languages exist, the only complete extant manuscript is a Portuguese translation. It is one of three copies made on the order of Nunes Barreto's secretary Luís Fróis in Malacca and sent to Europe (DocJ 1:743).

Buddhism) as a religion consisting of different sects with distinctive doctrines. 4. It first related different sects, scriptures, and specific teachings of Buddhism to phases of the founder's life. 5. It is the earliest Western source clearly distinguishing esoteric and exoteric Buddhist doctrines. 6. It contains the first detailed description of Zen practice. 7. It is the first known attempt to understand central tenets of Buddhist doctrine in terms of late medieval scholastic philosophy. The *Sumario's* identification of Buddhism by way of its Japanese name *buppō* (lit.

Buddhist law; Buddha dharma) represents clear progress from earlier documents such as the translation of the Duke of Yamaguchi's deed where the same word *buppō* was said to signify "the law that produces saints" (see Table 1). The *Sumario* distinguishes the Buddhist religion from Japan's indigenous Shinto in which kami (gods) are worshiped (DocJ 2:655),[13] and it specifies that Buddhism is a religion with "eight or nine sects" (p. 659). Its founder is identified as a Chinese man named "Xaqua" (Jap. Shaka, Shakyamuni Buddha), and "a certain scripture" that remains unnamed is connected with Buddhism's origin (p. 659). The fact that this "law" is said to have a number of sects, a founder, a founding scripture, and clergy in several Asian countries proves that Europeans already in 1556 regarded *buppō* (Buddhism) as a religion.[14]

Indeed, the *Sumario's* authors begin by discussing some of the features that justify the (modern) badge of "religion" for this *buppō*: it has priests who preach five commandments and hold ceremonies for the dead; monks and nuns in monasteries who pray day and night; and various religious orders with frocks "resembling those of Do-

---

13 For a translation and analysis of the Shinto part of the *Sumario* see Schurhammer 1923.

14 This stands in stark contrast with the view that Buddhism was first identified (or even "invented") as a religion by European orientalists in the first half of the nineteenth century. Among the proponents of this mirage are Almond (1988:11), Roger-Pol Droit (1997:36), Faure (1998:17), and Lenoir (1999:90). See also below.

minican and Franciscan friars." Moreover, some sects of this religion are said to hold notions of a soul continuing to live after death and of punishment in hell or happiness in the Pure Land, and even believe in a savior called *hotoke* (佛, Buddha; pp. 659-60). Depending on the sect, either Shakyamuni or Amida is worshiped. Amida is portrayed as the son of a king who became a *bonzo* after the death of his wife, meditated for a long time, and wrote forty-eight books in which he promised to save all those who recite "Nāo mo Amida Ambud" (Namu Amida butsu) and worship him (pp. 661-2).

While such information as well as the *Sumario's* description of three kinds of Pure Land clergy is interesting, the dynamite is packed into the following section. Exactly those teachings that the missionaries regarded as relatively sensible (i.e., that were similar to Christian doctrine) were called by the Japanese themselves "expedient" (Jap. *hōben*), which the Jesuits interpreted as "pious lie ("mentira virtuosa"; p. 663).[15] According to the *Sumario*, Buddhist clergymen preach to the people about punishment in hell and recompense in the Pure Land. In their hearts, however, they are said to believe that "the interior core of their law" states that "there is neither a soul nor life in the yonder, and that all ends with this life" (p. 663). This denial of a soul, a future state, and consequently of any possibility of recompense or punishment in the yonder were to gain a great echo in Europe as features of Shaka's (and later the entire Orient's) "inner" doctrine, as did the distinction between a false doctrine preached to the people and a different one that the preachers themselves believed to be true.

---

15    *Hōben* (Ch. *fangbian* 方便) is an important Buddhist term meaning "expedient means" or "skilful means;" see Pye 1978. It is also commonly used in everyday Japanese, for example in the saying *uso mo hōben* (lies can also be expedient means). In the religious context *hōben* is used for teachings that are adapted to the capacity and circumstances of the recipient—which resembles what Christian missionaries as well as modern scholars tend to call missionary "accommodation."

The *Sumario's* authors also used their newly-won knowledge to add detail to the biography of founder Shaka. Whereas Fernández's 1551 account features a single reversal at age forty-nine, the *Sumario* has no less than three major ones. First Shaka is said to have spent eight years writing a book explaining that there is nothing but birth and death ("declarava não aver mais que nacer e morrer") because all things consist entirely of the four elements and return to them (p. 663). This sounds like a materialist doctrine. When Shaka realized that the people could not understand this he reversed himself for the first time and began to teach that one should do good, avoid lies, pray to the *hotokes,* and worry about one's fate in the yonder (pp. 663-4). Having promulgated this second doctrine for a total of forty-one years and filled three texts with it, Shaka once more changed idea. Now he declared that all his former teachings had been *hōben* or expedient means and announced his decision to write a final book. After decades of talk about a Pure Land and hells etc., he regressed to his initial assertion that there is nothing but matter and the four elements. However, he now added explanations about a principle (*honbun*)[16] that "neither lives nor dies nor feels yet has formed the elements" (p. 664-5). Having finished his last book containing this doctrine, Shaka was ready to die. But as death's cold breath drew near he had one more surprise in store: he dictated on his deathbed a final text "which proclaimed that in his entire life he had not written a single word" because the origin and destination of man cannot be written or spoken about nor can they be taught in other ways (p. 665).

---

16 *Honbun* 本分 literally means "original part" or "fundamental share." It is an expression that was frequently used in Zen circles with the meaning of "what it is all about," "what is fundamentally at stake," "what is essential," "the gist of the matter," or "the original essence." In Jesuit interpretation it came to mean, as shown in the *Vocabulario* of 1604, "primeiro principio" (the first principle). See Chapter 4 for the *Sumario's* and Fróis's interpretation.

The founder's life as portrayed in the *Sumario* thus had five distinct phases:

1. *Youth.* Shaka's youth was marked by his mother's death which the *Sumario* attributes to the child's viciously ripping open his mother's belly with his teeth;[17] by his pointing at heaven and earth at age seven; by his marriage at age nineteen and the birth of his son; and by the departure from his royal home after the early death of his wife (DocJ 2:663).

2. *Training and first doctrine.* During the second phase, Shaka trained with a master who is said to have lived more than one thousand years. He then spent eight years writing a book that teaches that there is nothing beyond life and death and that everything consists only of the four elements to which everything will eventually return (p. 663).

3. *Second doctrine.* Frustrated by the people's incomprehension, Shaka then began to teach the exact opposite of his first doctrine. He spent thirty-six years writing three books that advocate good deeds, faith in the *hotoke*, heaven, hell, recompense or punishment in the yonder, prayers, and so forth. This "exoteric" phase lasted forty-one years, i.e. presumably from around age twenty-seven to sixty-eight (p. 663-4). During this phase he gained as many as eighty thousand disciples (pp. 663-4).

4. *Third doctrine.* Around the age of sixty-eight Shaka proclaimed that all he had hitherto proclaimed (i.e., the second doctrine) had merely been expedient teaching (*hōben*); but at least it had motivated people to read his final book whose redaction took twelve years. This book contained his initial teaching that everything arises from and returns to matter, that is, the four elements. However, he now

---

17 Legend asserts that the founder of Buddhism emerged from the side of his mother Maya and that she died after giving birth. The Jesuit portrayal of baby Shakyamuni's vicious matricide is an invention that lived on in many European sources. It sometimes was supplemented by the explanation that his decision to leave home and engage in ascetic practices was driven by remorse.

called this matter *fombum* (Jap. *honbun*)[18] and stated that it neither lives nor dies nor feels even though it constitutes all elements and forms (pp. 664-5).

5. *The final doctrine.* On his deathbed Shaka offered an even more radical teaching. He now claimed that in his entire life he had not written a single letter and that the origin and end of things cannot be described or explained by words (p. 665).

This is what the *Sumario's* authors understood of Paulo Chōzen's explanations. Paulo appears to have informed them about the standard Tiantai 天台 (Jap. Tendai) classification scheme of Master ZHIYI 智顗 (538–597) in which five phases and eight teachings (Jap. *goji hakkyō* 五時八教) are distinguished. According to Zhiyi, the Buddha conveyed to his first disciples the advanced, "sudden" teaching of the *Huayan* (Jap. *Kegon*, Skt. *Avataṃsaka*) *Sutra* designed for bodhisattvas. From the second to the fourth periods he employed expedient means (Jap. *hōben*) and delivered "gradual" doctrines in order to guide people of less advanced understanding: twelve years of Āgamas, eight years of elementary Mahāyāna sutras, and fourteen (in another account twenty-two) years of Prajñāpāramitā teachings. In the fifth and final period that lasted eight years he went on to proclaim the *Lotus* and *Nirvāṇa* sutras (the latter, according to legend, in a single day and night before passing away).

Though the missionaries' understanding of this classification scheme was in many ways flawed, they did grasp its overall aim of associating certain doctrines and scriptures with distinct phases of the founder's life. Some of the *Sumario's* data can be traced to specific texts. For example, the assertion that Shaka had after forty-one years portrayed his previous teachings as "tudo fombem" (all *hōben* or expedient means; DocJ 1:664) is based on a passage in the *Wuliangyi jing* 無量義經 or *Sutra of Innumerable Meanings*: "I knew that the natures and desires of all living beings were not equal. As their natures

18 This appears to be the first occurrence of this important term in Jesuit sources. For its meanings see the next chapter.

and desires were not equal, I preached the Law variously. In forty years and more, the truth has not been revealed yet" (Katō 1984:14). This phrase was later adduced by numerous missionaries including Alessandro Valignano as proof that Shaka had misled the majority of his disciples by withholding his real doctrine ( Jap. *jikkyō* 實教) and conveying merely provisional teachings ( Jap. *gonkyō* 權教). This distinction between outer / provisional and inner / genuine teachings was to have a great career in Europe—just like the Jesuits' interpretation of Zen doctrine that will be examined in our next chapters.

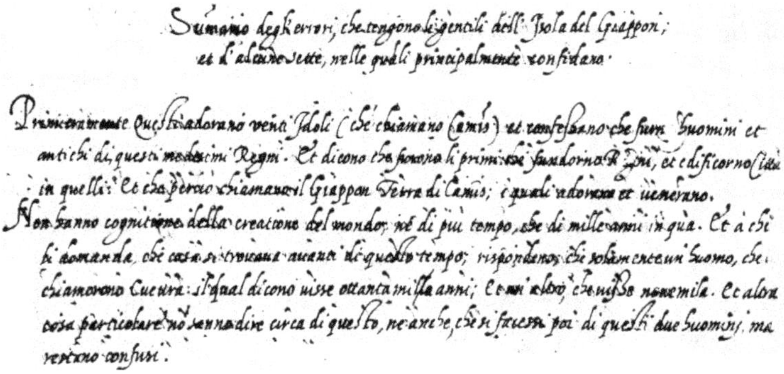

FIG. 6: BEGINNING OF SUMARIO DEGLI ERRORI (1556); BIBLIOTECA NAZIONALE ROMA, FONDO GESUITICO 1384, NO. 7

# Chapter Four

# CHAOS AND THE GOD OF ZEN

The *Sumario* of 1556 distinguishes three main categories of Japanese Buddhism: 1. sects that worship Amida; 2. sects that worship Shaka; and 3. the "sect of black-robed bonzes who follow what he wrote last" (DocJ 2:665). The third corresponds to the Zen sect whose clergy "engages in contemplations [fazem contemplações]," teaches it to the people, and provides them with "themes on which to meditate [ponto sobre que meditem]" (p. 665). The *Sumario's* five examples of such "bridges" or themes for meditation show that the missionaries wrote about *kōans* (公案, Ch. *gongan*). The use of these teaching devices—aptly defined by Richard DeMartino (1983:53) as "Zen presentations in the form of Zen challenges"—was booming in the twelfth and thirteenth centuries when Zen Buddhism was brought from China to Japan. What is of interest here is not only the fact that the *Sumario* furnishes five specific examples of *kōans* but that it uses them to explain the content of founder Shaka's ultimate teachings.

The Jesuits were interested in Zen Buddhism because of its popularity with the ruling class in important regions of Japan. In his letter of January 13, 1558 to the Jesuit General Lainez, the superior of Asian missions Belchior NUNES BARRETO (c. 1520–71) identified the Japanese "sect of meditators" as representative of the theology of Buddhism, He expressed his conviction that this religion exists not only in Japan but also in China and southern Burma (Pegu), and conjectured that its origin may lie in Pegu:

41

This is the pseudo-theology of Xaqua and Amida, which also reigns all over China and Pegu where this pest, to the best of my knowledge, came from. These are the devil's tricks [doli diaboli], this is the science that the bonzes and nobles discuss in their schools [in suis gynnasiis], and this is the kind of demonic deception of the prevalent sect that they call 'sect of meditators.' (DocJ 2:110-111)

This is, to my knowledge, the earliest Jesuit letter pointing to the presence both in East and Southeast Asia of the religion of Shaka and Amida, that is, of what we today identify as Buddhism. Not only that: Nunes even claims for the first time that the doctrine of the "sect of meditators," that is, the Zen sect, is not only prevalent among the bonzes and nobles of Japan but also in China and in the country where he surmised Buddhism had its origin: Burma. This projection of known Japanese circumstances on the unknown—Japanese Zen on the religion of China and Burma—was a feat Arlecchino could only dream of. Nunes Barreto thus pioneered a trend that, as later chapters of this book show, was pursued with great vigor by Valignano and especially by João Rodrigues (see Chapter 8) whose writings were to create the basis for the projection of that very doctrine on all of Asia: the "inner" doctrine of "Oriental philosophy" *par excellence*!

Nunes, the man who had ordered the redaction of the seminal *Sumario de los errores* during his brief stay in Japan in the summer of 1556, very much appreciated the help of Paulo Chōzen in uncovering this religion's diabolical doctrine:

Divine grace brought it about that some bonze who was quite an expert in all these errors was enlightened and, thank God, converted. He brought to light the poison of the old serpent. (p. 111)

In effect, the 1556 *Sumario* presents this most poisonous doctrine of the devil as a particular notion of "nothingness" which Zen adepts frequently meditate on:

| Sumario de los errores (DocJ 2:665-6) | Sumario degli errori, BNR Fondo Gesuitico 1384 no. 7 | English translation of Portuguese text (Urs App) |
|---|---|---|
| E dam-lhe outra meditação em que lhe perguntão: aquelle que está fora de todas as coussas visíveis, que coussa hé. E depois de bem meditado, acha que hé huma coussa que estáa cheio, a qual hé este espaço que há entre o ceo e a terra, a qual coussa acha que não vive nem morre nem crece nem minguoa nem vai nem vem, que hé nada. | Li propongono anche che pensino, che è quello che stà fuora di tutte le cose uisibili; et dopoi d'hauer ben meditato, ritruouano che è una cosa che sta piena; ò ueramente che è questo spatio, che è tra il cielo et la terra: il quale ritrouano che ne more ne uiue, ne cresce ne manca, ne ua ne uiene; ch'è un niente. | And they give them another meditation by asking: what is it that is beyond all visible things? And after having well meditated they find that it is something that remains full, like this space between heaven and earth; and they find that this something neither lives nor dies, neither grows nor diminishes, neither comes nor goes: that it is nothing. |

TABLE 2: THE *SUMARIO*'S VIEW OF NOTHINGNESS IN ZEN DOCTRINE

The *Sumario*'s fifth example of a Zen kōan, which asks what exists before birth and after death, ends with the same conclusion inspired by the old serpent: "In the end they find that all is nothing [por derradeiro acha tudo nada]" (p. 666). When Paulo Chōzen spoke to the missionaries about the central Mahāyāna concept of emptiness (Jap. *kū*) and the *mu* or nothingness of Zen, Arlecchino thus once more played his trick: the Jesuits interpreted the unfamiliar philosophy in terms of what they were familiar with. The familiar, in this case, was information gained in philosophy and theology classes at Jesuit colleges in Europe and Asia. To the authors of the *Sumario*, Shaka's ultimate doctrine resembled that of ancient Greek materialists and hylozoists, and its "crux" or *honbun* seemed the spitting image of what they had encountered in Aristotle textbooks from Coimbra as *chaos* or *materia prima*:[19]

> He [Shaka] declared very clearly that nothing exists other than matter composed of four elements, which he called fombun. He said that this fombun neither lives nor dies nor feels, and that it had formed the elements, which he calls Genpo. (pp. 664–5)

Based on what they gathered from Buddhist apostate Paulo's explanations, the *Sumario's* authors thus present their understanding of Shaka's cosmogony: a *honbun* (something like an eternal and nonsentient *materia prima*) forms the visible world (Jap. *genpō* 現法) that consists of nothing but the four elements (Jap. *shidai* 四大) and contains "all creatures of matter and form, called Xiquisso" (Jap. *shikisō* 色相; p. 665). Unlike the eternal and formless *honbun* 本分, these creatures "grow and decrease, die and are born again" (p. 665).

The background of such views becomes clearer toward the end of the *Sumario* where the Japanese "literati who are like philosophers" and other adherents of Shaka's "inner" doctrine are accused of "understanding neither the first cause nor the purpose for which we were created but only the matter and form of creatures without anything spiritual" (p. 667). They are furthermore berated for "occupying themselves exclusively with corporeal things, which is why they say that nothing exists except being born and dying" (p. 667). Such accusations are clearly based on the Aristotelian conception of four causes as interpreted by Thomas Aquinas and his scholastic successors (see Chapters 7 and 11). The first and fourth causes, the *causa efficiens* and *causa finalis*, pertain to the creator God who is the first cause of everything (*prima causa efficiens*) and equips each creature with its final purpose (*causa finalis*). The second and third causes, by contrast, pertain to the world where matter (*causa materialis*) receives form (*causa formalis*). The latter causes are said to be

19 See also Chapters 7, 11, and 17.

the only two known to Shaka and his followers. Even what they call *fotoque* (*hotoke*, buddhas) consists, according to the *Sumario*, merely "of matter and the four elements" (p. 667).

The *Sumario's* interpretation of Buddhism's first principle or *honbun* as a formless *materia prima* was possibly advanced by the very man who ordered the report and was most familiar with scholastic philosophy: Nunes Barreto. After his brief stay in Japan in the summer of 1556, Nunes carried the *Sumario* to India where it was copied under the supervision of Luís Fróis and sent to Europe in several copies. Nunes's Latin digest[20] of the findings of the *Sumario* about the "inner" teaching of Shaka confirms his interpretation of its first principle as "chaos," which in turn is defined as the *materia prima* or raw material of all things:

> Even their first principle of things is merely perceivable matter of the elements—what one can in truth call chaos, the raw material of all things [chaos rudem indigestamque molem]. Neither do they admit any first efficient or final cause. (DocJ 2:110)

Exactly like the heathen Greek and Roman philosophers that were criticized by the Christian commentators of Aristotle, Shaka and his followers thus exhibit their ignorance regarding God's *creatio ex nihilo* (creation out of nothing) and blindly assert that everything must have arisen by chance from a *materia prima* or "chaos" that is seen as eternal: "[They believe that] the world, at least in the form of chaos, has always existed; that it has by chance brought forth various forms; and that it will never vanish" (DocJ 2:110). Shaka's ultimate teaching thus fits the pattern that students of scholastic philosophy had learned to identify as typical of ancient Greek and Roman atheism: the denial of an omnipotent and omniscient creator God in favor of an eternal chaos or *materia prima* from which all beings, like

---

20  Letter to Diego Lainez, Goa, January 13, 1558; DocJ 2:109-111.

waves in water, arise by chance only to eventually dissolve again into chaos in an endless cycle of birth and death.

This appears to be the reason why the Jesuit missionaries accused the followers of Shaka's ultimate doctrine of asserting "that nothing exists except birth and death" (DocJ 1:667). Once again they appear to have interpreted Paulo's explanations about *samsara* (Jap. *shōji* 生死; literally, "birth-and-death") in Arlecchino-style: "This sect of the contemplators is the one which holds that there is nothing beyond being born and dying" (p. 666). For the missionaries this signified that Zen adepts reject the notion of paradise and hell in the yonder and believe only in the present life between birth and death. They saw proof of this in Paulo's explanation that Zen followers interpret "Jomdo" (Jap. *jōdo* 淨土, Pure Land) not as a concrete place but merely as a state of mind in this world characterized by "the absence of joy and sadness as well as any thought about good and evil" (p. 666). These "contemplators" reportedly aim at becoming a *hotoke*, that is, "an accomplished man in the sense of a being that neither lives nor dies nor feels" (p. 666). The meditation sect's belief that "there is nothing beyond being born and dying [que não hay nada mais que nacer e morrer]" (p. 666) thus echoes Shaka's immanentist, materialist initial and ultimate teaching which "states very clearly that there exists nothing other than matter composed of four elements" (p. 664).

Although neither the 1556 *Sumario* nor Nunes's 1558 letter saw publication until modern times, they played important roles in the missionary venture. Nunes was convinced that *hōben*, that "useful and holy lie" ("utile sanctumque mendacium") of the Buddhists, had also poisoned the Japanese vocabulary since words can have both an exoteric meaning for the people and an esoteric one for initiates (DocJ 2:109–10). He realized that the missionaries' ignorance of the "esoteric" significance of Japanese words had already led to terrible mistakes. The study of Buddhism thus became a crucial part of mission reform. Based on such newly gained insights, the missionaries instituted the use of "*deus* instead of *hotoke* and *anima* or *spiritus* instead of *tamashii* (soul)" (p. 112). Many Buddhist terms whose meaning the missionaries had hitherto ignored were blacklisted and replaced by "safe" Portuguese words. Thus the Japanese Christians had to learn that *Dios* rather than Amida is joined in the *paraiso* by his *sanctos, beatos, apostolos, confessores,* the *virgen* and of course also by the *animas* of men equipped with *fides* in the *divina graça* who regularly examine their *consciencia* and partake of the *santa eucharistia* while exerting themselves to the point of *martyrio* for the *gloria* of the *sancta ecclesia.*[21]

While these events were causing much commotion in the Japan mission during the 1550s, an old companion of Anjirō was patiently waiting in India for the call to join the Japan mission: Luís FRÓIS (1532-1597). In his function as Nunes Barreto's secretary, this gifted Portuguese Jesuit was well informed about the Japan mission's vexing problems. He had, among other things, organized the copying and transmission to Europe of Japan-related materials such as the 1556 *Sumario* (DocJ 1:743). Furthermore, after his arrival in Japan in 1563, Fróis had benefited from an eight-month crash course in Japanese language and culture from his old pal Juan Fernández while the two sat out a war on a small Japanese island. Fernández was at that time the best foreign speaker of Japanese and the mission's expert on Japanese religions who had played key roles, first as Torres's interpreter and subsequently as intermediary between Torres, Nunes Barreto, and Paulo Chōzen.

After this intensive introduction, Fróis collaborated closely with Japanese converts such as the half-blind bard Lourenço and later the knowledgeable doctor Paulo Yohō (see next chapter). In time he became an expert in all things Japanese whose detailed letters were

---

21 The words in italics along with many additional terms (see Schurhammer 1928:99-102) had to be used by Japanese Christians after the language reform based on Paulo Chōzen's revelations. Many of them replaced pre-reform Buddhist terms.

read with much interest throughout Europe. His letter of June 12, 1567 shows an interesting development in the Jesuit view of Zen doctrine ten years after the *Sumario*. Calling Zen the teaching that "the major part of the noblest and principal people of Japan follow" (Cartas 1598:240r), Fróis reports that the "Ienxûs" (Zen followers) possess magnificent monasteries with hundreds of monks as well as "extremely eloquent books written in a more elevated style than all the others"—books that only people "very versed in letters and familiar with the literature of China" could understand (p. 240r).[22] According to Fróis, these sectarians constantly meditate about "the first cause of the universe," spend several hours every day concentrating on problems posed by their superiors,[23] and often continue to do so for fifteen or even twenty years (p. 240r).

Fróis's 1567 interpretation of *honbun* differs substantially from Nunes's "chaos" and "materia prima" of 1558. According to Fróis, Zen adepts believe in an invisible and non-physical being called "Fombum" that is also called "Fonrai come mogui" (Cartas 1598:241r). We have seen that in Zen parlance the word *honbun* 本分 refers to the "gist" of their teaching (see note 16). But Fróis was convinced that his Japanese interlocutors discussed what was most important to him as a Christian missionary, namely, God. Hence he regarded *Fombum* or *Fonrai nome mogui* (whose meaning he did not explain) as the God of Zen. From the point of view of the Japanese Zen adepts, however, there was of course no God in play. Rather, they are likely to have explained to the Jesuits that the fundamental purport and basis (*honbun*) of their teaching consists in awakening (*satori*) to one's "original face" (*honrai no menmoku* 本來の面目 – Fróis's "Fonrai nome mogui") or "Buddha nature" (*busshō* 佛性 – Fróis's "Buxon"). Understandably, Fróis's Arlecchino-style interpretation

---

22  During the Muromachi period, major Zen monasteries (the so-called *gozan* 五 山 or Five Mountains) and monks played an important role in introducing Chinese literature and philosophy to the educated class of Japan. See Collcutt 1981.

23  This is one more reference to *koans*.

of the "gist" (*honbun*) of Zen teaching caused consternation among Kyoto's Christian converts who "wanted to know if Deos is the same as Fombum" (p. 241r).

Fróis's assertion that there is a Japanese sect (namely, the Zen sect) that worships "an eternal principle without beginning or end" evoked a substantial echo in Europe.[24] He claimed that the followers of this sect believe this principle to have "existed before the creation of the world, heaven, and earth" and that it had "created all things." This principle is also said "to govern and maintain all things" and to be the ultimate "source of all the perfections, good, and virtues that man and all other creatures possess" (p. 241r). In spite of such impressive qualities, however, these sectarians assert that it shows "no movement whatsoever" and "lacks a heart [cor]." Zen's "God" thus appeared to be "infinitely impassive" (p. 241r): an eternal first principle that created the world yet is in no way involved in it and remains in torpor.

This portrayal of Zen's "first principle" impressed not only Fróis's superior Valignano but also numerous later authors including Athanasius KIRCHER (1601–80) who quoted the entire passage from Fróis's letter in his *China illustrata* of 1667, thus lending it his megaphone exactly one hundred years after Fróis's missive:

> Jenxus [the Zen sect] has an invisible and subtle aspect not dependent on the elements of the physical world. This is called Fonrai Come Mongui. The wise men also say that he has attributes different from that invisible aspect. They say that Fombum has always existed and that he will have no end. He was created for himself alone. His being fills the earth and sky and he occupies everything physical to show his immensity in the infinity of his essence. They assure us that he doesn't work hard to govern his creatures. Without any difficulty he

---

24  See for example Cristoforo Borri's and Giovanni Filippo de Marini's portrayals of the Buddha's deathbed scene in Chapter 10. De Marini was one of Athanasius Kircher's main informants.

contains them in his own being. They say that he had no quality or color which can be seen by people. Finally, this Fombum has a thousand rare perfections and is the source of every good thing. (Kircher 1987:133)

# Chapter Five

# VALIGNANO'S LECTURES AND CATECHISM

W hereas the missionaries regarded the language reform after 1556 as a victory against the devil, the Japanese Christians were confused by the newly introduced Portuguese and Latin vocabulary. For reasons explained in previous chapters, representatives of various Buddhist denominations had initially shown much sympathy for the missionaries from *Tenjiku*, the motherland of Buddhism. In 1555 Duarte da Silva reported that the bonzes kept claiming that "the law of Deos and the sects of Japan are all one" ("a ley de Deos e as seitas do Japão eram todas huma"; DocJ 1:523), and five years later the Japanese brother Lourenço wrote:

> Those of the Shingon sect say that what we preach is their Dainichi; those of the Zen sect say that it is the honbun[25] which they assert, meditate on, and seek to know; those of the Hokke sect say it is the myō they preach;[26] for the Pure Land sect it is Amida; and the Shinto sect says it is the Kokuzo[27] they believe in. (DocJ 2:274)

The Arlecchino effect was obviously at work not only for the Jesuits but also for the Japanese: each group detected in the other what it was already familiar with. For the missionaries, Japan's religions (as

25 In reading "Fonbum" rather than "Fonbem" I follow the Coimbra Cartas text given in Bourdon 1993:269 instead of DocJ 2:274.

26 Myō 妙 (wondrous) is the first letter of the *Myōhō rengekyō* (Lotus Sutra of the Wondrous Dharma), the main scripture of the Hokke (Nichiren) sect.

27 For various identifications of this "Cocujo" or "Coquio" see Bourdon 1993:269, DocJ 2:274n, and Schurhammer 1923:106-7.

portrayed by Anjirō) had at first seemed planted by the very hand of the Judeo-Christian God; but now they appeared as intricate ruses of the devil. This mirrored their black-and-white worldview: it's us or them, salvation or eternal damnation, truth or lies. The Japanese, on the other hand, were far more accommodating; after all they had for a long time identified native gods (*kami*) as Buddhist bodhisattvas.[28] For example, the Kokuzo mentioned by Lourenço as a Shinto deity was worshiped not only as the Shinto Lord of the Land (enshrined in the sanctuary of Izumo) but also as a Buddhist Bodhisattva personifying wisdom and compassion (Kokuzo Bosatsu, one of the twenty-five Bodhisattvas).

This accommodative or syncretistic tendency found expression in a conversation between a Buddhist priest and Jesuit brother Lourenço:

[The Buddhist priest asked:] "What do you think of the most holy Shaka who is venerated and famous in all the regions of Japan, China, and Siam?"

[Lourenço] the Jesuit replied: "It seems to me that he was a mortal man like all of us and a creature, fashioned by the creator of heaven of earth. Who do you think this creator was?"

[The Buddhist priest] retorted: "This creator has many names. In China he is called Hangonowō[29] and in Japan Izanami Izanagi,[30] the first man and the first woman in this world; and in Siam, where the law originally came from, they say there is another creator." (Fróis 1926:90)

---

28  Only after the Meiji reform (1868) and on the background of imperialist ideology were Japanese sanctuaries required to register either as Shinto or Buddhist. See Ketelaar 1987.

29  This is a Japanese transliteration of Pangu 盤古(の王), the creator of the universe in Chinese myth.

30  The counterparts in Japanese myth of Adam and Eve.

From the Japanese perspective it was also reprehensible that these black-robed Buddhist monks from India—who of course must have taken the precepts—ate animal flesh. A Japanese thus accused a missionary:

> Even though it is strictly forbidden in all sects and orders of Japan for bonzes to eat any kind of meat or fish, the [Jesuit] Father usually not only partakes of pork and the meat of deer but even—and this is an even graver infraction [of Buddhism's monastic precepts]—of the meat of oxen, cows, horses, and dogs as well as all kinds of impurities that men abhor. (p. 92)

The more the Jesuits studied the Japanese language and the more they reformed their vocabulary based on their study of Buddhism, the clearer it became to the Japanese clergy that these monks from Tenjiku are heretics intent on destroying the Buddha dharma rather than (as the Yamaguchi edict had proclaimed and many faithful had initially believed) promoting it. And had some of them not instructed their followers to burn Buddhist statues?

Though the translation of Christian doctrine into "neutral" Japanese terms was a hazardous enterprise, the translation of Buddhist doctrines into a conceptual framework that a Westerner could understand was imperative. The missionaries needed again someone of the caliber of the much-regretted Paulo Chōzen who had died in 1557. The Japanese brother Lourenço, a former itinerant bard, was eloquent but half blind (Schurhammer 1982:4.230). But in the 1560s a well-educated Japanese doctor was baptized and showed extraordinary piety and devotion: Paulo YOHŌ or Yohōken (1509/14–96). He was prized for his profound knowledge of Japanese as well as Chinese literature. After his conversion he accompanied various Jesuit missionaries for almost twenty years and assisted them not only as a gifted preacher but also as co-author of grammars and copy editor of translations (p. 95). Paulo's son Vicente TŌIN, also a doctor, possessed equal gifts and was much praised for his deep familiarity with Japanese sects in general and Zen doctrine in particular.

When Alessandro VALIGNANO (1539–1606) arrived in Japan on his first inspection tour (1579–1582) as supervisor of all Jesuit missions in Asia, he was fortunate to gain the help of this father-and-son team (who for simplicity's sake I will henceforth call the Tōins). It was one of Valignano's primary objectives to open schools in order to form Japanese novices and offer promising young men a solid Christian education. For this enterprise, and for the conversion of upper-class Japanese such as strongman Toyotomi Hideyoshi's secretary Ai (who was baptized in 1583 just after Valignano's departure), Valignano was in need of solid information about the religions and philosophies of Japan and grateful for the help of the Tōins. Valignano admitted them to the Jesuit order in December of 1580 (Cieslik 1981:359) after delivery of their report in the course of 1580. This report was first used in a lecture course for Western and Japanese novices in January of 1581. Since Valignano "did not know Japanese"[31] we must assume that Luís Fróis (probably with the help of these Japanese informants) first made a Portuguese translation of the original Japanese report. This information was then used by Valignano as the basis for his lectures (and eventually for his catechism). These lectures were presumably held in Portuguese; but the presence of Japanese novices and assistants necessitated a Japanese translation. For this, Valignano's interpreter Fróis is likely to have collaborated with knowledgeable Japanese such as the Tōins who were familiar with Buddhist thought and terminology. At the time of Valignano's 1581 lectures there were thus in all probability at least four sets of new documents: ① The Japanese Tōin report about the country's religions; ② its Portuguese translation; ③ Valignano's Portuguese lecture manuscripts; and ④ their Japanese translation.

Valignano's Portuguese lecture manuscripts ③ and their Japanese translation ④ were designed for the instruction of both Western and Japanese pupils and novices and used at the newly constructed Je-

31 This judgment stems from João Rodrigues who knew Valignano very well and had served as his interpreter; see Schurhammer 1932:38.

suit *seminarios* and colleges around Japan's imperial capital Kyoto. In the spring of 1581 Vicente Tōin was among the first teachers at the brand-new Jesuit schools in Azuchi and Kyoto. As one of the authors of the original report on Japanese religions he was supremely qualified to lecture on this topic, and he had at his disposal not only the original Japanese report ① but also a Japanese translation of Valignano's lectures on Japanese religions ④. Japanese student notes ⑤ from Vicente's lectures found their way into the hands of the government official Ai ⑥ who in 1583, when Vicente Tōin still lectured around Kyoto (p. 361), was preparing for baptism. It remains unclear, however, how the Jesuit mission documents (including the Japanese lecture notes) and Ai's papers ended up in the ⑦ folding screen in Evora, Portugal (see Chapter 1).

The Portuguese lecture manuscripts ③, on the other hand, were subsequently used by Valignano for the Latin redaction of the catechism text ⑧ that in 1586 got printed in Lisbon and appeared under the title of *Catechismus christianae fidei* ⑨. This catechism was published without the knowledge of Valignano, who at the time was in India, and it clearly was not written with a European public in mind. Its entire structure and content leave no doubt that its purpose was to equip Japanese pupils, novices, and preaching assistants as well as European missionaries with a toolkit for the refutation of native religions along with a custom-made presentation of the Christian alternative.[32] The reliability of the information about Japanese religions was thus crucial, and the presentation's content suggests that the lawyer and theologian Valignano had in preparation for the 1581 lectures ordered his Japanese collaborators to gather reliable information from foundational texts. His intention was not to create straw men to shoot at but rather to offer a strictly rational and

32  In those days, the term "catechismus" was ordinarily used for catechetical writings based on natural theology, whereas "doctrina" was based on revelation. See Standaert 2001:608. However, sometimes "catechisms" (for example Ruggieri and Ricci's first Chinese catechism of 1584) contains both.

reliable presentation of the core religious teachings of Japan in order to use it as basis for a devastating refutation.

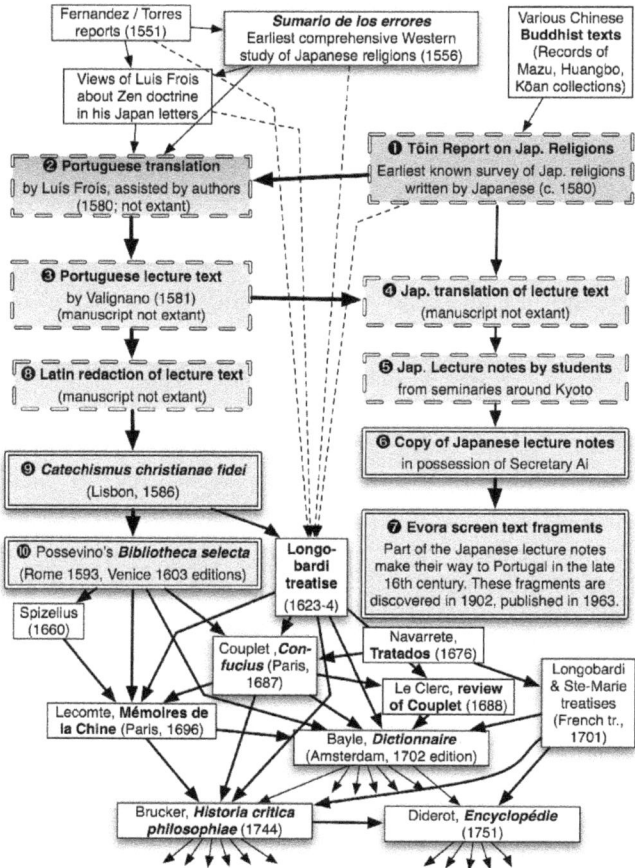

Fernandez / Torres reports (1551)

Sumario de los errores
Earliest comprehensive Western study of Japanese religions (1556)

Various Chinese Buddhist texts (Records of Mazu, Huangbo, Kōan collections)

Views of Luis Frois about Zen doctrine in his Japan letters

❶ Tōin Report on Jap. Religions
Earliest known survey of Jap. religions written by Japanese (c. 1580)

❷ Portuguese translation by Luís Frois, assisted by authors (1580; not extant)

❸ Portuguese lecture text by Valignano (1581) (manuscript not extant)

❹ Jap. translation of lecture text (manuscript not extant)

❽ Latin redaction of lecture text (manuscript not extant)

❺ Jap. Lecture notes by students from seminaries around Kyoto

❻ Copy of Japanese lecture notes in possession of Secretary Ai

❾ Catechismus christianae fidei (Lisbon, 1586)

❿ Possevino's Bibliotheca selecta (Rome 1593, Venice 1603 editions)

Longobardi treatise (1623-4)

❼ Evora screen text fragments
Part of the Japanese lecture notes make their way to Portugal in the late 16th century. These fragments are discovered in 1902, published in 1963.

Spizelius (1660)

Couplet , Confucius (Paris, 1687)

Navarrete, Tratados (1676)

Longobardi & Ste-Marie treatises (French tr., 1701)

Le Clerc, review of Couplet (1688)

Lecomte, Mémoires de la Chine (Paris, 1696)

Bayle, Dictionnaire (Amsterdam, 1702 edition)

Brucker, Historia critica philosophiae (1744)

Diderot, Encyclopédie (1751)

FIG. 7: THE TRANSMISSION OF THE TŌIN REPORT AND VALIGNANO'S CATECHISM (broken lines indicate inferred or lost manuscripts)

What I have earlier called "the Rosetta stone" texts for this study— the Japanese text fragments ⑦ in the Evora folding screen and ⑨ the published Latin catechism of 1586—permit our examination of the manner in which native information was understood and transformed by the missionaries. This is of major interest because of the Latin catechism's huge yet hitherto entirely ignored impact on Europe's perception of Asian philosophies and religions that will be explored in this book. Republished as part of Possevino's *Bibliotheca selecta* (1¹593, ²1603) ⑩, Valignano's *Catechismus* became a textbook for generations of missionaries as well as young Europeans studying at Jesuit colleges. Among the latter was Pierre Bayle who made extensive use of it in his bestselling *Dictionnaire critique* of 1702 (see Chapter 17). Thus relatively obscure mission materials from faraway Japan burrowed their way into European public consciousness and ended up furnishing major building blocks for the invention of "Oriental philosophy."

Since it was Valignano who commissioned the compilation of information about Japanese religions and defined its aims, the introductory part of his catechism ⑨ helps us understand what he wanted from the authors of the Tōin report. After underlining the importance of rationality in the preface (Valignano 1586:2r-3r), Valignano begins his first lecture ("concio") with a set of questions that he considers of primary importance for all humankind because they concern the right way to live: Whether there is a creator and author of the world who cares about his creation, administers it, guarantees that the good get remunerated and the evil punished, and hands out rewards and punishments in the present and future life (pp. 3v-4r). Valignano points out that the general interest of this inquiry is apparent from the great amount of pertinent writings in many languages (p. 3v) and from the general agreement of all peoples that there must be "a single, first, and supreme principle of all things" ("vnum primum, & summum rerum omnium principium"; p. 4r).

Valignano then defines the main areas of disagreement. They concern (1) the nature of the first principle; (2) the relationship of the first principle to all things; (3) the ultimate end of man and whether a future state follows the present life; (4) whether the creator of everything has providence, is involved in human matters, and watches over man's actions; and (5) whether acts in this life are rewarded or punished in the present life and a future state (p. 4r). The missionary then points out that the Japanese sects often disagree among themselves and hold such confused and changing opinions about these questions that it is difficult to figure out what they truly believe (pp. 4r-v). However, according to Valignano they all agree about one thing: "*Gonjit*,[33] which means 'truth' and 'the appearance of truth,' i.e. the true and the apparent" ("veritatem, et veritatis speciem, id est verum, & apparens," p. 4v). This distinction between "outer" expedient teachings for the common people and "inner" genuine teachings for the initiates, which will be further discussed below, was for Valignano the key to understanding Japanese religions. He accordingly divided these sects and their practitioners into two main categories: those who follow the outer "seemingly true teachings" (Jap. *gonkyō* 權教) and those who adhere to the inner "genuinely true teachings" (Jap. *jikkyō* 實教). Naturally, much of Valignano's effort is devoted to the presentation and refutation of these so-called "true" teachings, and it is this portrayal that interests us most because it furnished crucial building blocks for the European invention of Oriental philosophy.

Before presenting and criticizing these inner or true teachings, Valignano briefly discusses the outer teachings that only have the appearance of truth (pp. 4v-5r). Their followers hold that *Xaca* (Shakyamuni), *Amida*, and other *Fotoque* (Jap. *hotoke*, buddhas) live happily in four parts of the world, engaged in their own affairs. After death, those who lived according to the laws of the *hotoke* reach these happy places, are reborn as *hotoke* in thirty different forms and

---

33 Jap. *gonjitsu* 權實: provisional and real. See also Chapter 3.

58

with eighty qualities, and live forever in happiness. However, women are not admitted even if they observe the *hotoke's* laws and cult.[34] They must be reborn as living beings because they are by nature detestable (p. 4v). Those who violate the laws of the *hotoke* are after death demoted to inferior realms of which there are said to be six (p. 4v).[35] There they undergo six kinds of punishments until they are liberated from their tortures (pp. 4v-5r). According to Valignano, the entire Japanese clergy is in agreement about the need to preach such things to the common people. But in their hearts these priests as well as educated laypeople believe in the inner doctrine, and some even despise provisional teachings and dismiss scriptures containing outer doctrines (p. 5r).

Though Valignano's portrayal of "outer" teachings featuring Shakyamuni and Amida, paradises and hells, rewards and punishments, transmigration, etc.[36] also found its way into seventeenth- and eighteenth-century European sources, it was his far more detailed description and refutation of the "inner" teachings that had the deepest impact. It consists of an initial overview (pp. 5r-6v) that will be analyzed in our next two chapters along with Valignano's summary of the four core "inner teachings" (pp. 6v-7r). In the *Catechismus christianae fidei* this summary is followed by the missionary's

---

34  In traditional Buddhism it was widely believed that only males can attain *nirvana* and that therefore women need to be reborn as males to achieve this goal.

35  This appears to be a reference not to different hells, of which there are many more in Buddhist lore, but rather to the six different paths or realms of transmigration (Jap. *rokudō* 六道, "six ways"): 1. beings in hell (Jap. *jigokudō* 地獄道); 2. hungry ghosts (Jap. *gakidō* 餓鬼道); 3. animals (Jap. *chikushōdō* 畜生道); 4. half-gods or ashuras (Jap. *ashuradō* 阿修羅道); 5. humans (*nindō* 人道); and 6. heavenly beings or devas (Jap. *tendō* 天道).

36  The three core "outer" teachings are refuted on pp. 34r-40v (the power of *kami*, and of *hotoke* like Shakyamuni and Amida), pp. 40v-42v (the Buddhist Pure Land and hells), and pp. 42v-44r (transmigration and future state).

extensive refutation of each core teaching.[37] The fact that almost half of the total volume of Valignano's work is taken up by this presentation and critique of Japanese religions shows its importance to the author; but it also indicates why a Christian catechism designed for Japanese novices and preachers could become such an influential source for the European discovery of Asian religions and philosophies. I regard Valignano's catechism as the record of the West's earliest encounter with Buddhist philosophy. Our study of this encounter is immensely helped by the fortunate preservation of the Evora fragments (see Chapter 1). These fragments, consisting of student's notes taken during lectures by Vicente Tōin, contain original Japanese terminology. They permit the identification of a number of textual sources and allow us to study the translation process at the heart of this first systematic attempt by Europeans to come to terms with Buddhist philosophy.

---

37  The first main "inner" teaching is refuted on pp. 7r-18r, the second on pp. 18r-23v, the third on pp. 24r-34r, and the fourth on pp. 43v-44r.

## Chapter Six

## BUDDHIST PHILOSOPHY

Though the sheets found in the Evora screen only represent a small part of Brother Vicente's lectures about Japanese religions, they fortunately contain much of the initial presentation and critique of the "outer" and "inner" teachings—that is, precisely those sections of Valignano's presentation that were to elicit the most interest in Europe. In this chapter I will present a number of Chinese sources that Valignano's informants ostensibly relied upon. Their identification became possible because of the technical vocabulary of the Evora fragments. All of these sources are written in classical Chinese and can be considered representative of eighth- and ninth-century Chan (Chinese Zen) literature. Due to their clarity and brevity, they even today are favorites for introducing students to Zen doctrine.

The nature of these texts suggests that Valignano, a lawyer fond of reliable evidence, in 1580 asked Japanese informants and his interpreter Luís Fróis to furnish detailed and reliable information in order to gain a solid basis for his presentation and critique of Japan's "inner" doctrines. We know that in 1574, seven years before Valignano's lectures, Luís Fróis and Organtino Gnecchi-Soldo had devoted two hours per day to the study of the Chinese text of the *Lotus Sutra* under the guidance of a former Buddhist abbot and persisted for an entire year (Fróis 1926:452). In view of such a protracted effort, a translation for Father Visitor of a few short and far less complex texts with the help of Japanese experts such as the Tōins seems possible. Be this as it may, today we only have the Latin catechism and the Japanese Evora fragments at our disposal and must follow any hints they can provide.

The catechism's statement that philosophers such as "Coxiroxi" call the first principle "Quiobunodaido" (Valignano 1586:5v) contains such a hint. It leads to the first and arguably most important Chinese source: the *Yuanrenlun* 原人論 ("Inquiry into the Origin of Humanity") by the Chinese Zen and Huayan master Guifeng ZONGMI (圭峰宗密, 780–841). A century ago this Chinese Buddhist text was first published in a Western language (Haas 1909), and thanks to Peter Gregory (1995) it even today serves splendidly as an introduction to Chinese Buddhist thought. Zongmi's short text happens to address the very themes that most interested Valignano: the origin of man and the question of the first principle. Additionally, the text's preface stresses the importance of the very distinction between provisional and ultimate teachings that Valignano called the key to understanding Japanese religion. While Zongmi regarded Confucius and Laozi, the founders of Confucianism and Daoism, as consummate sages like the Buddha, he criticized their teachings as "just provisional" (Gregory 1995:74) and specified: "The two teachings of Confucianism and Taoism hold that human beings, animals, and the like are all produced and nourished by the great Way of nothingness" (p. 83). This "nothingness" charge was often raised by Buddhists against Daoism, but applying it simultaneously to Confucianism is a characteristic feature of Zongmi's short text. The Evora fragments show that the Latin catechism's "Coxiroxi" (Valignano 1586:5v) refers to Kōshi (Ch. Kongzi 孔子; Confucius) and Rōshi (Ch. Laozi 老子; Lao-tse) and that their common principle, which Valignano calls "Quiobunodaido," is what Zongmi called the "great Way of emptiness and nothingness" (Jap. *kyomu no daidō* 虚無大道).

Significantly, Zongmi bases his entire doctrinal classification of Confucianism, Daoism, and various forms of Buddhism on the distinction of provisional and ultimate teachings. Whereas Confucians and Daoists cling to provisional teachings as if they were ultimate

(Gregory 1995:87), Buddhists make use of both provisional and ultimate doctrines and have a highest teaching that "directly reveals the true source" (Ch. *zhixian zhenyuan* 直顯眞源). This teaching that "reveals the nature" (p. 177) is called "the true teaching of the ultimate meaning of Buddha" (佛了義實教). The nature that is directly revealed through awakening is called "true mind" (眞心), "Buddha-nature" (Ch. *foxing*, Jap. *busshō* 佛性), and "womb of Buddhahood" (Ch. *rulaizang* 如來藏, Jap. *nyoraizō*). Zongmi describes it as follows:

> The Teaching of the One Vehicle that Reveals the Nature holds that all sentient beings without exception have the intrinsically enlightened, true mind. From [time] without beginning it is permanently abiding and immaculate. It is shining, unobscured, clear, and bright ever-present awareness. It is called both the Buddha-nature and the tathāgata-garbha. ... The great enlightened one [i.e., the Buddha] took pity upon them and taught that everything without exception is empty. He further revealed that the purity of the numinous enlightened true mind is wholly identical with all Buddhas. (p. 178)

As Table 3 shows, the Evora fragments and Valignano's catechism describe this ultimate teaching in similar terms.

| English translation of Japanese text on the Evora screen (Valignano 1969:197; trans. Urs App) | Latin text of Valignano's Catechismus (Valignano 1586:5r-v) | English translation of Latin text of the Valignano Catechism (trans. Urs App) |
|---|---|---|
| This singular Buddha-nature 此一仏性, mind-Buddha, and sentient beings 衆生, all form One Mind 一心 without discrimination 無差別. | omnia item quaecunque sunt, quum dissoluuntur in vnum, & idem principium reuerti, quod ipsi dicunt *Ixin*, | Everything dissolves into and goes back to one and the same principle that they call *ishin*. |
| If one inquires about this singular Buddha nature 一仏性, [they say that] from the beginningless past it has manifested clearly. | quod fuit ab omni aeterniate vnum, clarum, & lucidum, | From all eternity [this first principle of all things] has been one, limpid, and luminous. |
| From ancient times to the present it has formed "a single numen that neither increases nor decreases" 不増不滅ノ一靈 and that always remains the same. | ab omni decremento, & incremento alienum, figura carens, | It knows neither decrease nor increase and has no form, |
| Utterly empty and tranquil 空々斎々, it is called "essence without thought or deliberation" 無念無想ノ本体. | ratiocinationis expers, vitam agens otij, quietis, & tranquillitatis plenißimam. | lacks reasoning, lives in idleness, and is quiet and full of tranquility. |

TABLE 3: BUDDHA NATURE AND VALIGNANO'S FIRST PRINCIPLE

This description of the first principle ("limpid and luminous," form-less, changeless, idle and tranquil without any activity and thought) will in the following be encountered again and again. The comparison of the Evora screen text with Valignano's catechism gives us a first taste of the translation effort involved. On the Sino-Japanese side the discussion turns around awakening to form- and timeless "Buddha nature" or "One Mind" from which everything arises and that is utterly beyond thinking and deliberation. In an introductory sentence that has no equivalent in the Latin catechism, the Japanese Evora text states that this is the realization attained "through the practice of seated meditation" (Jap. *zazen kufū* 坐禪工夫) by those who reject provisional explanations (Valignano 1969:197). In Valig-nano's catechism, Zongmi's "one Buddha-nature" and "One Mind" are understood in the Christian scholastic sense; but unlike the first principle of Christian theology, this principle is said to lack creative power, reasoning, and intelligence and is therefore without providence. Thus the enlightened mind with its tranquility and absence of discriminating thought—Zongmi's "empty tranquil awareness" that is "shining, unobscured, clear, and bright" (Gregory 1996:178–9)—was interpreted by Valignano and his readers as a first principle that, though "limpid and luminous," is characterized by a total lack of reasoning, by idleness, and by quietude. Valignano's description of this principle was extremely influential and destined to become a cornerstone of "Oriental philosophy" as it was repeated in countless Western sources. In the eighteenth century many authors were to cite Pierre Bayle's French translation of Valignano's argument:

> They maintain that there is only one principle of all things [...] It exists in all eternity, they add, and is unique, limpid, and luminous. Incapable of growing or diminishing, it has no form whatsoever, does not reason, and lives in idleness and perfect tranquility. (Bayle 1702:1628; see also Chapter 17)

The second Chinese Zen text whose identification appears possible on the basis of the Evora fragments stems from Pei Xiu 裴休 (791–864), a Chinese official of the Tang period who authored prefaces to several texts of Zongmi. After Zongmi's death in 841, this Chinese official became attached to Huangbo Xiyun 黃檗希運 (d. 850) who is known as the teacher of Master Linji Yiyuan 臨濟 義玄 (Jap. Rinzai), the founder of the largest branch of Zen Buddhism. In the mid-ninth century Pei Xiu had compiled notes from his conversations with master Huangbo in form of a short text titled *Quanxin fayao* 傳心法要 ("Essentials of the Teaching of Transmitting Mind").[38] It is all about the One Mind or *Ixin* (Jap. *isshin* 一心) that, according to Valignano, "forms the essence of separate things" and is the first principle of the Japanese doctrine. Pei Xiu's *Quanxin fayao* begins as follows:

> The Master said to me: All the Buddhas and all sentient beings are nothing but the One Mind, beside which nothing exists. From beginningless time this Mind is unborn and indestructible. It is not green nor yellow and has neither form nor appearance. It does not belong to the categories of things which exist or do not exist, nor can it be thought of in terms of new or old. It is neither short nor small, for it transcends all limits, measures, names, traces and comparisons. (Blofeld 1958:29; slightly amended)

In Huangbo's instructions the expression "your very mind is Buddha" (Jap. *sokushin sokubutsu* 即心即佛) is ceaselessly repeated. For Valignano, this "Soquxin, soqubut" formed the heart of the kind of meditation practiced by adepts of the "inner" or "real" teaching (1586:5r):

---

38 This text was translated into English by Blofeld (1958); for better translations see the Japanese rendering by Iriya (1969) and the French translation by Carré (1985).

| Valignano's Catechismus (Valignano 1586:5r) | English translation (Urs App) |
|---|---|
| Inter eos nonnulli sunt, qui praedictam de extrinsecus apparenti rerum specie, opinionem profitentur, | Among them there are many who differ from those who adhere to the above-mentioned appearance-based outer view of things. |
| alij tamen eam sententiam praetermittunt, & negligunt: suumque omne studium, & operam collocant in meditando, abijcientes omnem prorsus disciplinam, quae in verbis, & sermone consistit: | Some even make light of texts and neglect all study of them. Their practice consists in meditating, and they reject all practice involving words and sermons. |
| huic sese totos exercitationi addicunt, & dedunt, quam suo proprio vocabulo *Soquxin, Soqubut* vocant, quod significat cor, Paradisum, & infernos tollunt, hoc est beatam bonorum in coelis sedem, & sempiternam perditorum hominum apud inferos poenam. | They completely devote themselves to the exercise they call *Sokushin sokubutsu*, which means *heart*; and they reject paradise and hell, i.e., the happy realm of the righteous in heaven and the everlasting punishment of the damned in hell. |

TABLE 4: VALIGNANO ON ZEN PRACTICE

For masters like Huangbo and his teacher MAZU Daoyi 馬祖道一 (709–788), *sokushin sokubutsu* ("your very mind is Buddha") represented the core teaching of Zen. In Mazu's *Recorded Sayings*—the third text ostensibly used by Valignano's informers[39]—the beginning of the first instruction addresses this very theme:

> Each of you, be convinced that your own mind is the Buddha [*sokushin sokubutsu*]. This mind is the Buddha. The great master Bodhidharma came from South India to China to

---

39 The use of the *Records of Mazu* 馬祖語録 is indicated by expressions in the Evora fragments such as 森羅万像 ("the universe with its myriad phenomena"; Valignano 1969:197).

transmit the doctrine of the one mind of the Supreme Vehicle, so that you may become awakened. (Lievens 1987:85)

According to the official Pei Xiu, Mazu's disciple Huangbo also explained that Bodhidharma's doctrine is all about awakening to "pure Mind, which is the source of everything and which, whether appearing as sentient beings or Buddhas, or as rivers and mountains of this world," is absolutely free from "distinctions such as 'I' and 'other'" (Blofeld 1958:36, amended). By contrast, as Table 4 shows, for Valignano *sokushin sokubutsu* was linked to the dismissal of sacred texts, the rejection of the value of prayers and sermons, and most importantly to the denial of a yonder and thus of any punishment or reward in a future state.

Valignano was to some extent right about this, and the fourth short text inspiring his informers is extremely explicit in this regard. It is the *Bloodstream Treatise* (*Xuemailun* 血脈論) attributed to Zen's legendary founder Bodhidharma who, according to Mazu, had come to China precisely in order to spread the teaching of *sokushin sokubutsu*.

The Bodhidharma legend had the Indian monk arrive in South China in the year 475. Instead of proofs for the historical existence of this man, modern research has only uncovered evidence for the gradual growth and amalgamation of legends.[40] By the early ninth century, the major elements were finally in place: Bodhidharma was presented as India's twenty-eighth and China's first patriarch.[41]

This is where the ninth-century texts attributed to Bodhidharma come in. The *Bloodstream Treatise* features the twenty-eighth patriarch transmission line, and it completes the transformation of

40  See Faure 1986. John McRae's attempt to find, in the wake of numerous Japanese and Chinese researchers, a "historical kernel" of the Bodhidharma legend (McRae 2003) failed to produce anything beyond early traces of hagiographic legend.

41  See the introduction of Philip Yampolsky's study on the Sixth Patriarch's *Platform Sutra* (1967) for a summary of the genesis of this lineage scheme.

the colorless and somewhat pedantic meditation teacher of earlier "Bodhidharma" texts into a fiery orator with a compelling, radical message:

> Buddhas don't save buddhas. If you use your mind to look for a buddha, you won't see the buddha. As long as you look for a buddha somewhere else, you'll never see that your own mind is the buddha. Don't use a buddha to worship a buddha. And don't use mind to invoke a buddha. Buddhas don't recite sutras. Buddhas don't keep precepts. And buddhas don't break precepts. Buddhas don't keep or break anything. Buddhas don't do good or evil. To find a buddha, you have to see your nature. Whoever sees his nature is a buddha. (Red Pine 1987:11)

FIG. 8: BODHIDHARMA ON THE WAY TO CHINA (KAEMPFER 1906:221)

Such teachings from the ninth century became popular during the Song period (960–1279). In the twelfth century they already formed the doctrinal foundation of the earliest Japanese Zen movement, the Daruma sect (*Daruma-shū*, Sect of Bodhidharma) founded by Dainichi Nōnin 大日能忍), and subsequently also fed into the Rinzai and Sōtō branches of Japanese Zen.[42] The Bodhidharma of the *Xuemailun* is the prototype of "inner teaching" adepts whom Valignano describes as follows: "Some even make light of texts and neglect all study of them. Their practice consists in meditating, and they reject all practice involving words and sermons" (1586:5r). This was indeed taught in texts attributed to Bodhidharma, and the *Xuemailun* presents this with characteristic vigor:

> If you know that everything comes from the mind, don't become attached. Once attached, you're unaware. But once you see your own nature, the entire Canon becomes so much prose. Its thousands of sutras and shastras only amount to a clear mind. Understanding comes in midsentence. What good are doctrines? The ultimate Truth is beyond words. Doctrines are words. They're not the Way. The Way is wordless. Words are illusions. They're no different from things that appear in your dreams at night, be they palaces or carriages, forested parks or lakeside pavilions. (Red Pine 1987:31).

The Bodhidharma of the *Xuemailun* preaches precisely the doctrine that Valignano calls "*sokushin sokubutsu*, which signifies heart." Though the Jesuit missionary was, as we shall see, associating such teachings with early Greek philosophy and criticizing them based on Christian theology and scholastic philosophy, he understood that in this doctrine "the single first and supreme principle of all things"

---

42 The *Bloodstream Treatise* is included in both collections of Bodhidharma texts that were best known in Japan, the *Daruma sanron* 達磨三論 (translated into English by Red Pine [Bill Porter], 1987) and the *Shōshitsu rokumon* 少室六門. For the *Bloodstream Treatise*, the history of collections containing it, and their impact in Japan see Yanagida 2001:6.48–57.

is regarded as "the essence of separate things" and that "man's own heart does not differ at all from it" (Valignano 1586:5r). Founder Bodhidharma of the *Xuemailun* put it this way:

> Through endless kalpas without beginning, whatever you do, wherever you are, that's your real mind, that's your real buddha. 'This mind is the buddha' [sokushin sokubutsu] says the same thing. Beyond this mind you'll never find another buddha. To search for enlightenment or nirvana beyond this mind is impossible. ... You might think you can find a buddha or enlightenment somewhere beyond the mind, but such a place doesn't exist. (Red Pine 1987:9)

In his commentary on Zongmi's *Yuanrenlun*, Peter Gregory explains how much Indian and Chinese philosophy is packed into such seemingly simple statements. The very first phrase of the *Xuemailun* ("Everything in the entire universe goes back to the One Mind" 三界混起、同歸一心) would merit pages of commentary elucidating, for example, the connection to Yogacara idealism, to the doctrine of the *Lotus* and *Lankavatara* sutras, to the One-Mind teaching of the *Awakening of Faith*, and to early Chinese Zen texts. But here our focus must be on the translation of such notions into the mindset of Europeans who had not the slightest idea about all this. Familiar with Aristotle's critique of pre-Socratic Greek philosophers like Parmenides and Melissus, Valignano immediately detected the "absurd" monist doctrine of ancient Greece in Japan's esoteric doctrine. It holds that "the principle of everything is one and forms itself the nature and substance of things, such that all things have one and the same substance as the first principle" (Valignano 1586:18r). Valignano presents the teaching of Japan's adepts of the "inner" doctrine in similar terms (Valignano 1586:5r):

| Valignano's Catechismus (Valignano 1586:5r) | English translation (Urs App) |
|---|---|
| ... dicentes vnum esse principium rerum omnium primum, & summum: quod in rebus singulis inest: & tam ipsorum hominum cor, quàm reliquorum omnium intimum nihil ab eo principio differre: omnia item quaecunque sunt, quum dissoluuntur in vnum, & idem principium reuerti, quod ipsi dicunt *Ixin*. | They argue that there is only a single first and supreme principle of all things that is inherent in separate things; and both man's own heart and all other things do not differ at all from that principle. All that exists, whatever it may be, dissolves into one and the same principle that they call *isshin*. |

TABLE 5: THE ESSENCE OF THE ESOTERIC DOCTRINE OF JAPAN
(VALIGNANO 1586:5R)

Furthermore, these adepts claim that "in the other world they will all be reabsorbed into the principle of all things that they call *ichibusshō*" (p. 5v). For the Japanese, this term signifies "the one Buddha-nature" 一佛性. In Valignano's mind, however, it postulates an underlying unity and eventual resorption of all things into a kind of *materia prima*. He thus concluded that the Japanese adherents of the "inner" teaching lack the notion of an eternal soul that could undergo punishment or enjoy rewards after death. Such a doctrine had to lead to moral indifference, which is exactly what the missionary detected (p. 5v):

| English translation of Japanese text on the Evora screen (Valignano 1969:197; trans. Urs App) | Latin text of Valignano's Catechismus (Valignano 1586:5v) | English translation of Latin text of the Valignano Catechism (trans. Urs App) |
| --- | --- | --- |
| [They speak of the] non-duality of ordinary and holy 凡聖不二 and the oneness of right and wrong 邪正一如, and they say that "delusion is enlightened wisdom" 煩惱即菩提 and "samsara is nirvana" 生死即涅槃. | inter inscitiam, & sapientam nullum esse discrimen, inquiunt: & quum ad hoc inquirendum, & examinandum venitur, continuò dicunt, malum, & bonum non esse duo, inter prauum, & rectum nullam esse distantiam. | They say that there is no difference between ignorance and wisdom. To those who question them about this they further explain that good and evil are not two and that there is no distance between right and wrong. |

TABLE 6: MAHĀYĀNA NONDUALITY CONVERTED INTO MORAL INDIFFERENCE

These passages are particularly enlightening with regard to the translation process. The Evora fragment furnishes some examples of nonduality that are extremely common in Mahāyāna scriptures. Today we know that sutras popular in Zen circles such as the *Vimalakirti sutra*, the *Diamond Sutra*, and the *Lankavatara Sutra* are rich in statements that carefully distinguish non-duality from identity. They hail the highest, nondual wisdom (prajñāpāramitā) realized by the awakened ones, but they are by no means sanctioning the kind of moral indifference criticized by Valignano. This is clearly enunciated in the *Bloodstream Treatise*:

> People who don't see their nature and imagine they can practice thoughtlessness all the time are liars and fools. They fall into endless space. They're like drunks. They can't tell good from evil. ... Still others commit all sorts of evil deeds, claiming karma does not exist. They erroneously maintain that since everything is empty, committing evil isn't wrong.

Such persons fall into a hell of endless darkness with no hope of release. Those who are wise hold no such conception. (Red Pine 1987:19)

But since Valignano and his readers knew almost nothing about Mahāyāna Buddhism and its philosophy of nonduality, they could only shake their heads in disbelief that a religion would dare to teach that everything including man's soul simply melts back into "the common principle of things"—thus eliminating any possibility of reward and punishment in a future state— and even brazenly claim, as Bayle was to put it based on Valignano, "that knowledge is not at all different from ignorance; that evil and good are not distinct entities; and that one is not at all separate from the other" (Bayle 1702:1628). If this represents the "perfect glory of the *hotoke* [Buddha] and his successors," as Valignano claimed (1586:5v): could there then be any religion more worthy of condemnation?

Valignano's initial presentation of the "inner" doctrine of Japan shows that he was unaware of the philosophy behind *isshin* (One Mind) and *ichibusshō* (One Buddha-nature). Exactly how he interpreted what he learned will become clearer in the next chapter where his four-point summary of this doctrine will be presented. Though the Evora fragments reflect Valignano's take on things, their Buddhist terminology clearly shows that his Japanese informers were aware of the philosophical foundation of the texts they used for presenting One Mind or Buddha-nature as the ultimate source:

> Having realized that one's own nature is intrinsically the Buddha's state of mind [one understands that] the universe with its myriad phenomena comes from this one Buddha-nature and [that] mind-Buddha and sentient beings form One Mind without discrimination. If one inquires about this one Buddha-nature [they state that] from the beginningless past it has manifested clearly. (Evora fragment, Valignano 1969:197; translation from Japanese by U.A.)

Such teachings are based on the *tathāgatagarbha* doctrine of Mahāyāna Buddhism[43] that posits a "womb of Buddhahood" (Skt. *tathāgatagarbha*, Ch. *rulaizang* 如來藏)[44] as the ultimate ground of all phenomenal appearances and the perceiving mind. It is beyond the realm of subject-and-objecthood and all dualistic grasping, which is why it is often called "emptiness." Zongmi, the author of the *Yuanrenlun*, regarded this as the supreme doctrine and explained it as follows:

> This teaching says that all sentient beings possess the true mind of emptiness and quiescence, whose nature is without inception fundamentally pure. Bright, unobscured, astute, and constantly aware, it constantly abides to the end of time. It is called Buddha-nature; it is also called tathāgatagarbha and mind-ground. [Because] from time without beginning it has been concealed by false thoughts, [sentient beings] cannot realize it, and thereby experience birth and death. The Supremely Enlightened, feeling pity for them, manifests in the world to proclaim that all dharmas characterized by birth and death are empty, and to reveal the complete identity of this mind with all the Buddhas. (trans. Poceski 1992:20–21)

43  For descriptions of this doctrinal background of Zongmi's and early Chan teaching see Gregory 1991, 1995, and Poceski 2007.

44  See Ruegg 1969.

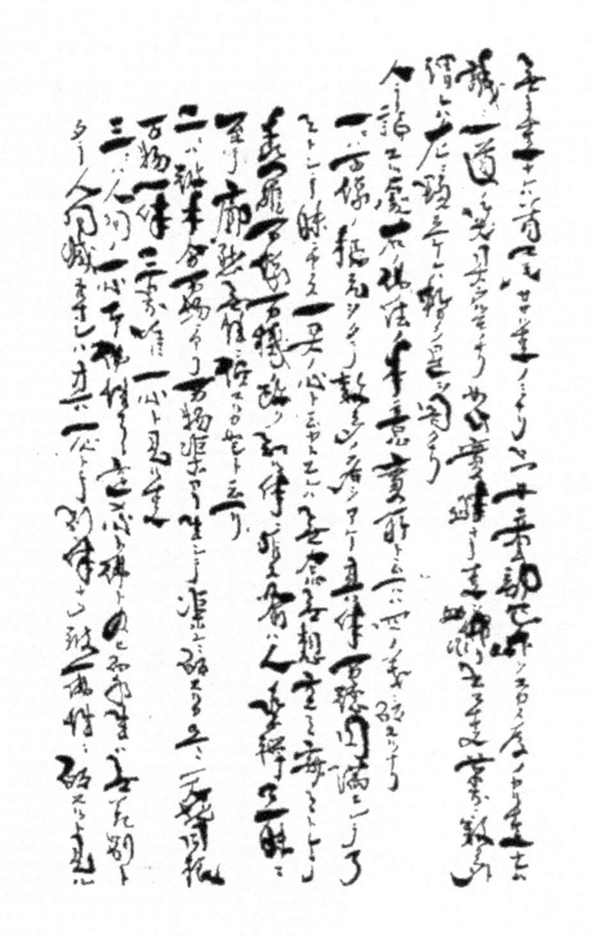

FIG. 9: EVORA FRAGMENT OF VALIGNANO'S MAIN POINTS REGARDING BUDDHISM'S INNER DOCTRINE (ITŌ 2000:166)

## Chapter Seven

## GOD'S SAMADHI

Valignano's four-point summary of Japan's "inner" doctrine is the most influential part of his presentation. It furnishes his answer to the questions posed in the introduction of the 1586 catechism, namely (1) whether this doctrine has a first principle corresponding to a creator God; (2) how it defines the relationship of this principle to all things; (3) whether it recognizes an immortal soul that is remunerated or punished in a future state; and (4) whether the first principle has providence and is involved in the world.

Though Valignano's Japanese informers had focused on One Mind and Buddha-nature as designations of the inner doctrine's first principle, they also mentioned other appellations (Valignano 1586:5r-v, 1969:197). Some of them clearly stem from Zen doctrine ("the protagonist" 主人公 and Master Linji's "true man without rank" 無位真人); but others represent general Buddhist doctrine ("the first principle of sacred truth" 聖諦第一義 and "the true form of suchness" 真如実相), Pure Land Buddhism ("Amida's genuine awakening of ten world-ages"), Shinto ("Kuni tokotachi no mikoto" 国常立尊) and, as mentioned above, Confucianism and Daoism ("the great way of emptiness and nothingness" 虚無大道). All of these designations are, according to Valignano, used for the same first principle. The character of this principle is described as follows in the first point of Valignano's summary of the inner teaching reigning in Japan:

| English translation of Japanese text on the Evora screen (Valignano 1969:197; trans. Urs App) | Latin text of Valignano's Catechismus (Valignano 1586:6v) | English translation of Latin text of the Valignano Catechism (trans. Urs App) |
| --- | --- | --- |
| [1] They posit a root-source 根元 of the myriad phenomena 万像 to which they give numerous names. | Primum est, secundum eam vnum esse primum rerum omnium principium, quod multis, & varijs nominibus appellant, vt etiam suprà diximus: | First: the first principle of all things is one, and it is referred to by many different names, as was also explained above. |
| They ascribe perfection and myriad virtues 万德円満 to this [root-source]. Though they call it a spiritual mind 一靈ノ心, | quod item principium aiunt esse omni ex parte perfectum, sapientia praeditum, | They say that this principle is in every way perfect and wise. |
| it is without thought and deliberation 無念無想, empty and aloof 空々斎々, and not involved in knowing and managing the world's myriad phenomena and functions 森羅万像万機, | sed nihil intelligens, eoque, in summa quadam quiete, & tranquillitate vitam traducat, nihil curans ea, quae in hoc mundo geruntur | But it does not understand anything and leads a life of complete quietude and tranquillity without caring about the affairs of the world, |
| just like someone who in seated meditation attains perfect concentration 坐禅三昧 and is "wide open and bare with nothing sacred" 廓然無聖. | instar hominis, qui quod acriter in rem vnam mentis aciem intendat, aliud non cogitat, nihil de reliquis aduertit. | just like someone who totally focuses his mind on a single thing, thinks of nothing but that, and pays no attention to anything else. |

TABLE 7: VALIGNANO'S VIEW OF EAST ASIAN "INNER" TEACHING'S FIRST PRINCIPLE

God's Samadhi

The closing phrase of this explanation in the Evora text gives away its Zen roots: "wide open and bare with nothing sacred" is one of the famous sayings attributed to Bodhidharma.[45] It forms part of a legendary exchange between Emperor Wu of the Liang dynasty (sixth century) and Bodhidharma in which the Indian sage informs the Chinese ruler that true merit consists not in striving for some petty reward but rather in "pure wisdom, marvelous and complete, whose essence is empty and quiescent." The famous dialogue ends as follows:

> The emperor then asked, "What is the first principle of sacred truth 聖諦第一義?" Bodhidharma replied, "Wide open and bare 廓然, there is nothing sacred [about it] 無聖."[46]

The phrase "without thought and deliberation" (Jap. *munen musō* 無念無想) is also frequently used in Zen texts and parlance, and the fact that the first principle is associated with perfect concentration (Skt. *samādhi*) achieved in seated meditation (Jap. *zazen sammai* 坐禅三昧) is a further sign of the Zen source of Valignano's information. What the Japanese tried to convey was a portrait of awakened reality unhampered by dualistic thought and clinging: "total clarity" without the least trace of sanctitude, and freedom from all attachment. In Zen parlance the realization of such clarity in which the ground and essence of everything becomes apparent is called awakening (Jap. *satori* 悟り).

45 The fact that the writer of the Evora fragment wrote "no nature" 無性 instead of "no holiness" 無聖 (as I corrected in the last section of Table 7) is one of the symptoms indicating that the Evora fragments are indeed based on lecture notes by a Japanese student. While the erudite lecturer Vicente Tōin certainly used the correct Chinese characters for this famous set phrase, the note taker must have been misled by the identical pronunciation (in Japanese both terms are pronounced *mushō*).

46 *Record of the Correct Lineage of Dharma Transmission* (*Chuanfa zhengzongji* 傳法正宗記), compiled in 1061. For the complete exchange see Taishō shinshū daizōkyō vol. 51, p. 742b27–c5.

Valignano, on the other hand, regarded this as a description of a dumb first principle and thus as a blatant contradiction. For a Christian theologian there was no question: God, the first principle, was omnipotent and omniscient by definition. Hence Valignano accused the Japanese "theologians" of being ignorant about the first principle and thought they have few dogmas worth discussing (Valignano 1586:7r). He found it "clearly ridiculous" that they would call their first principle "perfect" while maintaining that it "does not understand anything" (p. 7v). In his opinion the first principle had to be omniscient and the source of all perfection (p. 8r). If it "does not understand anything and lives in eternal quietude, like someone who does not think and comprehend," then it must be "like a stone or a rock" and thus a "stolid, stupid, and dumb principle" (p. 8v). Its lack of thinking also indicated to Valignano that this principle cannot be involved in the world and must be unaware of the difference between good and evil deeds. Hence it is in no position to apportion reward and punishment as befits its omniscience (p. 9r) and is deprived of the ability to create "our large, vast world that is so ornate and beautiful" (p. 9v). Valignano accused those holding such beliefs of regarding the world as a well-arranged house without a builder and householder, or as a ship without a captain (p. 10r). Their view thus left them unable to explain both the world's origin and its ultimate destiny (pp. 10v-11v).[47] All of this indicates, according to Valignano, that the inner doctrine with its thoughtless, idle, and aloof first principle is absolutely mistaken because the true first principle must by sheer logic be an omniscient, all-wise, om-

---

47 Valignano here refers to two of the four causes that Aristotle distinguished in his *Metaphysics*, the active cause (*causa efficiens*) and the final cause (*causa finalis*). The other two causes are the material cause (*causa materialis*) and the formal cause (*causa formalis*). Valignano had learned in his philosophy courses that God as the ultimate reason for all things should be referred to "only as the active and final cause" (Ricci 1985:87). The Japanese inability to explain the world's origin and destiny is blamed on their ignorance of God as the active and final cause of everything.

nipotent creator God (p. 12r). Valignano's God was by nature constantly involved in the world, watching and knowing everything—which is why the idea of a God lost in *samādhi* with a blank mind was an utterly revolting thought.

The second point of Valignano's summary addresses the relationship of the first principle to all beings.

| English translation of Japanese text on the Evora screen (Valignano 1969:197; trans. Urs App) | Latin text of Valignano's Catechismus (Valignano 1586:6v) | English translation of Latin text of the Valignano Catechism (trans. Urs App) |
|---|---|---|
| [2.] This very essence 彼本分 is present in all things 万物 and forms the pool 渠 from which everything is born and to which everything returns. They hold that "heaven and earth have the same root" 天地同根, that "all things are one" 万物一体, and that "the three realms are only One Mind" 三界唯一心. | Secundum est, hoc primum & summum rerum omnium principium in rebus singulis inesse: cum ipsisque suum esse communicat, ita vt res ipsae vniuersae cum illo primo principio sint idem: & in illud vnum principium cuncta, cùm finiuntur, & desinunt, revertantur. | Second: This first and supreme principle of all things is inherent in individual things and communicates its being to them in such a way that these individual things are identical with the first principle. As they form a unity with the one principle, they return to it when they end. |

TABLE 8: THE IDENTITY OF THE FIRST PRINCIPLE AND ALL THINGS

Valignano's theology dictated, in addition, that the creator had to be absolutely distinct from anything he created. To believe anything else was a sure path to idolatry, polytheism, pantheism, or even atheism. In philosophy courses, for which Jesuits of his generation used the Coimbra commentaries on Aristotle, he had read that Aristotle criticized Parmenides and Melissus for holding similar views about the oneness of everything.[48] In his catechism, Valignano mentions precisely these two philosophers as the main Greek exponents of the idea that "the principle of all things is one—which means that it also is the substance of things and their nature" (Valignano 1586:18r). The first principle of the Japanese, as Valignano understood it, is in essence identical with its productions. It is a monism with the "absurd" claim that "all things are one and the same thing, and that they are not many" ("res omnes eße vnam, eandemque rem, & non multas"), and that everything therefore has the same substance as the first principle (p. 18r). Valignano finds this notion of a single substance of all things absurd and combats it with some of the objections that had long been raised against Ionian monists and were a century later to be directed against Spinoza: it would imply that a horse is the same as a rock or that a house is identical with its architect, and so on (pp. 18v–19r). In Valignano's view, the creator of things is by necessity totally distinct from his creatures, just as a craftsman differs from his tools (p. 19v). Hence both an emanation from and a final resorption into the first principle are fundamentally mistaken notions (pp. 20r–v) that have their ultimate root in Japan's ignorance of the concept of efficient cause (p. 23r). Valignano's verdict about this second doctrine of Japan's "inner doctrine" is thus similar to the first: the true first principle can only be God, "the author and maker of everything, who created matter and the four elements that make up all bodies of nature, and fashioned these from nothing" (p. 23v).

The third point of the summary addresses the relationship between man and the first principle. If all things are one with the first principle, it follows that man's soul is also identical with the first principle. This was Valignano's understanding of *sokushin sokubutsu* ("your very mind is Buddha"). If the second main doctrine had reminded him of Greek advocates of monism, the third resembled the

---

48  *Commentariorum Collegii Conimbricensis Societatis Iesu, in octo libros physicorum Aristotelis Stagiritae* (Cologne ed. 1616:118–124)

teaching of some Pythagoreans and Stoics who taught that our soul forms part of a world soul and is at death reabsorbed into it:

| English translation of Japanese text on the Evora screen (Valignano 1969:197; trans. Urs App) | Latin text of Valignano's Catechismus (Valignano 1586:6v) | English translation of Latin text of the Valignano Catechism (trans. Urs App) |
| --- | --- | --- |
| [3.] They teach that man's one mind, as it is, is Buddha-nature 人間ノ一心即仏性, and that mind and Buddha 心ト仏 must not be discriminated 差別 from ordinary sentient beings 衆生. | Tertium est, intimum hominis cor esse vnam, & eandem rem cum illo primo rerum principio, | Third: the innermost heart of man is one and the same thing as this first principle of things. |
| When people die, their mind maintains no essence 則体; and though some say that it returns to Buddha-nature 仏性, they do not speak of rebirths 復生. | & cùm homines intereunt, ipsorum corda prorsus perire, & absumi, supereße tamen in eis illud primum principium, quod vitam ipsis anteà conferebat. | When people pass away, their hearts also completely perish and disappear; yet the first principle in them that had given them life persists. |
| and hold that after death neither pleasure nor pain await us. | Hinc consequitur secundùm hanc doctrinam non aliam huic vitae praesenti succedere: neque post hanc hominum vitam vllum esse benefacto-rum praemium, aut vllum malefactorum supplicium. | From this follows according to this doc-trine that there is no life after the present one, and that there is no recompense for the good or punishment for evildoers. |

TABLE 9: THE IDENTITY OF THE FIRST PRINCIPLE AND MAN'S HEART-MIND

The remark by a Zen monk that hell is right here in our present world and that there is nothing after death had already been communicated to Europe in the *Sumario de los errores* of 1556 (DocJ 1:666). Now such notions appeared as part of a coherent—though in Valignano's eyes of course mistaken—"world soul" rationale. If at death man's soul simply merges back into the world soul, there can be no recipient of recompense or punishment. The fact that some Zen adepts do not believe in heaven and hell after this life had already been noted in the earliest reports of 1551. In Valignano's presentation this tied in neatly with statements of Mahāyāna nonduality that he interpreted as a revolting ignorance of the distinction between good and evil: "[For them] there exists no difference between ignorance and wisdom. To those who question them about this, they further explain that good and evil are not two and that there is no gap between right and wrong" (Valignano 1586:5v).

The fourth and last point of Valignano's summary addresses a question that played a central role in medieval controversies about mysticism and had led to accusations of heresy against eminent mystics like Meister Eckhart. A century after the publication of Valignano's catechism it gained, as we will see in Chapters 12 and 13, renewed notoriety in the context of the disputes about quietism. At stake is whether man can, as some European mystics put it, achieve "union" with God in this life through contemplation and "mystical death," thereby becoming one with the first principle. Valignano formulates the fourth main tenet of Shaka's inner doctrine as follows:

| English translation of Japanese Evora text (Valignano 1969: 197; (trans. App) | Latin text of Valignano's Catechismus (Valignano 1586: 6v-7r) | English translation of Latin text of Valignano Catechism (trans. App) |
| --- | --- | --- |
| [4.] One must during this very life attain enlightenment, cut off the mind of delusion 妄心, and reach the state of buddhas and patriarchs 仏祖の果位. So one must be determined to reach the fruit of Buddhahood 本仏果 and practice by striving to reach perfect samadhi in seated meditation 坐禅三昧. | Quartum est, poße hominem in hoc seculo summum ipsum primi principij gradum, & locum adipisci, & tenere: ad amplißimam illius maiestatem, & dignitatem ascendere: eo quod poßit in hac vita meditando, & perfectè cognoscendo principium rerum ad summam illam vitae tranquillitatem, quam habet in seipso primum principium, peruenire: | Fourth: Man is capable in this life to attain the supreme degree and state of the first principle and to maintain it. He can ascend to that most ample majesty and dignity in this life by meditating. As he attains perfect knowledge of the principle of all things, he reaches the supreme quietude inherent in the first principle. |
| Unless one gets enlightened, one's deluded attachment 妄執 and transmigration 輪廻 will continue. | & hoc esse omne bonum, quod poßit homo consequi, & donec hoc adipiscatur meditando, & cognoscendo perfectè, continuo motu agitatur & ex vno inferno in alium subinde transfertur in nulla re quietem adeptus. | This is man's ultimate attainment; and unless he reaches this by meditating and knowing it perfectly, he will be constantly agitated and transferred from one hell to another, unable to find rest in anything. |

TABLE 10: UNION WITH THE FIRST PRINCIPLE IS ATTAINABLE IN THIS LIFE

For Valignano it is a "hallucination" to think that man, mortal and fallen as he is, can in this lifetime attain union with the supreme and first principle of all things, and he insists that no such perfection is possible on earth (p. 43v). As long as the soul is bound to a fragile, infirm, and mortal body, one can and must strive to love God and offer him appropriate worship; but "true tranquility" and perfection are only attainable in the future life "that consists in the clear vision of God and love" (p. 44r).

To summarize, Valignano presented the "inner" doctrine of Buddhism in form of four teachings that later came to be regarded as core features of "Oriental philosophy": (1) the existence of a first principle that is eternal yet lacks intelligence and remains aloof from the world; (2) the identity of this first principle with all things; (3) its identity with man's heart-mind; and (4) the attainability of perfection and of union with the first principle in this life through meditation.

Furthermore, Valignano asserted that the distinction between "inner" and "outer" doctrines is crucial. In his view, the outer doctrine is primarily concerned with traditional religious beliefs and activities such as ceremonies, recitation of prayers and sacred scriptures, worship of divinities, belief in heaven and hell, justice in the yonder, and so on. The inner doctrine, by contrast, is more philosophical and aims at explaining the first principle, its unity with everything, and the possibility of realizing this unity in one's lifetime through meditation practice. The heart of this inner doctrine is all-oneness.

Valignano's presentation of the "inner" teaching was predominantly based on the doctrine of the dominant form of Buddhism in the cultural centers of sixteenth-century Japan where Jesuits were active: Zen. The Evora fragments show that Valignano's informers consulted Chinese Zen texts whose philosophical outlook is shaped by Yogacara idealism and the "womb of Buddhahood" (*tathāgatagarbha*) doctrine of Mahāyāna Buddhism. As is to be expected, Valignano's religious and philosophical background played a decisive role in his appraisal. Ignorant of Buddhist philosophy, the European missionaries—again in classic Arlecchino manner—projected what they were familiar with onto the unfamiliar. Referring to Aristotle, Valignano interpreted the inner doctrine's "One Mind" and "Buddha-nature" from the standpoint of European scholasticism and criticized them as mistaken views of the First Principle akin to some Pre-Socratic doctrines rejected by Aristotle. His theology had no place for a thoughtless (Ch. *wunian* 無念) and inactive (Ch. *wuwei* 無為) first principle. The underlying unity of the first principle and the world (as in the Stoic notion of a world soul) was rejected because it disregards the distinction between the ultimate mover (creator) and the moved (created). Such doctrines were incompatible with Valignano's conception of an eternal God who willfully created the universe out of nothing. Instead of such a *creatio ex nihilo*, the Japanese appeared to believe in an eternal, all-encompassing substance resembling the *materia prima* criticized by European scholastics: formless, eternal prime matter. Like the ancient Greek and Roman philosophers who posited a chaotic *materia prima*, they seemed to think that everything unfolds out of a single substance and eventually merges back into it (see Chapters 4 and 11). This forms the philosophical background of Valignano's third point: the view of man's soul as consubstantial with the first principle, and death as resorption back into it. For the missionary this meant that adherents of the "inner doctrine" do not regard individual souls as immortal and consequently reject a future state with reward and punishment. Though Valignano explained this in much more detail, his view is in this respect fundamentally congruent with that of his predecessor Nunes Barreto as expressed in 1558 (see Chapter 4). The fourth doctrine with its seemingly Neoplatonic and mystical undertones—attainability of union with the first principle with true quietude of mind through contemplation—was also criticized on the grounds that it disregards the distinction between the creator and his creatures.

As mentioned above, Valignano's entire presentation and critique of the core teachings of Japan's "inner" doctrine in his *Catechismus christianae fidei* of 1586 was reprinted with minor changes in Antonio Possevino's *Bibliotheca selecta* (1593, 1603). In this form it reached a pan-European readership that included Pierre Bayle, the author of the bestselling *Dictionnaire historique et critique*.[49] But Valignano's vision also exerted more immediate influence on his subordinates in the Japan and China missions. Among them was a Jesuit whose writings on Asian religions and philosophies had a deep long-term impact: João Rodrigues.

---

49   The first edition of this work appeared in 1697 and the second in 1702. See Chapter 17.

# PART II

*Seventeenth Century*

.

# Chapter Eight

# ORIENTAL UR-PHILOSOPHY (RODRIGUES)

W hen Valignano in 1582 returned to Macao after his first three-year sojourn in Japan, Matteo RICCI (1552–1610) served for a brief period as Valignano's secretary before beginning his study of the Chinese language and joining Michele RUGGIERI (1543–1607), the first Jesuit China missionary. Valignano was at that time not only busy with reports about the Japan mission and his catechism but also with the redaction of a biography of Francis Xavier. In it he used an early report by Ricci about China. Valignano wrote:

> Concerning the religion and sects that they have—and they do have many of them—practically all are based on the same books of Xaca as the Japanese, who got them from China; but because the mandarins are given to letters, as I mentioned, and have by study and the light of reason [lumbre natural] understood the fabulations and lies of their sects, they hold them in very low esteem. (Valignano 1899:185)

For the given reason "the very great number of bonzes of diverse sects in China have neither the authority nor the power that they possess in Japan" (p. 185). If the mandarins "exhibit little faith in their idols," the common people praying to them in their homes and temples show not much more reverence as they punish these idols when they do not deliver (p. 185). "In the final analysis," Valignano concludes, "the principal idols they have are their mandarins whom they worship and revere with much more fear and respect than their idols" (p. 186).

FIG. 10: MANDARIN "WORSHIP" IN CHINA (DAPPER 1670:571)

Such observations led to the decision to have the missionaries thoroughly study the language of the mandarins and the imperial court—i.e. *guanhua* 官話 "which is among them like Latin for us"— in order to convert the king and his court and work from the top down (p. 186).

But the Chinese idolatry, and the "books of Xaca" on which all of its sects are purportedly based, were less easily disposed of than the Jesuits imagined. Their first Chinese catechism, the *Tianzhu shilu* 天主實錄 of 1584, was replete with Buddhist vocabulary, and history seemed to repeat itself: like the Japanese in the 1550s, the Chinese regarded the missionaries as Buddhist reformers. With good reason: the Jesuits called themselves "Buddhist monks" (*seng* 僧) from "*Tianzhu* 天竺" (India), dressed and shaved similarly to Buddhist clergy, and graced their first church with a door plate featuring the word *si* 寺 that the Chinese use for Buddhist temples.[50]

Of this first Chinese catechism of 1584 we have a handwritten Latin text[51] that differs substantially from the printed Chinese version (Gernet 1979). Among the significant differences is a section that has no counterpart in the printed Chinese text of the catechism. It is of particular interest because it signals the beginning of Ricci's and Ruggieri's study of Confucian texts and the emergence of Ricci's China mission strategy. This section of the Latin text is found in Chapter 7 of the manuscript where God's "three laws" are explained. The first is the "natural law" which "was not set down in written words but is inborn" and thus reigns in all nations on earth (Tacchi Venturi 1911: 1.519). This inborn law is what makes all peoples of our globe recognize by pure reason the existence of a single God, creator of all things, and the necessity of worshiping him. Furthermore, it teaches that man must not do unto others what he does not want others do to him (pp. 519–20). Hearing this explanation, the manuscript's Chinese interlocutor says: "I recognize that the second injunction has been transmitted in our books of Confucius, but I am not aware of any explanation [in the books of Confucius] about the first injunction [concerning the creator God and his worship]" (p. 520). The Christian teacher in this dialogue does not agree and suggests that "maybe he [Confucius] wanted to express this governing mind of heaven and earth by the word that you hold to signify 'heaven;' but I ignore if that is what he meant" (p. 520).[52] This last sentence forebodes the strategy that Ricci was going to adopt: the

---

50  This story requires separate treatment. For a recent survey of events and sources see Hsia 2010 and for the doorplate App 2010:20–1.

51  A transcription of this manuscript was published by Tacchi Venturi (1911: 1.498–540).

52  The printed Chinese text of 1584 (Standaert & Dudink 2002:52–53) contains none of this. It appears to be an addition to the Latin text from the later 1580s resulting from the Jesuit's early study of Confucian classics.

reinterpretation of ancient Chinese texts in order to present them as expressions of the "first law."

Another element of Ricci's strategy also stemmed from the early days of the China mission when Ricci was still collaborating with Ruggieri.[53] It is the claim that Buddhism was brought to China by mistake because the imperial embassy that imported Buddhism to China in the year 65 had in its search for true religion stopped short in India and failed to reach Judea.[54] The false religion of Indian origin that they brought to China bears the marks of ancient Greek philosophy such as Pythagoras's wrong notion of transmigration. Once ensconced in China, it caused the degeneration of ancient monotheism into idolatry and later the regrettable, Buddhism-influenced reinterpretation of ancient Confucianism by the Neoconfucians.

After Ricci and Valignano had recognized the grave problems of the first Chinese catechism, its printing plates were destroyed, and Ricci was ordered to write a better version focusing on the presentation and critique of Chinese views of the first principle. This necessitated Ricci's intensive study of Confucianism and Neoconfucianism as well as Buddhism and Daoism. The result was approved by Valignano and appeared in 1604 under the title *Tianzhu shilu* 天主實義: *The True Meaning of the Lord of Heaven* (Ricci 1985). Ricci clearly modeled his new catechism on the first part of Valignano's 1586 work and adopted his mentor's general line of argument. He also applied Valignano's 1586 critique of Buddhism to Daoist and

---

53 Rule (1987:10) mentions a similar scenario in a manuscript by Ruggieri, which means that this idea must have been conceived before 1589. According to Rule, Ruggieri writes that the golden youth seen in a dream by emperor Ming was really an angel announcing the birth of Christ to the Chinese, but the devil succeeded in preventing the legates from reaching Judea and diverted them to the land of idols.

54 In the scheme of three laws, Judea represents the second law conveyed by God to Moses and laid down in the Old Testament. The story of the mistake of the imperial embassy is told Ricci's published history of the Chinese mission (Ricci 1616:174–5) and the corresponding Italian original (Ricci 1942:123).

Neoconfucian conceptions of the first principle. While reinterpreting Chinese classics in line with his "first law" strategy, Ricci criticized Neoconfucian philosophers and their Buddhist mentors of having perverted Confucianism. Especially their doctrine "that man and all things in the universe are one" (Ricci 1985:225) is harshly criticized as "harmful to humanity and righteousness" (p. 231), and many themes and arguments familiar from Valignano's catechism are recycled and applied to Buddhism, Daoism, and Neoconfucianism. Among them is the critique of a first principle "devoid of intelligence and consciousness" (p. 117) for which the Chinese use "despicable [words like] 'voidness' and 'nothingness'" (p. 103). Ricci's 1604 catechism has the form of a dialogue between a Western and a Chinese scholar. Ricci makes the Chinese scholar characterize Daoism and Buddhism in the following manner:

> In our China there are three religions, each with its own teaching. Lao Tzu said: "Things are produced from nothing," and made "nothing" the Way. The Buddha taught that "the visible world emerges from voidness," and made "voidness" the end [of all effort]. (p. 99)

But the greatest problem of these sects is their shared belief that all things are one and form part of God—a notion that erases the fundamental difference between the creator God and his creatures. When the Chinese scholar states that it is possible "to say that the Lord of Heaven who is the Sovereign on High is within all things, and that he forms a unity with all things," the Western scholar throws a fit: "The error in what you have just said is greater than any I have previously heard you utter. How dare I hold a similar view? How dare I slight the dignity of our Sovereign on High in this fashion?" Was it not clearly stated in the Bible (called "the canonical writings of the Lord of Heaven") that such statements are "the arrogant words of the Devil, Lucifer"? (p. 203). This notion, which Ricci links to "canonical writings of the Buddha," is said to be not only contrary to the Bible but also to China's classics as interpreted by Ricci. Comparing it to Lucifer's rebellion against God, Ricci evokes the specter of a Buddhist rebellion against imperial authority:

> Because people do not ban the lying canonical writings of the Buddha they have become involuntarily infected with his poisonous words. Where in the teachings of the Duke of Chou and Confucius or in the ancient canonical writings of your noble country is there a person who cares to show disrespect to the sovereign or emperor and to insist that he is on an equal footing with him? (p. 205)

In a letter of 1609, the year before his death, Ricci openly described his strategy concerning Confucianism and the reinterpretation of Chinese classics:

> Your Reverence will have understood that in this kingdom there are three sects. One, the most ancient, is that of the literati who now as always have governed China; the other two [Buddhism and Daoism] are idolaters, although there are differences between them, who are continually under attack from the literati. Even though the [Confucian] literati do not set out to speak of supernatural things, in morals they are almost completely in accord with us. And so I commenced in the books I wrote to praise them [the Confucian literati] and to make use of them to confute the others [the Buddhists and Daoists], not directly refuting but interpreting the places in which they [the Confucian literati] are contrary to our faith. (Rule 1987:31)

Valignano's interpreter in Japan, João RODRIGUES (1561-1633), was among the early readers of Ricci's *True Meaning of the Lord of Heaven* after its delivery in Japan. Having arrived in Japan in 1577 at the age of sixteen, he was one of the Portuguese novices in Valignano's 1581 lecture course. At the turn of the seventeenth century he had already spent a quarter-century in the Far East and become—also thanks to the help of the Tōins—the best Western speaker, reader, and writer of Japanese of his time. Chosen as successor to

Luís Fróis as Valignano's main interpreter, he came to be esteemed as advisor to successive superiors of the Japan mission,[55] procurator of that mission, and court interpreter for Japan's autocratic rulers. When Valignano left Japan for the last time in 1603, Rodrigues was just putting the finishing touches on his remarkable Japanese grammar *Arte da Lingoa de Iapam* that was first printed in 1604 (Cooper 1994:228).

Like any educated Japanese of the time, Rodrigues had studied classical Chinese and sprinkled his grammar with examples from Confucius's *Analects*.[56] His grammar also features a treatise on Japanese poetry—hailed as "the first comprehensive description of Far Eastern literature by any European"—that includes a section on the translation of Chinese poetry into Japanese (Cooper 1994:229–30). Rodrigues was very much interested in the origins of Asian religions and peoples, and for this topic a firm grasp of chronology was needed. The third part of his grammar (Rodrigues 1604:232v–239r) contains chronological tables based on both Western and Far-Eastern sources.[57] In the section on Chinese chronology Rodrigues made the first known attempt to relate Japanese, Chinese, and Western chronologies. One of its major aims was to situate the founders of China's three major religions (Confucianism, Daoism, and Buddhism) within the framework of biblical history and traditional Western chronology (pp. 235r-236r).

---

55  Rodrigues was consultor of Valignano and subsequently of Pedro Gómez (1590–1612) and Francesco Pasio (1600–1612).

56  Fragments of the *Analects* are also found on the Evora screen; this was apparently a text used for language instruction in Jesuit colleges in Japan long before Ruggieri and Ricci began to study classical Chinese and Confucian texts. See Ebizawa 1963:94–100.

57  For the West, Rodrigues used Sebastião Barradas's *Commentaria in concordiam et historiam evangelicam* (Coimbra, 1599-1611) and Benito Pereira's *Commentariorum et disputationum in genesim* (Rome, 1591-9). See Rodrigues 1955:853.

Even before reading Ricci's *True Meaning of the Lord of Heaven*, Rodrigues had thus exhibited familiarity with Confucian texts such as the *Analects* and showed interest in Chinese philosophy, literature, history, and Buddhist scriptures. In 1607 Rodrigues accompanied Francesco PASIO (d. 1612)—the experienced Italian missionary who had witnessed the problematic beginnings of Ruggieri's and Ricci's China mission[58]—on a long inspection tour of mission stations. They were joined by a Japanese Jesuit called Fabian FUCAN 不干斎巴鼻庵 (c. 1565–1621) who in the following year was to leave the Jesuit order and eventually became a well-known critic of Christianity.[59] Fabian was known for his rhetorical prowess and had studied the religions of Japan as well as Confucianism. In an extant text of 1605, the *Myōtei mondō* 妙貞問答, he had criticized the Buddhist notion of first principle using terms that we recall encountering in Valignano's catechism[60] and the corresponding Evora fragments:

> Firstly, they hold that in the far distant past, this not discernable far off thing called Buddha was the same as emptiness, in other words that it wasn't anything at all. In Zen they call this honbun 本分 or busshō 仏性, and in Tendai they call it shinnyo 真如. The heart/mind of Buddha, if such a thing is said to exist, is in all cases said to have come from emptiness (kū 空) ... the Buddha of old is in other words "emptiness," it is nothing at all. (tr. Paramore 2008:238)

If Rodrigues had not heard about this event before, he must have learned during this trip that Fabian had in 1606 held a debate with the young Neo-Confucian thinker HAYASHI Razan 林羅山 (1583–1651), a man who later became secretary of the Tokugawa

58  For Pasio's connection with the early China missionaries Ruggieri and Ricci, see Brockey 2007:31–33.

59  Partially translated in Ellison 1991:165–174. For a more recent assessment and literature see Paramore (2008).

60  Ide (1995:284) has identified Valignano's catechism as one of Fabian's main sources. See Paramore 2011:248.

shogunate and was involved in the official expulsion of missionaries (1614) and cruel persecution of Christians. During this debate, Hayashi had ridiculed Fabian's understanding of Confucianism using passages of Ricci's *True Meaning of the Lord of Heaven* to support his argument.[61] The Japan mission's supervisor Pasio was taken aback by this and sought clarification from the Jesuits in China. This request was sent off to China in 1610, the year of Ricci's death, just when Rodrigues was expelled from his beloved Japan and had to move to Macao.

During his first years in Macao and the neighboring China, Rodrigues still hoped to return to Japan; but soon the persecution of Christians in Japan moved into higher gear and the Jesuit Macao residence teemed with expulsed members of the Japan mission.[62] Thus it came about that, having lived a total of thirty-three years in Japan, Rodrigues spent another twenty-three in Macao and China. No Westerner of his time could match his deep knowledge of the religions and philosophies of Japan and China. Soon after his arrival in Macao, he alerted his superiors about a number of "grave issues" in Jesuit mission methodology that were directly related to Ricci's reinterpretation of Confucianism as first or natural law and explained:

> These things arose on account of the lack of knowledge at that time and the Fathers' ways of speaking and the conformity (as in their ignorance they saw it) of our holy religion with the literati sect, which is diabolical and intrinsically atheistic, and also contains fundamental and essential errors against the faith. (Cooper 1981:277)

Rodrigues's opposition to Ricci's view of "true" Confucianism as a monotheistic and profoundly moral "natural law" grew more strident after two entire years (June 1613 to June 1615) of travel

---

61  See Ellison's translation (1991:149–53) of Hayashi's notes.

62  The entire area east of India formed part of the "Japan province" of the Jesuit mission whose headquarters were in Macao.

and research in China during which he "deeply investigated all these sects" that he "had already diligently studied in Japan" (p. 314). He studied "three sects of philosophers"—Confucianism, Daoism, and Buddhism—not only in books but also through observation and extensive field research: "To this end I passed through most of China and visited all our houses and residences, as well as many other places where our men had never been so far" (p. 314). Unfortunately, a new catechism compiled by Rodrigues (pp. 306, 315) as well as his voluminous treatise (pp. 310, 277) about Far Eastern religions appear to have vanished. But the gist of Rodrigues's views relevant for our inquiry can be reconstructed based on a number of extant manuscripts and printed sources:

1. Rodrigues's two published Japanese grammars (*Arte da lingoa de Iapam* of 1604 and the *Arte breve* of 1620);
2. nine Portuguese *letters* written between 1611 and 1633 from Macao and China;
3. extant parts of his *História da igreja do Japão* (1620s);
4. the *Longobardi Treatise* (1623–24) which reflects the essence of Rodrigues's view of the core doctrine of Confucianism, Daoism, and Buddhism (Spanish in Navarrete 1676; French in Longobardi 1701; also excerpts in French in Alexandre 1699);
5. Rodrigues's description of Buddhism as adopted by Navarrete (1676; see Chapter 11);
6. Rodrigues's description of Buddhism as employed by Prospero Intorcetta in the introduction to *Confucius Sinarum Philosophus* (1687; see Chapter 10).

We have seen that Ricci portrayed ancient Chinese religion, if suitably interpreted, as an excellent example of "natural law" and a strategic stepping stone to Christianity (which constitutes the "third law"), and that he attributed the degeneration of China's ancient monotheism to the influence of Buddhist and Daoist idolatry. By contrast, Rodrigues regarded the inner essence of all three major Chinese religions as profoundly atheistic. Far from being an example of the natural, monotheistic "first law," Rodrigues held that ancient Chinese religion is an outgrowth of the "evil" transmission line going back to Noah's flawed son Ham.

In the *Historia* of the 1620s Rodrigues identified the Chinese people as descendants of Belus who "is the same as Nimrod, the grandson of Ham." The reign of Belus was thought to have begun just after the Confusion of Tongues in Babel, and Rodrigues thought that the Chinese had soon afterwards settled in their land and were thus "the first to develop ... astrology and other mathematical arts and other liberal and mechanical arts" (Rodrigues 2001:355). Especially the "science of judicial astrology," which Chinese Confucians still practice "after the fashion of the Chaldeans with figures of odd and even numbers," was "spread throughout the world by Ham, son of Noah" (p. 356). Such data led Rodrigues to the conclusion:

> According to this and the other errors that they [the Chinese] have held since then concerning God, the creation of the universe, spiritual substances, and the soul of man, as well as inevitable fate, the Chinese seem to be descendants of Ham, because he held similar errors and taught them to his descendants, who then took them with them when they set off to populate the world. (p. 356)

It appears that Rodrigues experimented with different ways of linking China to Ham alias Zoroaster. At any rate, Longobardi wrote around 1624 that Rodrigues's treatise identified the legendary founder of China, *Fohi* (Fuxi 伏羲), as Zoroaster and regarded Confucianism, the "sect of the literati," as his heirs:

> In the treatise composed for these debates, Father Juan Ruiz [João Rodrigues][63] shows with great probability that Fo Hi [Fuxi] was the great Zoroaster, king of Bactria and chief of the Chaldean magi, who is the source of all sects in the Occident,

---

63    In many sources João Rodrigues is called "Ruiz," which is how he signed his letters.

and who after his arrival in this region of the Orient founded the kingdom of China and the sect of the literati. Because the sect of the literati and the sects of other heathen have the same source and are the work of the same devil, they show such great resemblance with one another and lead men to hell by the same path, art, and contrivance. I do not pursue this argument because the aforesaid Father [Rodrigues] has done so amply and learnedly in his treatise. (Navarrete 1676:250)

The association of Zoroaster with the origin of heresy and anti-religion began—according to Stausberg (1988:1.441 ff.) on whom I rely in this paragraph—in the Pseudo-Clementine texts of the third century that identified Zoroaster with Nimrod and made him into "a kind of arch-heretic" (p. 443). A century later, St. Augustine (354–430) denounced Zoroaster in *De civitate Dei* as the inventor of magic arts (p. 449); but it was not until the twelfth century that Zoroaster was directly identified with Ham by Hugo of St. Victor (1096–1141). In the thirteenth century, Ham = Zoroaster began to be regarded as the originator of heathen philosophy (pp. 456–7) by Roger Bacon (1220–1292) and others; and fifty years before Francis Xavier's arrival in Japan, the identification of Zoroaster with Ham was confirmed in the supposedly very ancient texts cooked up by Giovanni Nanni (Annius; c. 1432–1502; see next chapter). It is possible that Rodrigues was also familiar with other sources such as the *Silva de varia lección* by the Spaniard Pedro Mejía (c. 1499–1552) who credited Zoroaster = Ham with the invention of "el arte Mágica y encantamentos" (pp. 470–1).

The realization that China's founder Fuxi must be Zoroaster alias Ham was of central importance to Rodrigues since his goal was the redaction of a catechism for the entire region between India and Japan with a comprehensive analysis and refutation of the "inner" teaching common to all religions of this vast area. His research on Far Eastern chronology forced him to reject Ricci's "degeneration" scenario. In response to Ricci's claim that Greek philosophy had influenced Buddhism, Rodrigues wrote:

> Our [European] philosophers who held the same opinion probably took it from the sages of these parts, just as they took other theories, principally from the Indian sect and that of the Chaldeans, which is the same as the sect of the Chinese astrological scholars. The reason for this is that the philosophers of these parts lived long before the others and even before the Greek philosophers. (Rodrigues 2001:358)

Having already in 1593 debated with Buddhist monks about the existence of multiple worlds in the presence of Japan's ruler, Rodrigues effectively turned Ricci's scenario on its head: "Democritus, Metrodorus, Anaximander, Anaximenes, Archelaus, Aristarchus, Xenophanes, Diogenes, Leucippus, Epicurus, and the Indian gymnosophist Anaxarchus" were all born long after "Shaka or Shakia, also called Buddha, the founder of the sect of the gymnosophists of India" who "advocates three worlds, and afterwards three thousand, and finally a quasi-infinite number of worlds" (p. 358). Hence it appeared "most likely" to Rodrigues "that those who postulated many worlds took the theory from Shaka's doctrine" (pp. 359–60).

This was a revolutionary view in more than one sense. Rodrigues portrayed Greek philosophy as a relatively late development influenced by far older Chaldean, Egyptian, and Indian doctrines. But this oriental ur-philosophy was neither a "natural law" in Ricci's sense nor a "philosophia perennis" with a genealogy of wisdom reaching via Noah's good sons back to Adam. Rather, he regarded it as an atheistic disease spread by Ham alias Zoroaster from Mesopotamia to Persia, Egypt, and India, and from these regions westward to Greece as well as eastward to China. In his scenario, Confucianism was founded by "the sect of the Chaldean diviners" who (like the Chinese in their *Yijing*) philosophized with odd or even numbers and hieroglyphic symbols and were obsessed with light and darkness (Cooper 1981:239). Rodrigues described Daoism as "the sect of the Magicians and Persian evil wizards" and thus saw it as another "branch of the ancient Zoroaster" (p. 238). By contrast, Buddhism—"the sect of the ancient Indian gymnosophists"—is said also to show traces of Egyptian doctrine and to have reached China by way of India (p. 238).

Overall, Rodrigues's genealogy of Chinese religions was diametrically opposed to Ricci's. For Rodrigues, the texts commonly attributed or linked to Confucius did not constitute a precious repository of "natural law" that could serve as stepping stone to Christianity, but rather a remnant of Hamite atheistic philosophy. He detected its vestiges not only in India and the Far East (where they are best preserved) but also in Egypt, Persia, and ancient Greece. It is this ancient Oriental philosophy that Rodrigues regarded as the mother of all atheism, Ionian monism, Zoroastrian dualism, Buddhism, Daoism, and Confucianism. This was the fundamental reason for his adamant opposition to Ricci. The core "inner" doctrines of this oriental ur-philosophy were identified by Rodrigues—and in his wake by Ricci's successor Longobardi—exactly along the line of Valignano's critique of Buddhism:

1. *Public "outer" and encoded "inner" teachings*
Long before he forged what he had learned in Japan and China into a coherent system, Rodrigues had heard Valignano explain that the master key for the understanding of Japan's religions lies in the distinction between provisional (outer) and real (inner) teachings. Rodrigues detected these two types of doctrines not only in Buddhism but in all three major religions of China (Cooper 1981:311–2). For example, the oldest "Confucian" classic *Yijing* or *Book of Changes*—reportedly praised and commented upon by Confucius—showed a "Zoroastrian" dualism of light and darkness and betrayed its rotten origin by the use of numbers and symbols as well as rampant oracular superstition. In his letter to the Jesuit General of January 22, 1616, Rodrigues states that the China missionaries' and

Father Ricci's problems were a result of their failure to understand this basic distinction between outer doctrines and practices and the underlying ancient philosophy:

> Until I entered China, our Fathers of China knew practically nothing about this [distinction between outer and inner teachings] and about the speculative [inner] doctrine. They knew only about the civil and popular [outer] doctrine, for there was nobody to explain it to them and enlighten them. The above-mentioned Fr Matteo Ricci worked a great deal in this field and did what he could, but, for reasons only known to Our Lord, he was misled in this matter. All these three sects of China are totally atheistic in their speculative teaching, denying the providence of the world. They teach everlasting matter, or chaos, and like the doctrine of Melissus, they believe the universe to contain nothing but one substance. (pp. 311-2)

What Rodrigues calls the "speculative" teaching of Confucianism, Daoism, and Buddhism is the "inner" teaching forming their common philosophical core. Whereas the outer doctrines of China consist of a variety of religious beliefs and observances "for the people and adapted to their needs" that the "literati and sages" had invented "for the political administration and peaceful well-being of the populace" (pp. 312–3), their doctrinal kernel is philosophical:

> The other method is speculative and deals in a philosophical way with what sort of thing is God, and how this world was made, and everything else related to this. This entire doctrine is hidden in various very obscure symbols that only a few people understand and profess to be the greatest secret. (p. 312)

The use of symbols such as the trigrams and hexagrams of the *Yijing* or *Book of Changes* was in Rodrigues's and Longobardi's eyes a symptom of "the birth in all nations of two kinds of sciences, one true and secret, and the other false and public" (Longobardi 1701:24). In India, the naked sages (gymnosophists) and their founder Buddha had misled the common people by making them believe in the transmigration of souls into animals (p. 25). Though this was not their inner or real teaching, it was considered effective in seducing and guiding the mass of people. The "political" logic was that the people's fear of transmigration into a lower animal state would motivate them to avoid evil deeds out of self-interest. According to Rodrigues and Longobardi, the ploy of a double doctrine was employed by all three religions of China:

> The three sects of the Chinese follow entirely this manner of philosophizing. They have two kinds of doctrine. The one they regard as true is secret, and only the literati understand it and teach it by way of symbols. The other, vulgar one ... is regarded by the literati as false in the ordinary sense. They make use of it for the divine as well as the civil and fabulous cult, and by these means they lead the people to the good and turn it away from evil. (p. 26)

This view applies to Asia what Rodrigues and Longobardi had learned in philosophy lessons at Jesuit colleges. Longobardi quotes from the Coimbra textbook on Aristotle's Physics a passage that inspired both Valignano and Rodrigues:

> The antient custom of Philosophers taken by Pherecydes, Pythagoras his Master, from the Egyptians and Chaldeans, was, either not to write down the Precepts of Philosophy at all, or to write them obscurely, that is, under the obscurity of a deep hidden sense, and shrouded under Mathematical Figures, and Enigmatical Expressions. (Navarrete 1704:193)

## 2. First Principle, Emanation, and Resorption

Like Valignano's critique of Buddhism (1586) and Ricci's critique of Buddhism, Daoism, and Neoconfucianism (1604) in their respective catechisms, much of Rodrigues's and Longobardi's argument revolves around the view of the "first principle." They interpreted the Neoconfucian "principle" (*li* 理) along the line traced by Valignano: "According to them [the Chinese], this great and universal cause has neither life nor knowledge nor any authority; but it is pure, quiet, subtle, limpid, and without body or form" (p. 32). The Chinese regard it not only as "the physical principle of heaven and earth and other corporeal things" but also as "the moral principle of virtue," and they call it "first principle and final end because all things have emerged through emanation from it and will return to it when the world ends" (p. 74). Among other appellations, this first principle is called "great emptiness and immense capacity because in this universal essence all particular essences are included, like the waters of various rivers are included in the water of the single source from which they spring" (p. 75). The term emptiness is also used "because it can store in itself all things and there is nothing that is outside of it" (p. 76). This is the "full emptiness" that was mentioned in Chapter 4: an emptiness that signifies nothing other than "everlasting matter, or chaos," that is, an eternal *materia prima* out of which everything unfolds and to which everything returns (Cooper 1981:312).[64]

### 3. Monism and everlasting matter

The third fundamental aspect of this inner teaching, "the famous Chinese axiom *Vuen-Vue-Iety*" (Ch. *wanwu yiti* 萬物一體; the myriad things are one), constitutes—as in Valignano's catechism of 1586 and Ricci's catechism of 1604—the heart of the problem. It postulates that, though things may appear to be manifold, they in reality and substance are one (Rodrigues 2001:41), and that "one" is emptiness = chaos = *materia prima*. Inspired by the Jesuit order's standard "Coimbra" philosophy textbooks that had also shaped Valignano's view of Buddhism's "inner" teaching, Rodrigues detected vestiges of an ancient oriental monist doctrine in Greek thinkers such as Parmenides and Melissus. He accused them of holding the very same view as the Chinese, namely, that "the universe contains nothing but one substance:" an "everlasting matter" (*materia prima*) appearing

---

64 This interpretation of emptiness was, as we saw in Chapter 4, already advanced by Nunes in the 1550s.

in different modalities (Cooper 1981:312). Whereas Valignano and Ricci had argued that Indian and Chinese philosophers had inherited this belief from the Greeks, Rodrigues reversed this genealogy. Based on his intensive research on Japanese, Chinese, and Western chronologies he concluded that the Greeks flourished long after the Indian gymnosophists, and that these Indian "followers of Buddha" as well as the Daoists and Confucian literati must have adopted their core doctrine of all-oneness long before the philosophers of ancient Greece:

> These three sects [of China] are older than the Greek philosophers since they have their origin in Zoroaster, the magus and prince of the Chaldeans who taught and disseminated it in the world, established an eternal chaos, etc. This demonstrates what meaning the ancient Greek philosophers and the philosophers of China attach to the words all is one, and that they all agree in their interpretation of them. (Longobardi 1701:42–3)

Major parts of the old Orient thus seemed in agreement that there is no spiritual substance because the whole universe is but "a single universal substance, immense and infinite" (p. 47). One of the dire consequences of this monistic and materialistic doctrine was that entities such as souls are regarded as temporary condensations of a single *materia prima*. These condensations eventually dissolve again and "return to their principle just like all other things" (p. 53).

### 4. Modifications of a single Substance instead of Creation

Instead of God's creation of everything out of nothing, Zoroaster's ur-philosophy (which, according to Rodrigues, is best preserved in East Asia's "inner" doctrines) teaches an initial "infinite chaos" that the Buddhists call "emptiness" or "nothingness" and the Confucians "*li* [理]." It posits a condensation and dissolution process resembling that of Greek philosophers. The Chinese therefore possess "no knowledge whatsoever of a creation by an infinite being." More than that: they "even ignore what true generation is" (p. 46) and believe that the myriad things are nothing but "different modifications" of a single substance that adopts countless fleeting shapes (p. 44). Until a copy of Rodrigues's original report is located in some archive, we cannot be sure to what degree Niccolò LONGOBARDI (1559–1654) refined and systematized Rodrigues's vision. However, Longobardi's remarks about his indebtedness to Rodrigues as well as Rodrigues's extant letters and manuscripts indicate that Rodrigues's role in the invention of this fundamentally atheistic ur-philosophy of oriental origin was central. When Rodrigues informed the Jesuit General about his compilation of "a long treatise ... about all this, describing their fundamental doctrines," he explained his aim as follows:

> It will afford much light to our men here and will enable them to refute the errors against the faith (of which the Orient is full); it will also give much light to the Fathers of India for indeed up to now they have not realized the secrets of the Brahmin sect, which is the same as that of Shaka, about whose teachings even our Japanese Brothers here have also been deceived. The treatise will be full of interest in Europe, because as a result of it many things concerning the ancient and first philosophers will be understood; for over there such things are explained very differently from what in fact they are, and thus the true doctrine of the symbols of the ancients, which continues over here in all its vigour, is not understood. (Cooper 1981: 309–10)

Rodrigues thus insisted that his research on Japanese and Chinese doctrines had laid bare the foundations of the world's oldest atheistic philosophy: the philosophy of Ham alias Zoroaster. Though his treatise vanished in the course of the "Chinese rites and terms" controversy, his promise to throw light on "many things concerning the ancient and first philosophers" was fulfilled in strange and unexpected ways. His notion of a thoroughly monistic and atheistic oriental ur-philosophy as the common root of Asian as well Greek philosophies and religions first convinced several prominent Jesuits in China including Ricci's successor Longobardi who adopted it in his treatise of 1623–24 and credited Rodrigues with having found it. After the reaffirmation of Ricci's mission strategy in the Jesuit mission conference at Jiading in 1627 (Brockey 2007:87), both Rodrigues's and Longobardi's reports were officially suppressed. We will see, however, that their findings and ideas continued to be influential in the underground of Far Eastern missions and reemerged with great fanfare in late seventeenth-century Europe.

## Chapter Nine

## PAN-ASIAN RELIGION (KIRCHER)

The incorporation of newly discovered Asian peoples into the medieval Christian worldview was a difficult task. Countries like Japan, China, and even India were absent from the biblical world, as were the Americas and the fabulous "terra australis" called "land of parrots" that in Matteo Ricci's world map of 1602 still covered the entire southern end of our globe (Bertuccioli 1990). Given that only Noah and his family had survived the universal deluge, the question inevitably arose: which son of Noah is the ultimate ancestor of the inhabitants of newly discovered regions?

After Columbus's discovery of the New World (1492) the need for a comprehensive, Bible-compatible genealogy of the world's population became so urgent that the papal theologian (Magister Sacri Palatii) ANNIUS of Viterbo (Giovanni NANNI, c. 1432–1502) felt compelled to adopt drastic measures. He worked for years on the creation of a collection of forged texts that were published together with his learned commentary in 1498 under the privilege of Pope Alexander VI. The overall aim of this famous forgery (known as *Antiquitates*) and its tailor-made commentary was the incorporation of secular history into the biblical narrative. To this end Annius spun an elaborate tale that had Noah retire in Italy, made his offspring colonize the world (including regions ignored by the Old Testament's authors), and gave a very prominent role to Egypt as hub of ancient civilization. Under Annius's pen, the Egyptian Osiris became the descendant of Noah's least favorite son Ham. After defeating the giants with the help of Hercules the Egyptian, Osiris ruled Annius's Italian home town of Viterbo for ten years before returning to Egypt (Curran 2003:112). Annius's mind-boggling narrative (which even had Noah visit Annius's home town of Viterbo) also identified specific members of Noah's offspring as founding fathers of various European nations and thus created much-appreciated links to biblical genealogy as well as ramparts against secular historical speculation.

Noah's predilection for Italy was not just a sign of chauvinism but had profound theological significance: Noah, the unique heir and transmitter of antediluvian wisdom, had been determined to retire precisely in the future homeland of the Vatican! Long before Annius invented his scenario, church fathers and apocryphal texts had created a similar link between Ur-religion and Christianity. In one colorful narrative, Noah recuperated Adam's mummy, stored it on the ark, and had it buried on Mount Golgotha, that is, at the very spot where Adam's sin was to be redeemed by Jesus on the cross (Malan 1882:161–171). Such tales had the aim of portraying Christianity as the natural successor and fulfillment of the world's oldest religion (App 2010:256). Exactly this was also the overall goal of missionaries like Matteo Ricci in China and Roberto de Nobili in India as well as Jesuit scholars in Europe. Best known among the latter was Athanasius KIRCHER (1602–1680), the protagonist of the present chapter, who from his perch in the vicinity of the Vatican attempted to press not only all of the world's peoples into the fold of the biblical narrative but also all religions and philosophies.

When Kircher was born at the beginning of the seventeenth century in a small German town near Fulda, Europeans were familiar with only about half of the earth's surface. As shipbuilding and navigation techniques improved and both Christian missions and commerce boomed, a flood of new information inundated Europe. Much of it seemed incompatible with the biblical narrative, and this led to a variety of attempts to reinterpret the biblical account. For example, Isaac LA PEYRÈRE (1596–1676) argued in his *Prae-Adamitae* of 1655 that the Pentateuch's story of Adam and Eve describes only the origin of the Jews and that gentiles such as the natives of the West Indies must stem from forefathers far older than Adam. Much of Kircher's work, culminating in the spectacularly illustrated *Arca Noë* (1675) and *Turris Babel* (1679), was devoted to shoring up biblical authority and proving once and for all that the ultimate roots of all human culture lie in the blessed region between Mesopotamia and Egypt. To my regret the discussion must here be limited to a single facet of Kircher's grand enterprise: his invention of a singular pan-Asian religion of Egyptian origin.

The idea that some Asian religions are of Egyptian origin was not new. When Kircher was a schoolboy, the learned philologist Lorenzo PIGNORIA (1571–1631) of Padova proposed this in his enlarged edition of Cartari's famous book on the gods of antiquity entitled *Le vere e nove imagini de gli dei delli antichi* (The genuine and new images of the gods of antiquity; Pignoria 1615). Whereas Vicenzo CARTARI (c. 1531–69) had limited his descriptions and illustrations to Greek and Roman deities, Pignoria added a second part about the deities of the West and East Indies. In it he claimed that the inhabitants of the newly discovered regions "did no more than imitate the images of Egyptian deities" (p. IV). Pignoria explained that they worship, like the Egyptians, heavenly bodies such as the sun and the moon, and that this is "the oldest form of idolatry ever seen in the world" (p. IV). His examples include Mexican and Peruvian gods (pp. IV–XIX) and the elephant-headed Ganesha of India with three arms and noses (pp. XXVII–XXVIII), but most numerous are Pignoria's descriptions and depictions of Japanese "idols." He was particularly fascinated by representations of Amida (Amitābha Buddha) who is described as "a foreign God not of Japan but introduced by the Chinese Xaca" (p. XXIX). In a letter from the Jesuit Japan mission, Pignoria had also read about the statue of a half-naked Amida with pierced ears who sits on a large rose. In his imagination, this statue was so similar to a statue of the Egyptian Harpocrates that he found it "unnecessary to prove" their common Egyptian background (p. XXXI):

FIG. 11: HARPOCRATES AND AMIDA SITTING ON FLOWERS (PIGNORIA 1624:567)

Apart from a few woodcuts in the style of Figure 11 that seem inspired by descriptions rather than depictions, Pignoria's supplement also included woodcuts of more than a dozen drawings sent to him by Girolamo Aleandro (1480–1542). They depict Japanese statues brought by missionaries to Italy which are, to my knowledge, the earliest printed representations of genuine Buddhist statuary in the West.[65] Pignoria was particularly struck by the dignified and pious expression of drawings featuring Japanese Buddha or Bodhisattva

65 The first edition of Cartari's book that contained these images is the Padova edition of 1615 (not the 1626 edition, as Pastine 1978:82 claims). The Venice edition of 1624 contains three additional images (pp. 569–571), as does the Padova edition of 1626.

statues with folded hands and a halo—statues in which "the devil seems to have employed the manner of our images in order to impress by his deceptions the souls of the heathens of those lands" (Pignoria 1615:XXXIX).

FIG. 12: JAPANESE BUDDHIST STATUE FROM PIGNORIA (1624:573)

Pignoria's detection of Egyptian influence in the Far Eastern and American pantheon (Baltrušaitis 1997:232–42, 274–7) pointed in a direction that Kircher was to explore throughout his life. Though

Kircher's work covered an extremely broad range of topics, the search for origins and the construction of genealogies in tune with the Bible forms a common denominator. For Kircher, true religion, true science, and true philosophy are connected at the root. Their genealogy inevitably leads back to Noah and from there via the antediluvian patriarchs to Adam who was instructed by angels and by God himself. Apart from this "good" transmission line—which for him, as we will see, also included Greek philosophers such as Pythagoras and Plato—Kircher was also very interested in the origin and transmission of "bad" or degenerated religion, science, and philosophy. This is the genealogy that underpins his conception of a pan-Asian religion. Both genealogies form part of a typical "ancient theology" or *prisca theologia* scheme based on the notion of a pure original teaching (God's gift to Adam) whose degradation and perversion is periodically reversed through regeneration of the original teaching. In "ancient theology" movements (or, more broadly, Ur-tradition movements)[66] such regeneration is possible because of a special line of transmission of the original teachings that often involves secrecy and some form of encoding.[67] Such three-step schemes—original purity, degeneration, and regeneration based on reliable transmission of an original doctrine—are legion in the history of religions. They characterize many religious reform movements in East and West, for example the Mahāyāna reformation of Buddhism (where the basis of regeneration is the purportedly original teaching of the Buddha), the Zen reformation of Chinese Mahāyāna with its claim of an unbroken patriarchal lineage of "mind-to-mind" transmission starting with founder Buddha, or Luther's Reformation with its re-

---

66 See App 2010:8–9, 254–61 for the use of this term that—unlike "ancient theology" or "prisca theologia"—can also be used for movements that lack God and thus have no theology.

67 For descriptions of ancient theology in the Christian / Neoplatonic context see for instance Walker 1972 and Schmidt-Biggemann 1998; for Kircher's variant Stolzenberg 2004; and for Asian or Orientalist variants App 2009 and 2010.

generation of original Christianity based on the biblically transmitted, pure and genuine word of God.

Seen from this vantage point, the logic of Kircher's Egyptology and genealogy of religion is quite straightforward. Roman Catholicism is directly linked to the antediluvian wisdom of Egypt and from there to Adam's god-given wisdom. The Egyptian obelisks in Rome do not just symbolize but rather embody this link because their hieroglyphs, according to Kircher, are codes for the most ancient theology and express central doctrines of the Catholic church. Hence these obelisks furnish extraordinary "historical" proofs of the divine roots and legitimacy of the Catholic church. Their study, restoration, and erection in Rome thus justified any expense of money, even if that necessitated raising a new unpopular tax. Guided by such convictions, Kircher in his early work *Prodromus Coptus* (1636) prepared the ground for an elaborate genealogy of religions that he subsequently developed in the *Obeliscus Pamphilius* (1650) and the *Oedipus Aegyptiacus* (1652–54). With the exception of *China illustrata* (1667), later works such as the *Arca Noë* (1675) and *Turris Babel* (1679) added little to the scheme. Kircher's invention developed in three stages:

In the first stage (1636, *Prodromus Coptus*) Kircher explained that Osiris had brought Egyptian religion to India and claimed that all cults of Asia and the Americas have Egyptian roots. However, he did not furnish any explanation as to when and how Egyptian religion had spread to the Far East and Far West.

In the second stage (1650–54, *Obeliscus Pamphilius* and *Oedipus Aegyptiacus*) Kircher presented a transmission scenario that linked Cain via Noah's son Ham (alias Zoroaster) to all idolatries and philosophies of Asia. To the first transmission of Egyptian religion by Osiris, Kircher now added a second transmission by Egyptian priests who fled to India after Cambyses's invasion of Egypt in the sixth century B.C.E. Though Kircher listed similarities between various

Asian religions and Egyptian religion, the dissemination of Egyptian idolatry in Asia remained unexplained.

In the third stage (1667, *China Illustrata*) Kircher extended his previous scenarios by explaining in detail how Egyptian religion had conquered not just India but all of Asia. After the restoration in India of Osiris's ancient religion by the Egyptian refugee priests, an "Indian brahmin" called Xaca or Buddha began to propagate a doctrine with Egyptian and Greek elements that rapidly became the reigning religion of India. Xaca's very numerous Brahmin disciples subsequently disseminated his religion throughout Asia. The religions we today call Hinduism and Buddhism were thus presented as a single pan-Asian religion founded by Xaca, a brahmin influenced by Egyptian religion and Greek philosophy.

*Stage 1: The Egyptian cradle*

The *Prodromus Coptus* (1636) contains the first translation and description of the Nestorian stele of Xian that had been discovered in 1625.[68] Unaware that it stems from a branch of the church that is considered heretical by Roman orthodoxy, Kircher used this stone inscription from the eighth century as proof that teachings such as Christianity could in ancient times find their way from the Middle East to China. He concluded that "it is obvious that Egypt was the nursery [seminarium] not only of the propagation of Christianity to faraway regions but also of all superstition to the entire world." (Kircher 1636:86). Given that Jesus' favorite disciple Thomas had converted India to the Christian faith (p. 106), Kircher saw no reason to doubt that there were much earlier contacts between Egypt and India: "Since expeditions from Eritrea via the Red Sea to Ophir or India had been frequent, the same opportunity certainly presented itself not only to the Christian religion but also to the hieromants and philosophers of ancient Egypt" (p. 119–20). Had Diodorus of

68 On this inscription see Pelliot / Forte (1997).

Sicily not reported that Osiris was the first to reach India and to found cities (p. 120)? Such scant evidence was sufficient for Kircher to conclude:

> It is certain that the Persian magi, the Brachmanes of the Indians, and other sages of Asia have received all of their philosophical reasoning as well as their entire cult of the gods along with all their rites and ceremonies from the Egyptians by way of reciprocal commerce (Kircher 1636:121)

Kircher included both the East and West Indies (i.e., most of Asia plus the Americas) in his Egyptian cradle scenario and claimed that "all cults not only of India, China, Japan, and Tartary or Cathay but also of America itself" have their origin in Egypt. So do their statues, "mystical pyramids," and magnificent temples that are said to imitate Egyptian models (pp. 121–2).

*Stage 2: The two-track genealogy*

In the *Obeliscus Pamphilius* (1650), Kircher first presented an elaborate genealogy of pure and contaminated teaching. On the basis of a bewildering array of Coptic, Hebrew, Syriac, Hebrew, Arabic, and Greek sources as well as much apocryphal material, Kircher identified three key biblical figures as transmitters: the pious antediluvian patriarch Enoch as the first Hermes, Noah's son Ham as the first Zoroaster, and Ham's son Chus as the second Zoroaster. In Kircher's scenario the hermetic and orphic traditions formed part of the "pure" transmission line bound for the Vatican. By contrast, the contaminated Zoroastrian (hamitic) tradition was presented as the source of all oriental idolatries and of flawed philosophies stretching from Greece to Japan.

| Genealogy of pure teaching | Contaminated teaching |
|---|---|
| Adam | |
| Seth (books, pillars of Seth) | Cain |
| Enoch (books of Enoch) = first Hermes | antediluvian descendants of Cain |
| Noah | |
| Sem & Japhet | Ham = first Zoroaster (Egypt, Persia) |
| Hermes Trismegistos (second Hermes) inventor of hieroglyphs, restorer of true religion in Egypt | Chus = second Zoroaster (Chaldea, Bactria) |
| Orpheus (transmission to Greece); Pythagoras, Plato and some other Greek philosophers | Some Greek philosophers and all philosophers of Asia, Americas |
| Christianity | all idolatry |

TABLE 11: KIRCHER'S GENEALOGIES OF PURE AND CONTAMINATED TEACHING

Kircher based Ham's identification as Zoroaster mainly on Hebrew, Syriac, and Arabic sources (Kircher 1650:11–16) and regarded him as "the inventor of all magic and idolatry who transmitted to his descendants the illicit arts and sciences he had learned from the wicked descendants of Cain before the deluge" (p. 16). "Infected with superstitions and sacrilegious arts," it was Ham who first "converted to profane use what was piously transmitted" (p. 4) and smuggled written information about this onto the ark (pp. 4, 8). Ham also taught the cult of fire to the Persians and Chaldeans (pp. 16–18). But it was Ham's son Chus (Kircher's second Zoroaster) who brought such degenerate practices and beliefs to Bactria in today's northern Afghanistan and established the bridgehead for further dissemination to Central, South, and East Asia (pp. 16-19, 100, 107).

In the three-volume *Oedipus aegyptiacus* (1652–4) Kircher provided an extended genealogy of superstition and idolatry. Tracing everything back to Ham (Kircher 1652–4:1.164 ff.), he explained that the Egyptian cult of the sun (Osiris), moon (Isis), cows (Apis) and so forth infected not only Hebrews and Persians but inhabitants of countries as far away as Sumatra (1.172, 201). In the chapter on "imitators of Egypt" (*simia Aegyptiaca*) Kircher, who still lacked a concrete transmission scenario beyond India, blamed the devil's "propaganda idolatrica" for the infection of China, Japan, Tartary, Vietnam, the Philippines, Africa, and even Mexico (1.396–424).

Though the execution was typically Kircherian in its monomaniacal comprehensiveness, the inspiration for this view appears to have come from Pignoria's claim that the Far Eastern and American pantheons were clearly based on Egyptian models.[69] This view had found expression in Pignoria's juxtaposition of Amida and Harpocrates (the child Horus, son of Isis and Osiris, worshiped as victorious sun god; Fig. 11) which rested on descriptions of Harpocrates's flower seat by Iamblichus and Clement of Alexandria. Pignoria had detected its similarity with a description by Luís Fróis featuring Amida sitting on a rose with pierced ears and rays around his head.[70] While Pignoria's artist depicted Amida roughly along these lines, Kircher upstaged him by not showing images of Harpocrates and Amida next to each other but dreaming up an Amida whose very face expresses his sun-god identity. Ignorant of the fact that the Japanese actually have a great sun Buddha—the very Dainichi that Fran-

---

69 Another possible source of inspiration were the observations and theories of Pietro della Valle (Baltrušaitis 1997:207–210). In Rome, Kircher might have had access to some of della Valle's manuscripts even before publication.

70 These three sources were later on also adduced in Kircher's *China illustrata* (1987:132–3).

cis Xavier had mistaken for God—Kircher gave Amida this role in an image that states the "parallel to Harpocrates" only in its caption:

FIG. 13: AMIDA, PARALLEL OF HARPOCRATES (KIRCHER 1652:1.406)

This was only one of many examples used by Kircher to support his claim that all idolatry—whether Greek, Roman, Indian, Chinese, Japanese, or American—had its roots in Egypt, the adopted home of Ham. The Japanese *hotoke* and *kami*, for example, are nothing but "manifest vestiges of Osiris and Isis" (1.397). But in 1654, when Kircher's last volume of *Oedipus Aegyptiacus* went to press, the question how Egyptian idolatry could reach such remote regions remained unsolved.

*Stage 3: The pan-Asian dissemination*

To the learned South-German theologian Gottlieb SPITZEL (Theophilus Spizelius; 1639–91)—an avid reader of Kircher's works and of the atlas and history of China published by Kircher's pupil Martino MARTINI (1614–61) in 1655 and 1658—the data about the culture of China and its neighboring countries seemed sufficient for the redaction of a first summary. Spitzel's *De re literaria sinensium commentarius* appeared in 1660 and shows that he was impressed but not overwhelmed by Kircher's egyptomania. Rather than pressing everything into the service of an Egypt-based genealogy, Spitzel presented various philosophies and religions based on available sources. Instead of jumping to conclusions about their common origin and presenting data in support, he produced a tightly formulated and broadly based overview of knowledge that emphasizes variety and differences rather than uniformity. For example, in Section IX he juxtaposes European, Chinese, and Japanese ideas about the origin of the world. After analyzing and criticizing the cosmogony of the Nestorian stele of Xian (citing Kircher's *Prodromus Coptus*), Spitzel devotes five pages to the Japanese view of the principle of all things. The first two pages summarize Valignano's view and his four main points (see Chapter 7): a first principle that is called wise yet lacks intelligence and involvement in the world; the emanation and return of all things to this first principle; the identity of the human heart with this principle; and the possibility of reaching the perfection of this principle in this lifetime (Spizelius 1660:161–2). Spitzel presents this specifically as the basis of *Japanese* thought rather than some pan-Asian doctrine, and after discussing divergent views of

Japanese sects he returns to the exposition of Chinese cosmogonies (165 ff.). Egypt plays no role in most of his explanations. Spitzel's approach stands in stark contrast to that of *China illustrata* (1667), Kircher's popular work that was expeditiously translated into French and German. A major purpose of this book was the confirmation of the Egypt-based genealogy of the *Oedipus Aegyptiacus*, pages upon pages of whose explanations are repeated almost word for word. Once more the apostle Thomas, the Xian stele, Prester John, and Marco Polo are called upon as proof that communication between Egypt and Asia was possible, and we also meet again Osiris who allegedly first brought Egyptian religion to India. Also present are the priestly Egyptian refugees who are credited with the restoration of that religion in India after a long period of degeneration. However, Kircher also furnished new data in order to explain the dissemination of Egyptian cults to China, Japan, and the Americas. These additions merit special scrutiny because they contain Kircher's vision of a pan-Asian religion. Repeating his fifteen-year-old argument, Kircher states:

> There is no cult of the ancient Egyptians and their descendants which isn't followed today by our modern barbarians, who have changed the worship of sun and moon, or Isis and Osiris, into that of Foto and Chamis. You can find Bacchus, Venus, Hercules, Aesculapius, Serapides, Anubides, and other similar Egyptian gods, whom they worship under various other names. (Kircher 1987:121).

Kircher applied this kind of conviction to new information that he received from China and India missionaries visiting Rome in the 1650s and 1660s. Among them was the Austrian Johann GRUEBER (1623–1680) who in 1664 reached Rome after an astonishing overland journey from China via Tibet, Nepal, India, and Persia. Apart from numerous sketches used by Kircher in *China illustrata*, the Austrian Jesuit appears also to have furnished authentic Chinese prints for Kircher's increasingly well-stocked museum of exotica.[71]

FIG. 14: MAJOR CHINESE DIVINITIES (DETAIL FROM KIRCHER 1667:140)

Having spent only a relatively short time in China, Grueber was unable to enlighten Kircher about the figures depicted in the print that Kircher decided to publish in his *China illustrata*. But Kircher had the reputation of being able to solve just about any riddle and identified the main divinity in the center of Figure 14 (marked in the halo by the letter A) as "the Lord of Heaven, whom they call Fe or Fo, which means savior who ought to be worshipped." Buddha was thus called the Lord of Heaven and identified as the "Chinese Jove" and Osiris (Kircher 1987:126). His sidekick on the left (marked by the letter B) is "the deified Confucius," and on the other side is "Lauzu, whom the Chinese call the Old Philosopher, apotheosized and adorned with divine honor as the founder of the Chinese

---

71  Such prints were not only used by Kircher (1667) but three years later also more extensively by Dapper (1670).

religion" (p. 126; Laozi is marked by the letter C). One would think that these two deified Chinese natives would lack Mediterranean equivalents, but Kircher was quick to offer a solution:

> This is the belief of the Chinese about the highest gods. These are clearly vestiges of the Egyptian and Greek mythology. For what can the God Fe, with his attendants at B and C, signify except Jove with Apollo and Mercury? (p. 127)

It is of interest to observe that modern researchers are not much closer to the mark. Kircher expert Joscelyn Godwin, while criticizing Kircher's associations as "facile," finds his identifications "correct, up to a point"—the point being Kircher's Buddha (Fo) who, according to Godwin, ought to be the deified emperor Fuxi or Fohi (Godwin 2009:247).[72] In fact the engraving is certainly Daoist and shows Daoist deities, probably the "Three Pure Ones" (Ch. *sanqing* 三清) or the "Three Officials" (Ch. *sanguan* 三官).[73]

But with regard to Kircher's contribution to the invention of a single Oriental philosophy, two visitors to Rome who were far more knowledgeable about China than Grueber played a role. The first was Martino MARTINI (1614–1661), Kircher's former student who had spent nine years in China before being dispatched to Rome in the 1650s in order to convince the pope and Church authorities that Ricci's strategy did not threaten orthodoxy. As the official Jesuit delegate in this important matter, Martini must have had all relevant documents at his disposal, and a failure to study Rodrigues's and Longobardi's critical reports would have constituted a dereliction of duty. But of more importance to Kircher was information gained from a second Jesuit, Giovanni Filippo DE MARINI (1608-77), an

---

72 This identification appears to be based on a misguided correction (Kircher's "Fo" replaced by "Fohi") by Rivosecchi that compounds Kircher's mistake (Rivosecchi 1982, note to Fig. 91).

73 For a brief explanation of these deities and relevant literature see Kleeman and Kohn (2008). I am indebted to my wife Monica Esposito for her help.

Italian Vietnam missionary who visited Rome in the early 1660s and in 1663 published a very interesting description of Vietnam and other Southeast-Asian countries (see Chapter 11). Following de Marini's lead, Kircher identified the central figure of Grueber's print as Fo (Buddha) and portrayed him as the founder of an enormous religion that "is found not only in the regions of India far and wide, but was also propagated in Cambodia, Tonchin, Laos, Cochin China [Vietnam], as well as all of China and Japan" (Kircher 1987:141).

> This first creator and architect of the superstition was a very sinful brahmin imbued with Pythagoreanism. He was not content just to spread the doctrine, but even added to it so much that there is scarcely any one who is able to describe the doctrine or write about it. (p. 141)

This "sinful brahmin" called Buddha or Xaca supplied the missing expansive element to Kircher's genealogy. Kircher speculated that the brahmins had infected most of Asia with their founder Buddha's toxic mixture of Egyptian religion, Pythagoreanism, and some new inventions. This explains the title of the *China illustrata* chapter containing Kircher's ultimate scenario: "Brahmin institutions and how an Egyptian superstition passed by means of the Brahmins to Persia, India, China, and Japan, the farthest kingdom of the East" (p. 141).

In spite of a somewhat different take on the Buddha's role and the ultimate origin of heterodoxy, Kircher's vision shares crucial characteristics with that of Rodrigues. Both Rodrigues and Kircher saw Asian religions and philosophies as branches of a single root-heresy. For Rodrigues it was lodged in Mesopotamia and for Kircher in Egypt; but both posited a fundamental unity of doctrine not only embracing much of Asia but also the Greek and Roman world. In *The Birth of Orientalism* I traced some of the spectacular effects of this invention on eighteenth-century Europe's perception of a pan-Asian religion comprising not only the religions of the Far East but also those of India (App 2010). Here we are less interested in the gradual emergence of fault lines in that picture than in the source of the perception of unity. Both Rodrigues and Kircher held that all heresies and superstitions go back to a single root and classified the world's religions and philosophies accordingly. Kircher's vision of an Egyptian origin of this pan-Asian system remained influential far into the eighteenth century and seduced men of the scholarly caliber of Mathurin Veyssière de La Croze (1661–1739), Engelbert Kaempfer (1651–1716), Denis Diderot (1713–84), and Johann Gottfried Herder (1744–1803) (see App 2010). As late as the nineteenth century, Kircher's fantasies about Buddhism's founder as a refugee priest from the African continent were considered corroborated by depictions of incense-blackened Buddha figures with curly hair.

FIG. 15: BLACK BUDDHA IN F. MAJER'S MYTHOLOGICAL LEXICON
(1803; PLATE 8)

# Chapter Ten

## BUDDHA'S DEATHBED CONFESSION

João Rodrigues and Athanasius Kircher were not the only clerics concerned with the genealogy of creeds as they confronted an increasingly complex religious landscape. During the first centuries of the common era, when Indian and Central Asian Buddhism took root in China, Chinese Buddhists also created classification schemes (Ch. *panjiao* 判教). Their intention was to bring a semblance of order into a bewildering variety of Buddhist doctrines and texts. Some of these classifications evoked the Indian Buddhist "two-truths" scheme which asserts that, apart from the absolute truth of the awakened, there is also a provisional truth designed to accommodate deluded beings and to help them reach enlightenment. Others attached particular doctrines and texts to phases of the Buddha's life; and naturally those of one's preferred sect tended to be associated with particularly poignant events of the founder's life such as the first sermon after his enlightenment or his ultimate instructions before passing away. Such schemes often employed, in one form or another, the distinction between a "provisional" (Jap. *gonkyō* 權教) and a "genuine" or "real" teaching (Jap. *jikkyō* 實教)—a distinction that also underlies Zongmi's *Yuanrenlun* whose influence we detected in Valignano's catechism (see Chapter 6). It is also a central feature of major Mahāyāna texts such as the *Lotus sutra* (Skt. *Saddharma-puṇḍarīka-sūtra*) and associated texts such as the *Wuliangyi jing* 無量義經 or *Sutra of Innumerable Meanings*. As mentioned above, already in 1574, five years before Valignano's first arrival in Japan, the visitor's designated interpreter Luís Fróis had for an entire year studied a Chinese translation of the Lotus sutra (Fróis 1926:452). This sutra presents itself as the ultimate teaching of the Buddha. In reality, though, it is "not so much about doctrines in an assertive sense, but rather about the inner method of the Buddhist religion" (Pye 1978:20). Indeed, both the sutra's discussion of Mahāyāna doctrine and its famous parables revolve around the distinction between "provisional" and "ultimate" teachings and describe the Buddha's use of skilful or expedient means in leading the faithful to the One or Great Vehicle, that is, the ultimate doctrine of Mahāyāna represented by the very Lotus sutra. The sutra summarizes the Buddha's approach as follows: "First he preaches the three vehicles to attract and guide living beings, but later he employs just the Great Vehicle to save them" (Watson 1993:62). Realizing "that our minds delight in lesser doctrines," the Buddha is said to have "employed the power of expedient means to preach in a way that was appropriate for us" (p. 86). The Lotus sutra thus appears to be "the summation of the Buddha's message, superseding his earlier pronouncements, which had only provisional validity" (p. xvii).

We have seen in Chapters 2 and 3 that the Jesuits created their own narratives about classes or phases of Buddhist teaching. The 1551 Fernández report divided the Buddha's life into two parts: before age forty-nine he wrote books, but subsequently he rejected his previous teachings and advocated solely meditation. In this report the Buddha is for the first time accused of having lied. The 1556 Sumario de los errores featured a materialist phase with nine books, an exoteric phase with three books, an esoteric phase with a single book (in which the Buddha called all his former teachings expedient), and finally a deathbed announcement denying the usefulness of words and writings.

Valignano offered an interesting variant. In his biography of St. Francis Xavier[74] he asserted that Xaca's disciples authored many books filled with their master's teachings and that these books were as highly esteemed as the Bible in the West (Valignano 1899:1.112). Rather than first teaching one thing and later another, Valignano claimed that Xaca formulated his doctrine in a clever way so that it could be interpreted both literally and allegorically. Some people thus thought that he taught recompense in paradise and punishment in hell; but others believed that they must attain *satori* [satorar] and realize that "all things have the same substance as their principle, Amida, from which they themselves do not differ" (pp. 112–3). According to Valignano, the Buddha's final book stated that earlier on he "had only accommodated himself to the stupidity [rudeza] of the people" and "had reserved the most profound and excellent doctrine for this last work" (p. 113) which contains the only "ultimate and true doctrine" (p. 114).[75] Valignano did not mention any deathbed announcement by the Buddha; and what he presented as ultimate teaching is not based on the *Lotus sutra* but on the Zen-inspired "inner" teaching as explained in the 1586 *Catechismus*: no heaven and hell, no reward or punishment in the yonder, attainment "through *satori*" of "the perfection and truth of their principle," and so on (p. 115).

To summarize the innovations related to Buddha's deathbed confession tale in the second half of the sixteenth century in Japan: Fernándes's founder of Buddhism stopped writing at age forty-nine

74 According to Schütte (1951:2.433), this book is a product of the early 1580s. Bernard dates its completion to June 13, 1583 (Bernard 1941:286).

75 As mentioned above, this remark by Valignano is based on the *Wuliangyi jing* 無量義經 or *Sutra of Innumerable Meanings*, a short text that was widely regarded as an introduction to the *Lotus Sutra*. The passage in question reads: "I knew that the natures and desires of all living beings were not equal. As their natures and desires were not equal, I preached the Law variously. In forty years and more, the truth has not been revealed yet" (Katō 1984:14).

and thereafter only taught meditation. This account of 1551 contained neither the transmission of a secret nor a deathbed scene but first speaks of a lie (DocJ 1.257). The *Sumario de los errores* of 1556 first mentions a deathbed scene, but the founder did not confess anything to his disciples; instead he dictated a text that denied the possibility of saying or writing anything about the origin and destination of man (DocJ 2.665). His use of expedient means, however, is called a "pious lie." Valignano's account of the early 1580s featured neither a deathbed announcement nor a secret or lie; instead the founder had throughout his career made use of double meanings and explained this tactic in his ultimate book (Valignano 1899:112–4).

It was during the first half of the seventeenth century that more specific elements of a deathbed confession story emerged. The Milanese Jesuit Cristoforo BORRI (1583–1632), a resident of Saigon between 1610 and 1623, reported in his 1631 book about Cochinchina that Xaca is a great metaphysician from Siam, much more ancient than Aristotle but equally gifted, who at age thirty realized while contemplating the appearing and vanishing star Diana that all things are "nothing, from nothing, and for nothing [nulla, da nulla, e per nulla]" (Borri 1631:201–2). After returning home, he wrote "many books about this including large volumes titled 'Of Nothing' [Del Nulla]" in which he reduced everything to the basic elements and then the elements to a "pure potency and indeed to nothing" (pp. 202–3).

> From all this he concluded that, since these things are nothing, they have their origin in a cause that is not efficient but material: from a principle that, though it is nothing, is an eternal nothing that is infinite, immense, unchanging, and omnipotent, so that finally God is nothing and the origin of nothing. (pp. 203–4)

Borri's explanations indicate that such information came from Japan. Indeed, Borri explained to his European readers that Xaca's doctrine of nothingness had first taken root in Japan where it had formed a "Sect of Nothingness [Setta del Niente]" that the Japanese call "Gensiù" (Jap. *zenshū* 禪宗, Zen sect; p. 206–7).

Borri furnished an entertaining tale about Xaca's swerving between "inner" and "outer" teachings. While the Chinese only wanted the "outer" teachings, the Japanese Zen sect accepted the "inner" teaching of "nothing." This success in Japan played a key role in Borri's narrative of Xaca's death:

> The fact that the Japanese and others made much of this doctrine of nothing was the reason why its author Xaca called together his disciples when approaching death and proclaimed on the word of a dying man that he had during his many years of life and speculation found nothing more true and well-founded than the [inner] doctrine of the Sect of Nothing; and though his second [outer] doctrine may seem to differ from it, he did not regard it as a contradiction or recantation, but rather as a proof and confirmation of the first [inner teaching], though not in plain terms but by way of metaphors and parables that are entirely compatible with the doctrine of nothingness, as his books plainly show. (pp. 207–8)

Borri's creative tale displays a breathtaking lack of historical perspective since he has the Buddha make decisions based on events (the introduction of Buddhism to China and of Zen to Japan) that took place many centuries later. But several of its elements are found in later accounts such as that by Borri's successor in Vietnam, Alexander DE RHODES (1591–1660). Chosen to serve in the Japan mission, de Rhodes spent an entire year studying Japanese in the very residence in Macao where Japan veteran João Rodrigues was then living. Prevented from going to Japan because of the closure of Japan's borders, de Rhodes ended up missionizing Vietnam and became known as the author of a Vietnamese-Latin catechism and a history of Tonkin that were both published in 1651. In de Rhodes's scenario, the Buddha first taught a purely atheistic doctrine. This was rejected by the people who instinctively knew that there must be "a first being and a supreme cause" (de Rhodes 1651:66). Frustrated, the Buddha then decided to introduce "a certain fabulous genealogy of gods" and "the belief in multiple divinities" (p. 66). During four decades he thus taught polytheism and idolatry. But on his deathbed he declared to a few select disciples that he had all along been an atheist and crude materialist:

> The devils governing the mind of this unfortunate prince did not ignore that atheism is worse and more pernicious than idolatry, and they convinced this impious mind to recant at the end of his life. He did this not before the people but only to the most ingenious and cunning of his disciples. To them he declared that the doctrine of idols taught by him for forty years had only served for the amusement of simple people. Everything that he had said and taught had in fact only been a veil and cover for the secrets of anatomy. He explained this summarily by saying that the idols he had shown symbolize the five senses and the principal internal and external body parts. (p. 67)

In the first half of the seventeenth century there are thus two major accounts related to the Buddha's last moments. Both stem from missionaries to Vietnam—another country that, like China and Japan, had a strong and at times dominant Zen tradition. The first by Borri (1631) features a deathbed scene of Buddhism's founder in which no new teaching, no secret, no lie, and no recantation are mentioned; rather, Buddha simply confirmed before dying that his old teaching adopted by the Japanese Zen sect is the true doctrine. The story by de Rhodes (1651) was thus the first to mention an oral deathbed recantation of Buddhism's founder in which a long-held secret was revealed to his closest disciples. This secret consisted not really in a new doctrine but rather in a new way to interpret earlier teachings.

In the second half of the seventeenth century de Rhodes's successor in the Vietnam mission, Giovanni Filippo DE MARINI (1608–1682), furnished some new elements. He explains that Xaca, "having arrived at the end both of his life and his deluding [ingannare], summoned his disciples and told them with great secrecy that he wanted in this hour at last reveal another mystery and a new doctrine" (de Marini 1665:215–6). Because this doctrine was "too sublime," he had never spoken about this to anyone, not even to his closest disciples. But on the verge of death he told them:

> You must know that the doctrine I hitherto taught was fable; nevertheless you must present it to the people as if it were true and maintain it in good faith inasmuch as it is sufficient for their good and their understanding. (p. 216)

De Marini then comments on the content of the "sublime and interior doctrine that Xaca revealed to those ten chosen scholars"—a teaching that "consists of such abstruse mysteries and subtle matters that it vanishes into nothing [un nulla]" (p. 218):

> In the first place, he maintained that the principle forming both man and all other things is a kind of most subtle air whose substance cannot be perceived by the senses ... nor even by the sharpest and most perspicacious intellect.... The Chinese tried hard to devine the meaning of this new philosophy, and after extensive speculations ... they arrived at the truth by calling it, in their language, Cūm kiū, and the Tonkinese khaù, which in Italian means Emptiness [Vacuo] or Nothingness [Nulla], into which at death everything dissolves. (pp. 218–9)

In order to further clarify this doctrine, de Marini uses the analogies of water taking various forms depending on its container and of golden objects of multiple shapes that, when sufficiently heated, melt and reveal their common essence of pure gold (p. 219). Then a conversation between the dying Buddha and his closest disciples ensues:

> When asked who first gave diverse forms to this subtle air and endowed them with specific qualities, his answer came down to a true nothing [un uero nulla]. Hence this new Democritus knows neither God nor good and evil nor recompense, and

neither punishment nor an immortal soul ... He added that this air that is so subtle possesses no heart that moves it, no thought that bothers it, no intellect that discourses, no power by which it operates—yet that it is pure, delicate, and subtle to such a degree that it cannot be created [ingenerabile], altered [inalterabile], or corrupted [incorruttibile]. In addition, one feels obliged to add, it also is impossible to understand [inintelligibile]. (pp. 219–220)

De Marini's account of 1665—which reached a broad European readership also through long excerpts in Dutch translation (Dapper 1670)—for the first time has the Buddha reveal a truly new doctrine to a small number of followers before passing away and reports that he admonished them to keep this strictly secret. Another innovation is that this doctrine concerns the "first principle," which is defined as "subtle air." The Indian founder himself does not yet speak of emptiness or nothingness; rather, these concepts are said to be the result of extensive speculation at a much later time by Chinese Buddhists who were puzzled by this doctrine of "subtle air."

The first "classical" version of the deathbed confession tale was published in Domingo Navarrete's *Tratados* of 1676. It reads:

He preached his doctrine [ley] for forty-nine years and died at age seventy-nine. Before his death he said: During more than forty years I have not made known [manifestado] the truth of what I know, because I have only preached the exterior and apparent part of my doctrine by means of diverse comparisons that I held all to be false, rather than the interior which I judged to be true. And so he then declared that the first Principle and ultimate end is the materia prima [materia primera], or Chaos, which they express by the two letters Kung and Hiu, which are the same as emptiness [vacuo], and that apart from this there is nothing else to be strived or hoped for. (Navarrete 1676:86; cf. Navarrete 1704:86).

We have seen that already in 1558 Nunes Barreto had argued that Buddhism's founder taught that *materia prima* or *chaos* is the first principle, and we recall that his teaching in metaphors for over forty years was also known to the authors of the 1556 *Sumario de los errores*. Furthermore, it was discussed at length in Valignano's *Catechismus* of 1586, a text that Jesuit novices bound for Japan such as de Rhodes, Borri, and de Marini were obliged to study. But now this idea was wrapped in a concise, striking story destined to become widely known in Europe in the *Confucius sinarum philosophus* version that differs in some significant respects from Navarrete's account. In Navarrete's version, the Buddha's ultimate teaching has a scholastic odor since it consists in the equation materia prima = chaos = emptiness. The *Confucius sinarum philosophus* version published in 1687, on the other hand, obfuscated the scholastic background of Buddha's last words by replacing "materia prima" by *vacuum* and "chaos" by *inane* (emptiness). The much-quoted Buddhism-related section of the *Confucius* introduction also presents the Buddha in a strident tone as a fraud, liar and coward who needed to be prodded by the cold breath of death to "vomit forth" his nihilistic atheism. Instead of simply "saying," "declaring," or "proclaiming" something to his disciples in his last moments, the "horrible impostor" now makes a deathbed *confession* that seems addressed not only to his immediate disciples but also to their successors among Europe's freethinkers and atheists:

> At the age of seventy-nine, this newly manufactured god felt that he was not among the immortals, sensed that his powers were waning, and knew that his hour had come. Never had anybody been more pernicious for humankind ... Already on the verge of death, he vomited forth the foul poison of atheism and, as one might expect, openly confessed that during more than forty years of preaching he had not told the truth to the world and had concealed the naked truth under the veil of metaphorical teachings by way of figures, analogies, and

parables; but that now, as he approached death, it was time to declare its arcane meaning: "There is nothing to be sought and nothing to pin our hopes on other than vacuity [vacuum] and emptiness [inane]—called Cum hiu [空虛] by the Chinese— which is the principle of all things." These are the last words of this horrible impostor, and they constitute the principal root of Atheism—a root that even today is lurking in the murkiness of falsehoods and superstitions as if buried underground, which is why it escapes the attention of ignorant people. (Couplet 1687:xxix)

The numerous journal reviews of *Confucius sinarum philosophus* citing this striking confession story naturally attributed its authorship to Philippe Couplet who had signed the introduction. However, the recent examination of its extant handwritten text[76] and of related materials by several scholars showed that this introduction (Declaratio proëminalis), though signed by Couplet, had in fact been written by several authors (Golvers 1998). Its entire first part (which includes the section on Buddhism with the deathbed confession tale) is attributed to Prospero INTORCETTA (1626–1696), a Jesuit of Sicilian origin who wrote it during the Canton detention in 1665–66.[77] By contrast, the second part of the introduction was later added by several authors including Couplet.[78] Here we focus on the introduction's portrayal of Buddhism and the deathbed confes-

76  Bibliothèque Nationale in Paris, Ms. Lat. 6277.

77  Meynard (2011:3) dates it to 1668; but in a remark by Intorcetta (Bibliothèque nationale Ms. Lat. 6277, vol. 1, §7, fol. IIIv) which was struck out by Couplet and therefore not published in *Confucius Sinarum philosophus*, the Sicilian mentions his teacher da Costa's *recent* death. Da Costa died on March 25 of 1666.

78  See Golvers 1998. In the printed edition of 1687, for which Couplet had heavily edited the original manuscripts mainly by eliminating numerous sections, the first part occupies 44 (pp. ix–liiii) and the second part 61 pages (pp. liiii–cxiv).

sion tale in the first part. Like Golvers and other authors[79] I used
to believe that it was authored by Intorcetta and revised by Couplet. But when I examined the manuscript (marked Latin 6277) at
the Bibliothèque nationale in Paris in the summer of 2010, I was
struck by a very interesting remark by Intorcetta which proves that
the Buddhism part of the *Confucius sinarum philosophus*, which is
what interests us here,[80] stems from a different author. This handwritten remark, which all previous investigators of Manuscript 6277
including Golvers and Meynard appear to have overlooked, is one of
the passages that Couplet decided to omit in the printed version of
*Confucius sinarum philosophus.*

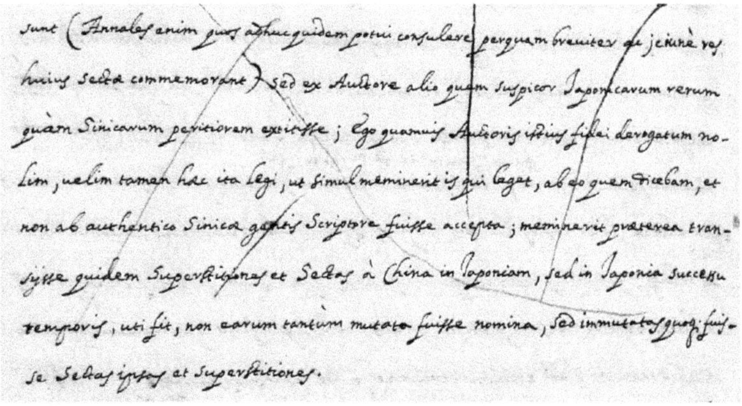

FIG. 16: MS. LAT. 6277, INTORCETTA'S EXPLANATION ABOUT HIS SOURCE OF
INFORMATION ABOUT BUDDHISM

79 Most recently, Meynard (2011:6), who apparently was not aware of the work
of Golvers (1998) and Dew (2009), also attributed the first half of the *Confucius
sinarum philosophus* introduction to Intorcetta and the second half to Couplet.

80 Meynard calls this part "probably the most comprehensive account of the seventeenth century" and "a landmark for the wealth of information it contains and
also for its intellectual engagement with Buddhism" (2011:5).

Like most of his predecessors and colleagues in the China mission, Intorcetta had concentrated on the study of Confucian texts and neglected Buddhism—which is why he admits at the very beginning of the introduction's section on Buddhism that he only briefly consulted annals about this religion and therefore decided to use data "from another author whom I suspect of having been more familiar with Japanese than Chinese things."[81]

Intorcetta justifies his reliance on this unnamed author by explaining that he does not intend to question that author's expertise and that the superstitions and sects of Japan, which are of Chinese origin, have at any rate remained unchanged in Japan except for some differences in terminology.[82]

There is no doubt that this unnamed author "more familiar with Japanese than Chinese things" is João Rodrigues who had studied Buddhism for decades and whose writings were stored in the Jesuit archive in Macao. Hence this "landmark report" on Buddhism (Meynard 2011:5) seems not to reflect Intorcetta's knowledge about Buddhism around 1666 but rather that of João Rodrigues in the early 1620s. We recall that Rodrigues's report on Chinese religions was such a revelation to Ricci's successor Longobardi that he ordered his missionaries to carefully study it before he wrote his report in 1623-4. Intorcetta's remarks suggest that none other than Rodrigues could be the ultimate source of the deathbed confession story. Borri,

---

81 The beginning of this passage reads in my transcription: "(Annales enim quos adhuc quidam potui consulere perquam breviter ac jeiunè res. huius secta commemorant) sed ex Auctore alio quam suspicor Japonicarum rerum quàm Sinicarum peritiorem extitisse" (Ms. Lat. 6277, vol. 1, §33, fol. XIVv).

82 Intorcetta continues: "ego quamvis Auctoris istius fidei derogatum nolim, uelim tamen haec ita legi, ut simul meminesit is qui leget, ab eo quem dicebam, et non ab authentica Sinica gentis Scriptore fuisse accepta; meminerit praeterea transijsse quidem Superstitiones et Sectas à China in Japonicam, sed in Japonica successu temporis, usi fit, non earum tantùm mutata fuisse nomina, sed immutatas quoque fuisse sectas ipsos et superstitiones." (Ms. Lat. 6277, vol. 1, §33, fol. XIVv)

de Rhodes, and de Marini had all stayed in Macao and could have picked up bits and pieces of the story. Intorcetta and Navarrete had during their leisurely Canton detention access to holdings of the Macao mission archive that had been brought to Canton, and they appear to have made use of João Rodrigues's manuscripts. Their tales are so similar that one must assume a common source, and Intorcetta's remark in the *Confucius sinarum philosophus* manuscript points to this source: Rodrigues.[83] Navarrete's tale of Buddha's deathbed confession clearly puts the essence of Valignano's, Rodrigues's and Longobardi's view of the "inner" teaching of Buddhism into the Buddha's mouth: the first principle of Buddhism, so he declares, is the *materia prima* or *chaos*, called by the Chinese *vacuum* or *emptiness*. Navarrete's account has the Buddha formulate his ultimate teaching in line with the interpretation of "chaos" and "emptiness" by Nunes Barreto, Valignano, Rodrigues, and Longobardi, that—as I have observed above and will further document in the next chapter—was inspired by Coimbra textbooks on Aristotle. The Buddha's ultimate teaching thus was a tailor-made target for the Jesuit attack line as formulated in Valignano's influential catechism. The *Confucius sinarum philosophus* version, which is the one that became the "golden" standard, removed the tell-tale terminology of scholasticism and provided modern atheists with a rotten, lying, and nihilistic Oriental ancestor. The inventors of this story had thus committed with a vengeance what reformers of all creeds are fond of doing, namely, to insert their own ideas and agenda into a founder's mouth.

The complete tale of the founder's deathbed confession deftly combined a striking tale of his last moments with a pithy presentation of his horrible doctrine. The *Confucius sinarum philosophus* version was enormously successful and found its way not only into many scholarly journals but also popular China books such as

83 De Marini had lost all his manuscripts in a shipwreck and in 1658–9 spent four months in Macao collecting materials before departing for Rome where his 1663 book was published. He thus worked on this story independently from Intorcetta.

Lecomte's *Nouveaux mémoires sur l'état présent de la Chine* (1696) and du Halde's four-volume *Description géographique, historique, chronologique, politique et physique de l'Empire de la Chine et de la Tartarie chinoise* (1736). In addition it is found in travel account collections, histories of philosophy, popular encyclopedias, and books by the likes of Pierre Bayle, Johann Jakob Brucker, and Denis Diderot, thus furnishing crucial elements to the flowering of "Oriental philosophy" in the eighteenth century. Even in the nineteenth century the tale was repeated *ad nauseam*, and the philosopher Hegel was in good company when he wrote in his *Enzyklopädie der philosophischen Wissenschaften* of 1830 about "the nothingness that the Buddhists consider to be the principle of everything as well as the final purpose and goal of everything" (Hegel 1991:107). He read about this in his main source for such matters, Abbé Grosier's synthesis of missionary reports (Grosier 1787: 2.147–246), where the (by now standard) story of the Buddha's deathbed confession from the *Confucius* introduction was presented as follows:

> When he had attained the age of 79 years he felt by the weakening of his forces that his borrowed divinity would not prevent his having to pay tribute to nature like other men. He did not want to leave his disciples without revealing the secret to them, along with all hidden profundities of his doctrine. Having gathered them, he declared that until this moment he had always believed that he should only make use of parables in his discourses; that for forty years he had hidden the truth under figurative and metaphorical expressions; and that on the verge of disappearing to their gaze he wanted to finally manifest his real feelings and reveal to them the mystery of his wisdom. You must realize, he said to them, that there is no other principle of all things than emptiness [le vuide] and nothingness [le néant]; it is from nothingness that everything arose, and it is to nothingness that everything must return; this is where all our hopes end up. (Grosier 1787: 2.205–6)

Thus it was not at all poor Hegel who "installed in the philosophical imaginary the link between the Buddha and nothingness," as Roger-Pol Droit (1997:91) claims in his book *Le culte du néant* (The Cult of Nothingness), but rather *the Buddha in person*, reclining on his deathbed in the "imaginary" of Christian missionaries. Like Ma Ferguson's Jesus who spoke English (see Chapter 1), the Jesuit's Buddha now uttered what was in the Jesuit missionaries' mind. But unlike Ferguson's statement and Arlecchino's antics that make people laugh because of the obvious incongruity of imagined and known reality, the story of Buddha's confession was no laughing matter. After all, this was not a clown amusing his public on a comedy stage but the founder of a religion expressing the heart of his doctrine on his deathbed. And that religion was—as we will see in the next chapter—considered by some to be the largest on earth. Europeans had read in Alvarez de Semedo's famous China book that the monasteries *in China alone* had formerly housed "up to three million monks" (1643:113)[84]—a number that Dapper (1670:123) used to describe the state of affairs in his own time. Dapper claimed that there still are "two to three million" monks inhabiting China's huge monasteries. The enormity of this number only hits home when one realizes that in 1570 the entire population of England was 3 million and that of Portugal 1.5 million! (Hsia 2010:37)

To return to seventeenth-century China: given that the Jesuits had in 1627 decided to suppress Rodrigues's and Longobardi's viewpoint and to follow Ricci's strategy, it comes as no surprise that Rodrigues's name is seldom mentioned after that date. But half a century after the suppression of Rodrigues's and Longobardi's reports, their views did find a vociferous champion among the critics of Ricci's approach: Domingo Navarrete. It was thanks to Navarrete that these ideas escaped in 1676, eleven years prior to the publication of *Confu-*

---

84 Semedo's work on China, which first appeared in Spanish in 1642, was translated into many European languages and had an enormous impact rivaling that of Ricci's book of 1615 (translated, edited, and published by Trigault).

*cius sinarum philosophus,* from the exotic confines of the China mission into an entirely new arena: Europe's Republic of Letters whose members were very eager to learn more about the world in general and China in particular.

## Chapter Eleven

## THE COMMON GROUND (NAVARRETE)

While Father Kircher in Rome was busy preparing his *China illustrata* for publication, nineteen of his fellow Jesuits in the China mission were deported to Canton and put under house arrest for almost four years. Only four missionaries were allowed to remain at the imperial court in Beijing. The same deportation order also brought a handful of Dominican and Franciscan missionaries into a cramped house in the southern Chinese city of Canton. From their arrival in March 1666 until June 1668 the conditions of detention were most severe as the missionaries were forbidden to leave their residence and were closely guarded. Subsequently the inspections gradually became less frequent until official visitations stopped and the detainees enjoyed limited liberty of movement (Cummins 1993:144–5). The Canton detention prevented the missionaries from catechizing; thus they used their time for intensive study, translation of Chinese texts, writing, praying, and quarreling among themselves. It is in this house that—with the help of books and manuscripts brought from the Macao Jesuit archive—the missionaries collected and synthesized much of what they had so far learned about Chinese religions and philosophies.

Among the nineteen detained Jesuits was Prospero INTORCETTA (1626–1696), the Sicilian Jesuit whose introduction to *Confucius sinarum philosophus* was discussed in Chapter 10. Intorcetta was a typical product of the Ricci-inspired China mission strategy. In 1659 he had accompanied Martino Martini—his countryman and author of the China Atlas (1655) and history (1658)—to China as a new mission recruit. Tutored by the Jesuit Vice-Provincial Inácio DA COSTA (1603–66), Intorcetta first studied the basics of *guanhua* 官話, the language of Chinese officials, and then took da Costa's course in Chinese philosophy which consisted, as was the rule among Jesuit missionaries, of the study of the four Confucian classics (the *Great Learning, Doctrine of the Mean, Analects of Confucius,* and the *Book of Mencius*). In 1662 Intorcetta published a textbook that in several respects is a sign of the times. Other than being the first printed translation of a sample from these so-called Four Books (*sishu* 四書) into a Western language, it was a symptom of severe personnel problems. Instead of preparing for their mission duties by taking intensive two- or three-year courses in the Chinese language and Confucian philosophy under the guidance of native tutors and experienced missionaries, recruits now received "no more than a crash course in speaking Chinese" (Brockey 2007:279) and were almost immediately dispatched to regional centers where they had to fend for themselves. Intorcetta was lucky to have a knowledgeable instructor of the old school who himself had studied Chinese classics under Gaspar FERREIRA (1571–1649) and decided to make what he had learned accessible to less fortunate missionaries in form of a reader entitled *The Meaning of Chinese Wisdom as explained by Fr. Ignacio da Costa, Portuguese, of the Society of Jesus, and made public by Fr. Prospero Intorcetta* (Jiangxi, 1662).

Brockey's fine analysis of the Jesuit China mission's education system (2007:207–86) shows that the Jesuit curriculum toed Ricci's line in stressing the study of a selection of Confucian texts. The tactic of cuddling up to Confucianism had the odd effect that the study of the religion commonly identified as Christianity's greatest enemy and rival, Buddhism, was from the beginning of the China mission largely neglected—which is why Intorcetta felt obliged to rely on a report by João Rodrigues that was almost half a century old.

Severely outnumbered by these nineteen Jesuits, the four Franciscan and Dominican friars seemed to be in a losing position regarding differences in mission strategy. But the Spanish leader of the Franciscans, Antonio a Santa Maria CABALLERO (also known as Antoine de Sainte-Marie; 1602–1669) had a trump card up his sleeve: he was in possession of part of the report that Fr. Longobardi, Ricci's successor and critic, had written in 1623–24. This document was supposed to have been burned, but Caballero (who had met the aged Longobardi twice during the 1650) had obtained part of the report through Jean Valat, a maverick Jesuit (Cummins 1993:159). The fact that Caballero had clandestinely sent a copy of this document to the Propaganda Fide in Rome around 1662 (Brockey 2007:133) may explain his long silence and unwillingness to share it with his fellow detainees in Canton. But in the summer of 1668 he handed this clandestine copy of Longobardi's treatise to his Dominican countryman Navarrete. It crashed like a bomb into the missionaries' detention center since it showed that learned Jesuits had entertained similar misgivings as the Franciscan and Dominican friars and had severely criticized Ricci's views and mission strategy. In essence, Longobardi's treatise argues that Confucianism, Daoism, and Buddhism share a profoundly atheistic inner doctrine that originated with Ham alias Zoroaster and had radiated not only to Egypt and ancient Greece but to India, China, and Japan. While ostensibly focusing on Confucianism and Neoconfucianism, the treatise presented Rodrigues's invention in a well-documented, scholarly form. Its entire core logic thus stems from Rodrigues and can be found in his extant writings (see Chapter 8).

Once the cat had escaped from the bag in the summer of 1668, there was no return: Caballero immediately sat down to write a treatise with the aim of destroying the entire Jesuit rationale for the tolerance of Chinese rites. Meanwhile, Navarrete collected whatever materials he could get hold of and escaped from Canton determined to inform the authorities in Rome and to publish all relevant documents. The first volume of Navarrete's explosive *Tratados* was published in 1676 and contains the Spanish translation of Longobardi's treatise, thus serving as a bullhorn for Rodrigues's invention in Europe. Publication of the second volume was stopped midway and prohibited. But the published first volume and the manuscript of the second volume were used in attacks on the Jesuit society by Antoine Arnauld (1682) and by the noted French church historian Noël Alexandre, who translated numerous sections from both volumes (1699). But the greatest impact was due to the publication of a French translation of Longobardi's and Caballero's treatises in 1701 which appeared at the height of the *Querelle des rites* (Controversy about Chinese rites) in Paris (Longobardi 1701). They became central documents in the raging controversies about quietism, Chinese rites, and atheism, which is why they were discussed and commented upon not just by scores of missionaries and theologians but also by the most famous philosophers of the time: Bayle (1702), Malebranche (1708), and Leibniz.[85]

The second book of Navarrete's published *Tratados* is often overlooked because of the Longobardi treatise in the fifth, but it is important as it expresses Navarrete's view of the common ground of Asia's religions and philosophies. Right from the beginning, Navarrete makes it clear that in his opinion the "Learned Sect" (Confucianism) "professes down-right Atheism" (Navarrete 1704:81). Navarrete completely agrees with Rodrigues's and Longobardi's take on the common "inner" doctrine of Confucianism, Daoism, and Buddhism. But since it is Buddhism that is "the greatest Enemy we have to deal with in *Japan*, *China*, and many other Kingdoms" (p. 86), Navarrete focuses his discussion on this religion. He calls it the "sect of Foe" or "the Sect of the Idols of *India*" and explains that it was brought to China "about sixty years after the Birth of our Saviour" (p. 82). The consensus among the missionaries in Canton about the geographical spread and enormous size of Buddhism is reflected in Navarrete's relatively accurate description:

85  "Letter to Rémond;" see Leibniz 2002 and the English translation in Leibniz 1977.

This curs'd Sect has so spread, that it certainly far exceeds the *Mahometan*. From *India* it pierced as far as *Japan*, without leaving any Island or part of the Continent all that way exempt from it. This Hellish Infection has seized the *Laos, Lequios*,[86] *Tibet*, both *Tartaries*,[87] *Siam, Camboxa, Cochinchina, Tunquin*,[88] and all the Archipelago of *St. Lazarus*.[89] (p. 82)

This description was published in 1676, that is, fully two centuries before—according to Masuzawa (2005:122)—Buddhism was first "recognized as 'the same' tradition existing in diverse regions of South, South-east, East, and Central Asia." There is an even older source containing such a description along with very detailed information about Buddhist beliefs and practices in many Asian countries: the book published in 1663 by Giovanni Filippo DE MARINI (1608–1682). On his way to Japan, de Marini was from 1641–2 in Siam (Thailand), and after missing the ship to Japan he spent three years in Macao (1643–6) in the company of numerous Japan and China missionaries before joining the Vietnam mission where he stayed for eighteen years (1646–58). Apart from much valuable information about Vietnam, his book also contains pioneering descriptions of other Buddhist countries such as Laos and Cambodia. He informed his readers that the religion of the Indian founder Xe kia (Shakya) is found in India, Bengal, Pegu (Burma), Siam, Cambodia, and Laos in addition to Vietnam, China, and Japan, and he mentioned the Indian founder's diverse appellations in these countries (de Marini 1665:210–1). Apart from his detailed descriptions of Buddhism in China and the neighboring Southeast Asian coun-

---

86  The Ryūkyū islands south of the Japan archipelago including Taiwan.

87  The entire region to the north of China including Siberia, Mongolia, and Manchuria.

88  Tunquin corresponds roughly to North Vietnam and Cochinchina to South Vietnam.

89  The Marianas.

tries, de Marini furnishes a biography of the Indian founder based on Chinese sources (pp. 211–5), a description of his outer and inner teachings (pp. 216–41), and much more. But he was mistaken in assuming that this religion's founder is called "Rama" in India and had been a rival of the older "O My To" (Amitābha Buddha). The consequences of this misconception are an indication of de Marini's influence: it seduced Kircher (1667), Dapper (1670), La Loubère (1691) and many others to imagine Oriental pantheons that are truly mind-blowing. For example, Dapper took a Chinese print he probably obtained from Grueber as proof for Confucius's and Mencius's worship of "goddess Pusa": a Buddhist Bodhisattva!

FIG. 17: CONFUCIUS & MENCIUS WORSHIPING A BODHISATTVA (DAPPER 1670:107)

Apart from such overestimated boundaries, de Marini's book shows how much solid knowledge had around 1660 already accumulated in missionary circles. But now such knowledge became public and Europe's readers showed much interest. After the book's first Italian edition of 1663, three Italian reprints with different titles appeared in a single year (1665), followed by two French translations (1666 and 1683) and very extensive excerpts in Dutch in Dapper's spectacularly illustrated Dutch China volume (Dapper 1670). Even in the eighteenth century the interest did not abate, as is evident from the frequent quotations by authors like La Croze (1724), Brucker (1736), and compilers of popular travel account collections.

A major eye-opener was de Marini's statistic of the inhabitants of our world (one billion in total) of which Europe possessed barely ten percent, Africa a bit less, the Americas close to twenty percent, and Asia an astonishing fifty percent (p. xix). Since the religion of Rama = Buddha was said to reign in most of Asia, this religion was thought to be the largest religion on earth—much larger even than Islam, as Navarrete wrote: a true world religion if there ever was one!

De Marini described the "inner" teaching of this huge religion much like Navarrete (p. 216–21) a few years later, and he also offered—as we saw in the previous chapter—his version of the founder's deathbed scene. Hence Buddha's doctrine of "emptiness" and "nothingness" (*Vacuum, ò Nulla*; p. 218) became in one fell swoop the core teaching of the largest religion on earth: a gigantic cult of emptiness. Navarrete's relatively accurate description of this religion's geographical range is followed, as in de Marini, by a presentation of its inner teaching in China:

> The first Principle they assign and know does not go beyond the *Materia Prima*, wherein it agrees with the two former [Confucianism and Daoism], tho it differ in the names and terms. This is the opinion of most solid Missioners, of the *Chinese* Doctors, and of their Classick Authors. (Navarrete 1704: 82)

The "most solid Missioners" of course included Rodrigues and Longobardi whose views Navarrete presents both in the second and fifth book of his *Tratados*. After briefly describing the Indian founder's life, Buddhist temples, clergy, worship, etc., Navarrete returns to the discussion of the doctrine that in his opinion forms the heart of the inner doctrine not only of Buddhism but also of Daoism and Confucianism. It is presented in a nutshell by way of the last teachings of Foe alias Buddha to his disciples before passing away:

> Therefore he then declar'd, that the first Principle, or Beginning and ultimate End, was no other than the *Materia prima*, or *Chaos*, which they express by these two Letters *Kung* and *Hiu*, signifying a *Vacuum* or Emptiness, and that there was nothing further to be sought after of hoped for. (p. 86)

This teaching of emptiness was spread from its Indian homeland by thousands of disciples to most parts of Asia, written down "in above 50,000 several Gatherings" on "Palm-Leaves," and professed— among countless others—by "*Ta Mo* [Bodhidharma], a famous Idol in China" (p. 86).

> They report of him, that he was nine years in contemplation with his Face to a Wall. These Contemplations on the *Vacuum* or *Chaos*, which are directed to imitate that first Principle, they call taking the Degree of an Idol, and then returning to the *Vacuum*, or Nothing whence they came. (p. 86)

This famous exponent of the inner teaching, who is said to have come from India to China "over 300 Years after the Incarnation of the Son of God" (p. 87), is today known as Bodhidharma, the founder of Zen Buddhism. Since the eleventh century, his Zen sect made use of koans such as "What is your true face before your parents were born?"[90] Navarrete suggests the following answer:

---

90  On koans and their discovery see Chapter 4. This saying is associated with case 23 of the *Gateless Barrier* (*Mumonkan*) koan collection; see Aitken 1990:153.

The purport of the Interior Doctrine is, That as before my Parents were born, there was nothing but the *Vacuum*, which is the Being of all things, and gave us that which we have; so after Death all things return to, and are reduced to that *Vacuum*, or Nothing, without leaving any other distinction betwixt Creatures, but the bare Figure and Qualities they have. As for instance, the Water that is in several Vessels of sundry shapes, round or square, &c. (p. 87)

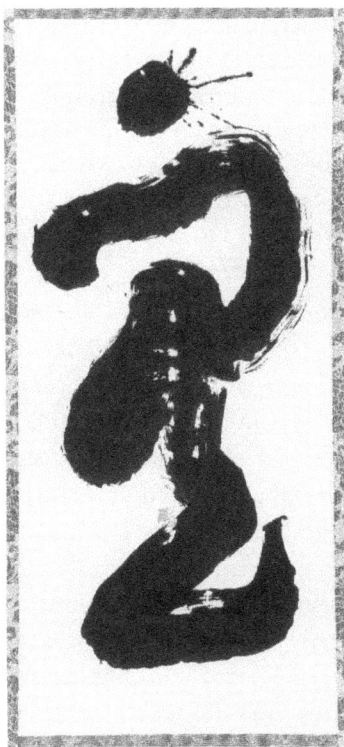

FIG. 18: *KŪ* 空 (EMPTINESS). CALLIGRAPHY BY SHIN'ICHI HISAMATSU

According to Navarrete, the "Learned Men" of China—the Confucians of his time—are said to have a doctrine that "is the same as the Interior Doctrine of the *Bonzes*" (p. 87).

> They also make use of the Simily of the Moon, which shows its Figure in the Water, or a Glass, and it looks like a Moon, but is only an Image of Resemblance, and mere Nothing. So they say of Creatures, that they are nothing but the first Principle, which the Being of them all, whose Substance they set down as a Rule, has no Understanding, Will, Virtue, Power, &c. Yet they describe it as pure, subtile, ingenerable, infinite, incorruptible, and most perfect. They place Beatitude in this Life, through Meditation and Mortification; so that their Bliss is obtain'd by meditating on that first Principle, and reaching to the height of Contemplation, wherein a Man is as it were beside himself void of Reflection, and without any operation of the Understanding, and further than this he has nothing to seek or hope for. (pp. 87–88)

In this manner, the very doctrine whose origins I described in earlier chapters of this book—the ultimate teaching of Buddha proclaimed on his deathbed—had by 1676 become not only the true teaching of Buddhism's founder but was presented to European readers as the philosophy of the world's largest religion and half of humanity, a philosophy professed since ancient times by Indian gymnosophists whose core teaching is identical with Confucianism and Daoism. Now "Oriental nothingness" had in a sense come home to Zen: born in the minds of missionaries in Japan, China, and Vietnam where the Zen tradition was strong or even dominant, Bodhidharma now represented not only the exact teaching of the dying Buddha but, true to Rodrigues's line of argument, a kind of ur-philosophy whose first principle is found not only in the entire Orient but also in the writings of ancient Greek philosophers and poets!

If we observe the first Principle assign'd by all the *Chinese* Sects, we shall find they do not much vary from other Antients, against whom the Saints writ much. *Hesiod* treated of the *Chaos*, and not of the Cause which produced it, as *Lactantius* observes, *de fals. Rel. lib. 1, cap. 5*. The same do these Sects we have mention'd. ... The Learned Men of *China* maintain the same. (p. 89)

A very interesting aspect of Navarrete's description of this ur-philosophy is that he constantly refers to theological views shared by Christian missionaries of all orders. Texts known and respected by all theologians are continually quoted in support of arguments: they formed their common ground and shared perspective. This was the lens through which missionaries like Nunes Barreto, Valignano, Fróis, Rodrigues, Ricci, Longobardi, de Marini, and Navarrete perceived and interpreted Asian philosophies and religions. In Arlecchino manner, they projected on Oriental philosophy what they were familiar with from their philosophy and theology courses. The opinions of Church fathers and theologians about ancient religions and philosophies are thus absolutely crucial for our understanding of the missionaries' portrayal of Asian phenomena.

I have already observed that the Coimbra textbook version of Aristotle's *Physics* played a central role. But texts by other Catholic "Saints"—particularly St. Augustine and St. Thomas Aquinas—are also often mentioned and quoted in the 1623–4 Longobardi report (first published in Spanish translation in Navarrete's fifth book of 1676) and in Navarrete's own comments and explanations. I will here mention only a few particularly instructive examples. With regard to the missionaries' view of the "first principle," the connected doctrine that "all is one," and their oriental origin, Longobardi adduces St. Augustine's *De civitate Dei* (City of God):

> We must observe in this place, that the *Chinese* Idolatry in a great measure resembles that of *Europe* ... S. *Aug. 4 de Civit. Dei, cap* 10, 11, 12 proves out of the antient Roman, Greek and *Egyptian* Writers, that several Gods the Old Philosophers introduced were in effect one and the same thing; that is,

that there is but one Thing, which is all things, all the Gods, the Soul of the World, and the World it self. Whence we may gather that the Antients thought all to proceed from the Infinite Chaos, as they imagin'd it to be the first Material principle, and *materia prima*, perswading themselves it was the same thing with the particular Parts of the World: and thus they grounded all their multitude of Gods and Idolatries on these Physical Notions. And it is evident, as the same Saint [Augustine] says, that this Opinion was receiv'd and current in *Asia*, thence communicated to the *Greeks* and *Egyptians*, and from them to the Romans. (p. 211)

This passage was certainly known to all missionaries involved in the invention of Oriental philosophy. Rodrigues frequently quoted this text, as did other missionaries. According to Longobardi (as cited by Navarrete), the Chinese thus have the very same notion of the first Principle as some ancient Greek philosophers—though they refer to it by other names such as *Li* 理 (principle), *Kung* 空 (vacuum), *Hiu* 虛 (emptiness), *Tao* 道 (way), *Vu* 無 (nothingness), and so on (p. 198). Explaining this first principle, he quotes a passage from Luis Vives's commentary on this passage in Augustinus's *City of God* that also throws light on Valignano's understanding of the Buddhist "One mind" in the 1586 *Catechismus*:

> *Lewis Vives* upon the words of the Saint, cap. 12. *If the Spirit of the World is God*, & c. says, it was *Pythagoras* his opinion, that all things were part of God, which implies that there is but one thing in the World, that is, the Chaos, or *Materia prima*, which they call'd God, or the Mind. (p. 211)

According to Longobardi's report published by Navarrete, the ancient monist view—that all things are "one and the same substance" and that multiplicity is illusory—has "much resemblance with that of some antient *European* Philosophers" (p. 200) who believe

> *That all things were continued, and are one and the same by nature, and the manner of their being, but various according to*

*sense, and no way differing.* In the course of *Coimbra, Fonseca* and others, relying on *Aristotle's* Text, say, those antient Philosophers knew nothing beyond the material Cause, and even that but grossly; for they imagin'd that the Matter it self was the whole essence of Natural things, and that they were all one continu'd thing, and very agreeable to outward Sense, without having any essential difference among themselves. ... Just as we say of artificial things made of Wood, that as to the Essence they are Wood, but are distinguishable by the artificial form. And in this sense *Parmenides* and *Milito* affirm'd that all things were one and the same, and accordingly *Aristotle* quotes and refutes them. See *Fonseca* in 1. *Physic.* from whom this is taken. (p. 200)

Another theme of Valignano's catechism and Rodrigues's writings that played an important role in their perception of oriental thought systems is, as we have seen, the distinction between an outer (exoteric) and inner (esoteric) teaching. In support of this view, Longobardi adduced the Coimbra text of Aristotle's *Physics*:

The antient custom of Philosophers taken by Pherecydes, Pythagoras his Master, from the Egyptians and Chaldeans, was, either not to write down the Precepts of Philosophy at all, or to write them obscurely, that is, under the obscurity of a deep hidden sense, and shrouded under Mathematical Figures, and Enigmatical Expressions. For the Poets darkened and conceal'd the Secrets of Philosophy under Fables, the Pythagoreans under Symbols, the Platonists under Mathematicks, and Aristotle under the conciseness of his Style. (p. 193)

Writings by Albertus Magnus were another favorite reference point of Navarrete, for example with regard to creation-and-destruction cycles that are obviously incompatible with the Christian God's singular act of creation.

Observe how true it is, that the *Chineses* hold the same Errors that were formerly in *Europe*, as the Author [Longobardi] proves in the sequel, and I [Navarrete] instanced in another place out of *F. Arias*, and *F. Kircher*. Our *B. Alb. Magnus tract. 2 de hom. quaest.* 89. art. 2. *in fine*, mentions the same that is writ in the first paragraph: *Some said there were infinite Worlds successively; the head of them was Empedocles, who said, that one motion of the Heaven being perform'd according to the motion of the World, all things return to the first Matter, and another motion beginning are regenerated in like number as they were before, and another World begins. But that motion of the Heaven is perform'd according to the progress or motion of the sixt Stars, & c. in 36000 years, and this space of time they call one great Year.* p. 198)

Navarrete often quotes writings of Thomas Aquinas and intersperses them with his own comments that show how he applied the Saint's views to all sects of China. Thomas Aquinas's interpretation of Greek monists and atomists is discussed as follows:

*S. Thomas, opusc.* 15, *cap.* 9. says, *For the first Philosophers set it down as a Maxim, concerning the nature of things, that it was only a change from one Being to another.* And therefore they *assign'd as the first Principle, A Matter without any Cause, for their Understanding did not extend beyond the distinction betwixt the Substance and the Accidents.* All this is plainly the Doctrine of the Sects we have spoken of. *But others proceeding somewhat further, search'd into the Origin of Substances themselves, assigning some Substance as the Cause of their Being; but because they could not frame a Conception of anything but Bodys, therefore they resolv'd Substance into some Principles; yet such as were corporeal, laying it down as a Rule that Bodys were fram'd by the gathering of others, as if the Origin of things consisted in only gathering and dispersing.* Which Doctrine the Chinese Men of Letters directly hold. ... (p. 90)

Even before the publication in French of Longobardi's and Caballero's treatises in 1701, the famous and prolific Dominican church historian Noël Alexandre (1699) published countless excerpts both from the published first volume of Navarrete and the manuscript of the second volume whose printing had been stopped midway because it contained too much incendiary material and risked causing an explosion in the cauldron of controversies involving Jansenists, deists, freethinkers, Jesuits, Dominicans, and philosophers. Alexandre played an important role in the quarrels about Chinese terms and rites, and his *Apologie des Dominicains* of 1699 became required reading. At the end of the seventeenth century it presented in French—a language virtually all European intellectuals could read—the views of Rodrigues, Longobardi, and Navarrete.

In the last decades of the seventeenth century not only missionaries and theologians were involved in the invention of Oriental philosophy. They were joined by secular philosophers and historians of philosophy such as the protagonists of our remaining chapters.

## Chapter Twelve

## PAN-ASIAN PHILOSOPHY (BERNIER)

The synthesis by François BERNIER (1625–1688) of a singular pan-Asian philosophy, which will be described in this chapter, echoed several earlier attempts in Persia and India to classify oriental religions and philosophies. After the death of his teacher, the philosopher Pierre GASSENDI (1592–1655), Bernier set out on a twelve-year journey to the Orient. After one year in Cairo he reached the trading port of Surat (India) in 1658 just when the succession struggles to the Mughal throne came to a head. Soon after his arrival he met the designated successor of Mughal emperor SHAH JAHAN (1592–1666), crown prince Mohammed DARA SHIKOH (1615–1659).

Prince Dara was the eldest son of the Mughal emperor SHAH JAHAN (1592–1666) and his favorite wife MUMTAZ MAHAL (1593–1631) whose mausoleum is the world-famous Taj Mahal in Agra. This monument's mixture of Persian and Indian elements echoes the crown prince's cultural and religious background. Since his youth Dara, whose mother tongue was Persian, had been interested in Sufism, and in his twenties he authored several books with biographies and teachings of Sufi masters. But after meeting the famous Muwaḥḥid (unitarian) Mullā Shah, Dara's interest in other religions and their sacred scriptures grew by leaps and bounds. So did his entourage of experts of religions such as Judaism, Christianity, and Hinduism that also included Yoga adepts, Islamic mystics, and other holy men. For his study of the religions of India the prince consulted with some of the country's most famous scholars and had them translate important texts such as the *Bhagavadgītā* and the *Yogavāsiṣṭha* into Persian. In 1656 Prince Dara finished a book called *The Confluence of the Oceans* that lays out what he regarded as the common core of Hindu and Sufi teaching (Mahfuz-ul-Haq 1990). Shortly thereafter the prince assembled a team of experts for the first ever translation of fifty Upanishads from Sanskrit into Persian. The result, titled *Sirr-i akbar* (The Great Secret), contained not only Upanishadic text but also Sufism-inspired explanations and Vedantic commentary.[91] Soon after this work's completion in 1657, Prince Dara became embroiled in the succession struggle with his younger brother Aurang-zeb, lost in battle, and had to flee.

It is during this flight in 1659 that Bernier, the protagonist of this chapter, briefly met the unfortunate prince and provided medical treatment for one of his wives. After Prince Dara's murder in 1659 by order of his brother Aurang-zeb, Bernier was employed by DANESH-MEND KHAN (also called Muhammad Shafi or Molla Shafi'a), a native of Persia who had been emperor Shah Jahan's secretary of state and under Aurang-zeb was in charge of the imperial treasury. Danesh-mend, who was familiar with the "mysteries of the cabal of the Sufis" (Bernier 1671:61), was very interested in philosophy and science, and for five or six years Bernier's principal occupation consisted in translating Descartes and Gassendi into Persian and philosophizing with his employer (p. 71). Prodded by Bernier who wanted to know more about Indian philosophy, his master employed a famous Indian scholar from the late Prince Dara's entourage. This is how Bernier came to spend no less than three years in the company of "one of the most famous pandits in the entire Indies" (p. 70–1) who had

91 In early nineteenth-century Europe the Latin translation of the *Sirr-i akbar*, Anquetil-Duperron's *Oupnek'hat* (1801–2), was regarded as an embodiment of a unitary, ancient Oriental philosophy. See App 2010:363-439 and App 2011.

been a member of Prince Dara's Upanishad translation team.[92] Bernier states that it was because of information provided by this man that he was able to convey "many things drawn from books in this [Sanskrit] language" (p. 70). Through him Bernier also got to know the "chief of the pandits" of Benares (p. 115) and other scholars of note who supplied him with information about Indian religion and various systems of Indian philosophy (pp. 115–26).

A second major informant of Bernier was the German Jesuit Heinrich ROTH (1620–68) who had traveled to India in 1652 and from 1654 taught at the Jesuit school in Agra.[93] In the year of his arrival in the capital of the Mughal empire, Prince Dara's father had just finished construction of the Taj Mahal; and while Roth was intensively studying Sanskrit, Prince Dara wrote his *Confluence of the Oceans* and assembled the high-caliber team for his 1656 Upanishad translation project. In the early 1660s Roth's study had so much progressed that he was able to redact a pioneering Sanskrit grammar that has been called "a masterpiece" (Hauschild 1988:13). Based on his research on Roth's Sanskrit manuscripts, Hauschild concluded that between Roth's arrival in Agra in 1654 and his departure for Europe in 1662 the German missionary had also become thoroughly familiar with the language and philosophy of the Upanishads (p. 19). On his journey to Europe, Roth carried his manuscript grammar (Camps 1988) as well as notes and drawings related to Indian religion. During a stopover in Shiraz (Persia) in 1663, some of those notes were copied by a Carmelite father who later showed them to Bernier (Zimmel 1988:20–1). In 1664 Roth spent two months in Rome and furnished information about Indian writing systems, languages, mythology, and philosophy to his compatriot and fellow

---

92 Though the evidence is scarce, various names have so far been proposed for this man, for example that of the poet Kavindracarya Sarasvati. See Pollock 2001:407–8, Dew 2009:152, and Busch 2010:291–3.

93 For biographical information about Roth see the study of Camps 1988 that also lists numerous primary and secondary sources.

Jesuit Kircher. Thus it came about that Kircher's *China illustrata* featured not only information about China but also about India. As we have seen in Chapter 9, Kircher (inspired by de Marini's overblown vision of Buddhism) regarded India as the Asian distribution hub of Egyptian cults and the homeland of Buddha's brahmin missionaries. For our inquiry, *China illustrata*'s paragraphs that are based on information by Roth are of particular interest. In his presentation of "the ridiculous Brahmin religion and the teachings about the origin of man," Kircher insists that "the brahmins take their origin according to the Indian writers from Cechian or Xaca" and mentions several "stupid fictions" upheld by these "Brahmin" missionaries of Buddha. One group of them is said to hold a particularly absurd doctrine about the beginning of the world:

> They say that a spider is the first cause, and he created the world by spinning a web with the threads coming from his stomach. Then he formed the heavenly spheres and he rules everything until the end of the world, which he will cause by pulling back into himself all of the threads in his web. I thought this ought to be included here since human imagination can scarcely conceive anything more discordant than these absurd doctrines of the blind pagans. Thanks be to God and to Christ our Savior, because he has taken us before innumerable others from such darkness and has shown mercy to us through the infallible light of his truth. (p. 145)

This appears to be the earliest occurrence of a variant of the "spider" allegory in Western literature. It is based on a passage of a principal Upanishad, Muṇḍaka (1.6–7) that Patrick Olivelle (1998:437) translates as follows:

> What is eternal and all-pervading,
> extremely minute, present everywhere—
> That is the immutable,
> which the wise fully perceive.
> As a spider spins out threads, then draws them into itself;

As plants sprout out from the earth;
As head and body hair grows from a living man;
So from the imperishable all things here spring.

Since no earlier trace of Western study of the Upanishads has so far been found,[94] we must assume that Kircher learned about this from Roth. It is possible that Roth had read the relatively short *Muṇḍaka* Upanishad in Sanskrit or heard about its content from someone— for example his Sanskrit teacher, some *pandit*, or even Bernier who lived in Agra and was in contact with Roth. Furthermore, the possibility cannot be excluded that Roth, who was fluent in Persian, got hold of the Persian translation of this Upanishad produced by Prince Dara's team in 1657.

Before turning to Bernier's presentation, the possible source of his second allegory needs to be briefly quoted: the water bubble allegory from the *Cūlikā* (Mantrika) Upanishad. Deussen (2004:2.681) translates the verses in question as follows:

Through the eye of knowledge
The Brāhmaṇas see the One alone
Extending throughout, from Brahman
Down to the world of plants.

In whom is woven this universe,
All that moves and does not move,
In Brahman also merges everything
As bubbles in the ocean.
In whom enter all the objects
Of world, in whom become invisible,
In whom they merge and emerge again
To view like so many bubbles.

---

94 Filliozat's arguments for third-century evidence of acquaintance with Upani-shadic thought (Filliozat 1956) were shown to be baseless by Ducoeur 2001.

Bernier's presentation of the spider and water flask allegories in his letter to the poet Chapelain of October 4, 1667[95] was not only much richer than Kircher's but also situated in a different context. Kircher's version in *China illustrata* forms part of his condemnation of the "ridiculous view" of the Brahmin disciples of Buddha that infected much of Asia. For Bernier, by contrast, it represents "the practically universal teaching [la doctrine comme universelle] of the gentile pandits of the Indies," a doctrine that "even today represents the cabal of the Sufis and of the majority of the educated people of Persia" (Bernier 1671:127–8). A weaker form of this doctrine is according to Bernier also found in the West, for example in writings by Western alchemists of the ilk of "Fludd whom our great Gassendi has so learnedly refuted" (p. 128). In Bernier's letter, as printed in 1671, the "grande cabale" that also infected the mind of Prince Dara and his brother Sujah (p. 127) is presented as the "strong" form of a doctrine that he regarded as prevalent in the Indies (i.e., in India proper and Southeast Asia) and in Persia.

While Bernier's description of the content of this doctrine varied little between 1671 and his death in 1688, the area of Asia in which it purportedly is dominant grew considerably. When Bernier first

95    This letter apparently made the round of Paris salons even before Bernier returned to France. He subsequently edited it, as is evident from passages such as a reference to Kircher's *China illustrata* that only appeared in 1667 (Bernier 1671:90). In the absence of the original letter or a copy thereof we cannot know to what extent Bernier edited his letter for publication in his *Suite des memoires du Sr Bernier sur l'Empire du Grand Mogol* (1671; separately paginated, pp. 1-137). See below for Bernier's recycling of part of this letter in several editions of his summary of Gassendi's philosophy. For a detailed bibliography of Bernier's writings see Archibald Constable's Bibliography of the Writings of François Bernier (Bernier 2005:xxv–xlii).

recycled his letter's description of the "strong" form of the doctrine in 1674[96] he wrote:

> I have noticed in Asia that the vast majority of the Dervishes of the Turks, of the Sufis and scholars of Persia, and of the Bragmanes of the Indies are infected with it, and I learn that this doctrine has penetrated as far as China and Japan. (Bernier 1674:xxix)

The 1678 edition of Bernier's Gassendi summary, which contains Bernier's third presentation of the spider and water flask allegories, shows only minor changes in the text.[97] But when Bernier presented his description of the "strong" doctrine with the spider and water flask allegories for the fourth time, the crescent from Turkey via Persia and India to China and Japan had expanded even further:

> I cannot be astonished enough how this opinion was able to so generally take hold of the minds of men—not to mention our cabalists and several of our alchemists who make an effort to return to it—and could infect a large part of Asia [une bonne partie de l'Asie]: because, while travelling in Asia, I noticed that the vast majority of the Dervishes of the Turks and the Sufis or scholars of Persia are enthralled by it, and I have also learned from trustworthy people that it has penetrated as far as China and Japan. Thus almost all those who are regarded as learned in Asia pride themselves to assert in various ways that they constitute parts of the divine substance and are in some way little Gods. (Bernier 1684:90)

Though Bernier presented the content of these teachings with little variation over the years, the area in which they are said to be

96  In the first edition of his *Summary of Gassendi's Philosophy* (*Abrégé de la philosophie de M. Gassendi*; Bernier 1674), Bernier included this description in an appendix to the third treatise ("On Generation and Corruption"; pp. 101–122) under the title "si le monde est animé" (whether the world is animated).

97  In the 1678 edition, the 1674 appendix about the question whether the world is animated (see previous note) was included in the main text as chapter VII.

dominant grew to such an extent that by 1684 practically all of Asia was covered: it had become the philosophy of educated people across Asia—the Oriental philosophy par excellence!

Let us now examine the content of these "strong" teachings as presented by Bernier. Unlike the area in which they supposedly reigned, the content of these doctrines varied little in Bernier's writings over the years. Here I will translate from the earliest printed version of 1671.

### 1. God as world; pantheism

The first major doctrine of Bernier's pan-Asian philosophy presents the world as the unfolded divine substance. The spider allegory is used to explain this emanation doctrine. In his Gassendi summary Bernier connects this doctrine with philosophies that posit a world soul.

> Now what I call these Cabalists or Hindu Pandits are more impertinent than all these philosophers and pretend that God, or that sovereign Being whom they call Achar—the immovable, unchangeable—has not only produced the souls from his own substance but also generally everything material or corporeal in the universe, and that this production was not brought about simply in the manner of efficient causes, but like a spider that produces a web from its own navel and withdraws it at pleasure. The Creation, say these make-believe doctors, is nothing other than an extraction and extension that God makes of his own substance, of those filaments that he draws, as it were, from his own bowels; and, in like manner, destruction is merely the reintegration of that divine substance and filaments into himself; so that the last day of the world, which they call Maperlé or Pralea, when according to their belief everything must be destroyed, will be but the general retraction of all the webs that God emitted from himself. (Bernier 1671:128–130)

## 2. *The illusion of multiplicity*

The second main doctrine of Bernier's pan-Asian philosophy states that multiplicity is only an illusion:

> They say that there is thus nothing real or substantial in all that we imagine seeing, hearing, smelling, tasting, or touching; the totality of this world is merely a kind of dream and a pure illusion, inasmuch as all that multiplicity and variety of things appearing to us are only a single, unique, and identical thing, which is God himself; in the same manner as all those different numbers, of ten, twenty, a hundred, a thousand, and so on, are but several repetitions of the same unit. (pp. 130–1)

## 3. *All-Oneness*

The third doctrine follows from the second: if all multiplicity is only an illusion, and if the variety of things we call "world" is like a dream, then true reality is characterized by oneness. The first allegory Bernier mentions for this underlying oneness is that of water flasks in the ocean.

> But question them a bit about reasons for this idea [that all seemingly varied things are in reality a single, unique, and identical thing], or about the mechanism of this emission and retraction of substance and about the appearance of variety, or how it can be that God—who has no body but is Biapek and, as they admit, incorruptible—can nevertheless be divided into so many portions of bodies and souls, then they will produce nothing beyond fine allegories: That God is like an immense ocean in which several flasks of water move. Wherever these flasks may float, they always remain in the same ocean and the same water; and when they break the water inside is united with the whole, that is, with the ocean of which they form part. (pp. 131–2)

The second allegory described by Bernier features light and objects:

> Or they will tell you that it is with God as with the light, which is the same throughout the universe yet does not fail to appear in a hundred different ways depending on the diversity of the objects on which it falls or according to the various colours and shapes of the glasses through which it passes. I tell you, they will produce nothing other than comparisons that are out of all proportion to God and serve only to throw sand in the eyes of ignorant people. Any hope for a solid answer is futile. (pp. 132–3)

Bernier had attempted to refute such views by logical argument, but apparently he failed to convince his Indian interlocutors.

> If one tells them that these flasks in fact only float in a water similar to their own but not identical, and that the light throughout the world is indeed similar but not identical, and so on to other strong objections to their argument, they keep resorting to the same allegories, to fine words, or, in the case of the Soufys, to the beautiful poems of their Goul-tchen-raz. (pp. 133-4)

Though Bernier did not include any direct quotations from the *Gulshan-i rāz* (Mystic Rose Garden) by Mahmud SHABISTARI (1288–1340), he was familiar with this famous Sufi text which (like Sufism in general) is deeply connected with the philosophy of IBN ARABI (1165–1240) and Neoplatonism. Many of the teachings that Bernier presented as the philosophy of "almost all learned Asians" are found in this text. In its first twenty verses the reader already learns that "the world is an imaginary thing, like as one diffused through many numbers," that "All are one," that "varied forms arise only from your fancy," and that the manifestation of the One takes place through emanation (Shabistari 1880:1–2). For all-oneness Shabistari uses such symbols as the ocean (p. 3), light (p. 10), and the number one (pp. 1, 14, 15, 32, 50, 70); and for illusory multiplicity that of the dream (pp. 18, 70), waves and drops of water (p. 51). He explains that "while you are cloaked in this self of yours, the world is always as a veil before your eyes" (p. 53) and points out that cessation of one's illusory dream can only be achieved through "stripping of 'self'" (p. 52). The goal of this emptying process and the awakening from the dream of multiplicity to the reality of all-oneness is expressed in verses like:

The glory of "The Truth" admits no duality,
In that glory is no 'I' or 'We' or 'Thou.'
'I,' 'We,' 'Thou' and 'He' are all one thing,
For in Unity there is no distinction of persons.
Every man who is as a void is empty of self,
Re-echoes within him the cry 'I am The Truth'. (p. 46)

Bernier's numerous European readers did not yet have access to a translation of Shabistari's *Mystic Rose Garden*—the only source text that Bernier mentioned by name—and had to take his word for the content of the philosophy of "almost all educated Asians." Unlike the reports by missionaries that were frequently criticized because of their bias and propagandist tendency, Bernier's "history" inspired confidence because of the author's excellent reputation as scientist and philosopher, his generally skeptical attitude, and his references to sources of information.

Since we have at present only Bernier's published writings at our disposal and no pre-publication manuscripts have so far been found, many questions about the genesis of his view of oriental philosophy are still open. There is no doubt, however, about the influence of his vision. In 1685, one year after the publication of Bernier's latest edition of his Gassendi summary, Noël AUBERT DE VERSÉ (c. 1642–1714) published a book in whose preface he distinguished three basic philosophical positions regarding the origin of all things. The first is the orthodox *creatio ex nihilo* position of theologians and Christian philosophers who believe in an eternal God who created matter from nothing. The second begins with two eternal beings, God and eternal matter, and is the position held by most philosophers. The third view rejects both the creation of matter and its eternity and instead proposes emanation:

> It is [the position] of all philosophers and theologians who hold that the world and its production are nothing but an emanation of divine substance. By emanation, a part of the divine substance has formed itself as world. This was the view of the ancient Gnostics, of Priscillanists, and it is that of the Cabalists, new Adamites or illuminists, and an infinity of philosophers of Asia and of the Indies. (Aubert de Versé 1685, unpaginated introduction)

This "infinity of philosophers of Asia and of the Indies" appears to be an early echo of Bernier's philosophy of "almost all educated Asians" and occurs in an intriguing context, namely, in the introduction to one of the first critiques of Spinoza's philosophical system. Though Aubert de Versé does not immediately associate Spinoza with this widespread philosophy of Asia, the body of his book presents the essence of Spinoza's philosophy in terms that echo Bernier's portrait of the reigning philosophy of the entire Orient. For example, Spinoza is accused of postulating that

> the universe is nothing but an emanation of God and can be nothing other than an emanation of God; that everything we see and perceive is only God; that God alone does everything that happens, that he himself is the entire action and the entire functioning found in the totality of nature: in a word, that God is all being and the only being. (p. 141)

Spinoza's cardinal sin, according to Aubert de Versé, was his belief that "all of nature is God and that everything that exists belongs uniquely to the substance of God" (p. 141). To my knowledge, Spinoza was here for the first time associated with a philosophy in tune with Bernier's reigning philosophy of Asia, and the association of "an infinity of philosophers of Asia and the Indies" with this philosophy in Aubert de Versé's 1686 introduction makes the link explicit. It was the first step in an ominous direction: the association of Oriental philosophy with Spinozism.

One of the classical Upanishads, the ***Muṇḍaka Upanishad***, contains the spider allegory

A later Upanishad, the ***Cūlikā*** **(Mantrika)** *Upanishad*, contains the water bubble allegory

Heinrich Roth S.J. studies Sanskrit, Upanishads (c. 1654–1662), meets Bernier in early 1660s

Prince Dara Shukoh's Persian Upanishad translation (1657): ***Sirr-i akbar*** (first Upanishad translation from the original Sanskrit)

Bernier meets Prince Dara after completion of Upanishad translation (1659)

On way to Rome, Roth's notes are copied by a Carmelite in Shiraz, Persia (1663)

Member of Prince Dara's Upanishad translation team, attracts Bernier's attention

Roth meets Kircher in Rome, copies his Indian notes for him (1664)

Bernier convinces his Indian master to employ this scholar, spends three years with him at the same court (1660s)

Bernier consults Roth's notes in Shiraz (1667)

Bernier combines information from Pandit, Roth in **letter to Chapelain** from Shiraz that includes spider and water bubble allegories (1667)

**ASIA**

Kircher uses spider allegory in portrayal of Xaca/Buddha's pan-Asian idolatry in *China illustrata* (1667)

**EUROPE**

After reading Kircher, Bernier revises and publishes Chapelain letter (1671). Describes an Indo-Iranian philosophy of all-oneness, God=world, emanation, illusion of multiplicity as Prince Dara's "strong" doctrine and uses the spider and water bubble allegories.

Bernier reuses the spider and bubble allegories and description of Prince Dara's "strong" doctrine in appendix (1674) and then text (1678) of his **Summary of Gassendi's philosophy**. This philosophy is now said to reign from Turkey to Japan.

Bernier's final edition of the Gassendi summary (1684) presents the spider and water bubble allegories and description of Prince Dara's "strong" doctrine as **"the philosophy of almost all educated Asians."**

Aubert de Versé's book against Spinoza (1685) associates Spinoza's philosophy of God=world and emanation with "an infinity of philosophers of Asia and of the Indies"

FIG. 19: THE SPIDER / WATER BUBBLE ALLEGORIES AND BERNIER'S PAN-ASIAN PHILOSOPHY (URS APP)

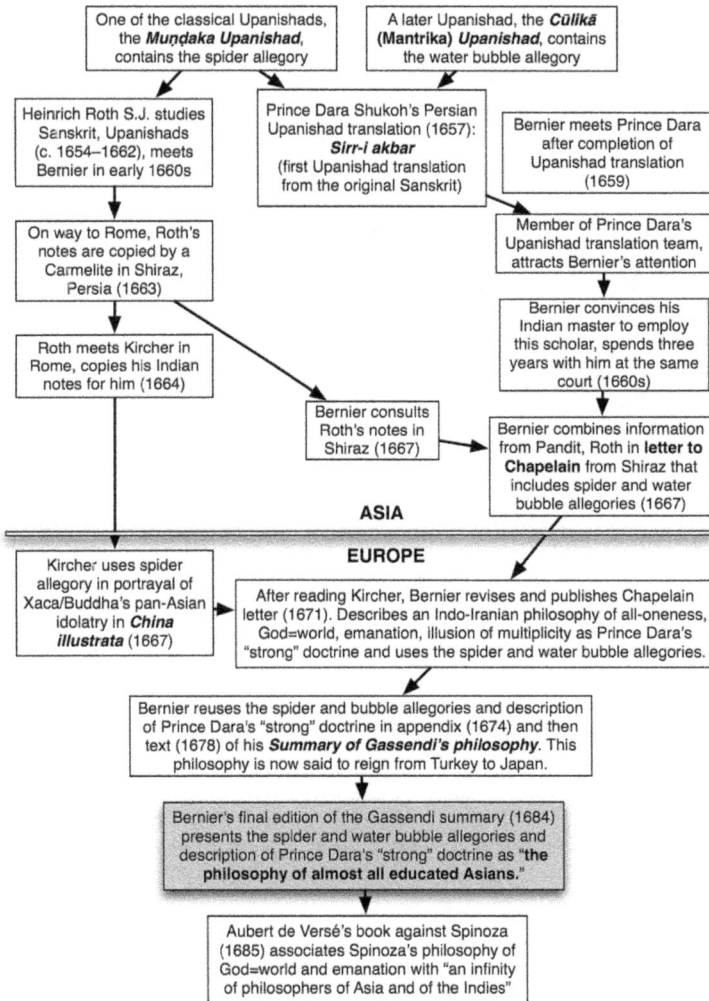

*Chapter Thirteen*

## THE MERGER (LE CLERC & BERNIER)

T he period between 1684 and 1688 can be compared to the late 1990s when the use of the internet triggered an information revolution. In the 1680s an analogous role was played by the explosive rise of scholarly journals containing "a new style of incisive 'critical' reviews" (Israel 2001:146). These journals almost immediately found a pan-European readership and became "incontestably one of the most potent agents driving the Enlightenment in its vital formative phase down to 1750" (p. 150). The French *Journal des Sçavans* and the English *Philosophical Transactions*, both established in 1665, were in the 1680s followed by a crop of new journals whose scope, content, and influence were nothing less than revolutionary. All of a sudden, a pan-European readership—the much-evoked "Republic of Letters"—felt connected to events and publications in faraway countries and was informed about new findings and perspectives in a wide range of fields. The case of *Confucius sinarum philosophus* is paradigmatic. Published in Paris at the end of May 1687, its appearance and availability at an Amsterdam bookstore was announced three months later in Pierre Bayle's *Nouvelles de la République des lettres* (founded in 1684). One month later, in September of 1687, the first review appeared in Basnage de Beauval's *Histoire des ouvrages & de la vie des sçavans* (newly founded in 1687). In October the *Philosophical Transactions* published a review, and in December Jean LE CLERC (1657–1736) discussed the book in his *Bibliothèque universelle et historique* (founded in 1686). Le Clerc's review is a good example for the new approach. Well aware that few readers had access to the Latin original of *Confucius sinarum philosophus*, Le Clerc presented its main arguments on no less than fifty-seven pages that contained not only perceptive summaries and analyses but also a massive amount of excerpts in French translation. The next review appeared in January of 1688 in the *Journal des Sçavans*, and before the first year after publication had elapsed, another important review of *Confucius* appeared in the *Acta eruditorum* (founded 1682). We will see below that such reviews had a long shelf life: unable to find a copy of Couplet's Latin *Confucius* (1687) while writing his *Dictionnaire historique et critique* (11697), Pierre Bayle included extensive quotations from the articles in *Bibliothèque universelle* and *Acta Eruditorum*.

The two last-mentioned reviews were not only the most interesting and voluminous ones but also the most relevant for the invention of Oriental philosophy. Both paid particular attention to Couplet's long introduction where China's religions and philosophies are listed and summarized, and both used a disproportionate amount of space for the discussion of the "inner" teaching of Buddhism.[98] In its presentation of Buddhism, the *Confucius sinarum philosophus* introduction combined various elements that we are familiar with from earlier chapters. Its biography of the Buddha features the classic legend of the Buddha's deathbed confession (see Chapter 10) in which he admits having withheld the truth for forty years and declares that emptiness and nothingness are the principle of all things (Couplet 1687:xxix). In his extensive review, Le Clerc summarizes the *Confucius* introduction's presentation of the inner or true doctrine as follows:

98  In the *Acta eruditorum review* (1688:254–265), the discussion of Buddhism's "inner" teaching alone (pp. 258–9) is longer than those of classical Confucianism and Daoism combined.

The interior doctrine, which is never unveiled to the common folk because they must be forced to virtue by the fear of hell and similar things, is in the words of these philosophers the only solid and true teaching. It consists in establishing as the principle and end of all things a certain emptiness [vuide, lat. vacuum] and a real nothingness [néant réel, lat. inane]. They assert that our first forefathers have come from this emptiness and returned to it after their death; that the same is true for all humans who at their death dissolve into this principle; and that we as well as all elements and creatures form part of this emptiness. (Le Clerc 1688:348–9; based on Couplet 1687:xxxi)

This is the teaching we encountered in Chapter 10. The likely author, whom I have identified as João Rodrigues, describes the inner doctrine in terms that betray the influence of Valignano's catechism: the pure and limpid first principle that is called perfect in spite of its total lack of thinking, understanding, and active involvement; the idea that by seated meditation and ecstatic absorption one can unite with this principle; the denial of providence, an immortal soul, and recompense or punishment in heaven or hell; and the substance shared by humans, animals, and even trees and rocks (Couplet 1687:xxxii).

However, the introduction to *Confucius sinarum philosophus* was not simply a rehash and synthesis of earlier publications. When Couplet edited and supplemented Intorcetta's introduction during his European tour in support of the Jesuit China mission, the Chinese rite controversy had already moved to a different level thanks to Navarrete's *Tratados* of 1676 and attacks on the Jesuits by theologians as well as Jansenists. Now Europe rather than China had become the stage of the controversy that was born with Rodrigues's opposition to Ricci's mission strategy. No wonder that editor Couplet felt the need of a particularly vigorous defense against Navarrete's *Tratados* that contained Rodrigues's and Longobardi's assertion of pervasive Chinese atheism. Couplet tried to achieve this by sharpening Intorcetta's arguments, a glowing portrayal of Confucius and China's original monotheism, and a newly written elaborate defense of Ricci's mission strategy in the second part of the *Confucius* introduction. But Navarrete, Longobardi, and Rodrigues were not the only enemies to combat. While editing the introduction, Couplet was just as concerned about the specters of Spinozism and quietism.

The association of worrisome European movements with China's most detestable doctrine—the atheistic rantings of the notorious liar Xaca / Buddha—was an elegant and effective way of attacking such movements without even once mentioning them by name. Why not associate Spinozism and its doctrine of a single substance whose modifications we perceive as our world with the Buddha's "inner" doctrine as described by Rodrigues / Intorcetta: "There is, therefore, only a single and identical substance, which only appears different in particular beings because of the figures, qualities or internal configuration, just as water is water whether it appears as snow, hail, rain, or ice" (Couplet 1687:xxxi). It is not surprising that some reader would triangulate Bernier's oriental doctrine (the Indo-Iranian stream), Shaka's inner teaching (the Sino-Japanese stream), and Spinozism. The learned Jean Le Clerc was the first to connect these dots when he suggested to his numerous readers:

> Those who would like to learn more about the philosophy of the Indians and the Chinese, which is not very different from the system of the Spinozists (if they indeed have one), can read the voyage to Indostan by Mr. Bernier. (Le Clerc 1688:349)

Le Clerc thus inserted the Sino-Japanese content as presented by Couplet into Bernier's pan-Asian philosophy and linked the result to Spinozism. We have seen in Chapter 10 that the "true" doctrine attributed to Buddha ended up as an episode of his life story. Our next chapters will show that the figure of "Zoroaster" (whom Rodrigues had identified as the father of Oriental ur-philosophy) had a comparable fate. But for the moment we will focus on the impact of the 1687 publication of *Confucius sinarum philosophus* and its link with another European controversy of the late seventeenth century: quietism.

Couplet prepared the *Confucius* introduction for publication at the very time when, according to Bernier, all of Paris was talking about nothing but quietism (Bernier 1688:47).[99] In this heavily charged atmosphere, Couplet renamed Intorcetta / Rodrigues's Indo-Chinese sect of the *meditantium de nihilo* ("those who meditate on nothingness"; Ch. *wuwei jiao* 無為教) first into a sect of *contemplantium de nihilo* ("those who contemplate about nothingness"), and on second thought into *nihil agentium secta* ("the sect of do-nothings")—which is what the readers of *Confucius sinarum philosophus* were in the end faced with.[100]

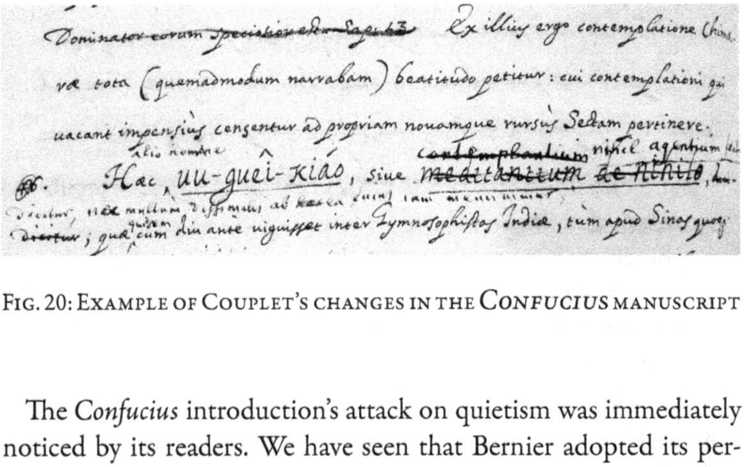
Ex illius ergo contemplatione (...) ra tota (quemadmodum narrabam) beatitudo petitur: cui contemplationi qui uacant impensius censentur ad propriam nouamque rursus Sectam pertinere.
Hac, uu-guei-kiao, siue ~~meditantium de nihilo~~ contemplantium nihil agentium
quæ cum diu ante viguisset inter Gymnosophistas Indiæ, tum apud Sinas quoque

FIG. 20: EXAMPLE OF COUPLET'S CHANGES IN THE *CONFUCIUS* MANUSCRIPT

The *Confucius* introduction's attack on quietism was immediately noticed by its readers. We have seen that Bernier adopted its perspective wholesale, but other readers exhibited a more critical atti-

99 For details about Couplet's activities in France see the chapter entitled "Printing Confucius in Paris" in Dew 2009:205–33.

100 This correction (see Fig. 20) is found in § 46 of the introduction in Ms. Latin 6277 at the Bibliothèque nationale; for the printed result of this change see Couplet 1687:xxxii.

tude toward Jesuit authors. For example, in his preface to a collection of Molinos's writings,[101] the anonymous editor (possibly Jean Cornand Lacroze) accused the Jesuits in general and Father Couplet in particular of surreptitious tactics in their fight against quietism: "They accuse the quietists, who say that one must empty oneself of everything in order to seek repose in God, of defining the essence of contemplation as emptiness," and they claim that the quietists "try to introduce atheism by contemplating an indeterminate principle, a true nothing [un vrai néant]" (Molinos 1688:24).

Readers interested in the forbidden writings of Molinos were thus treated to a critique of Couplet's anti-quietist tactics:

> In order to infiltrate people's minds with this calumny, Father Couplet has devised a tactic as discreet and malicious as possible. In a prologue to the translation of three books of Confucius that he made with the help of three Jesuit colleagues, he discusses the opinions of different sects of philosophers in China, and among others the adherents of Foe Kiao[102] that he portrays as political atheists. According to Couplet, these people teach two doctrines. The exterior one is for the people and entails diverse precepts and ceremonies. The second, the interior one, is described by the author in the very manner that the enemies of the quietists use for quietist doctrine. These philosophers, says he, recognize a first principle, pure, infinite, eternal, unmoving, perfect, and sovereignly tranquil since it does not think, does not want, and does not wish anything. (p. 24)

As we have seen, such information can ultimately be traced back to Jesuit mission reports from sixteenth-century Japan and to Valignano's catechism of 1586. The same can be said about the *Confucius*

101  The "quietist" writings by Molinos had recently been banned by the Catholic church, and publishers in Holland were not just willing but eager to supply clients throughout Europe with books listed on the index of forbidden books.

102  Ch. *fojiao* 佛教, Buddhism.

introduction's description of quietism (Couplet 1687:xxxii) as understood by the editor of the Molinos collection:

> Whoever wants to become happy must, according to them, try to render himself similar to this principle by reigning in his passions and smothering his feelings in order to not worry about anything and not feel any trouble. He thus passes into an ecstatic state and is completely absorbed in sublime contemplation. Without making any use of reason or of his intelligence, he reaches this divine quietude that constitutes supreme beatitude. (Molinos 1688:25)

The editor of the Molinos book correctly discerned that Couplet, without mentioning the Christian quietists by name, attacked their doctrine by associating them with the worst atheists of Asia. But this demonizing tactic had, not unlike Ricci's canonization of Confucianism, some unanticipated effects. One of them was that Valignano's description, which had gathered dust as Possevino's *Bibliotheca selecta* was replaced by other textbooks, was once more moved into the limelight. Even less anticipated was perhaps that some eighteenth-century defenders of mysticism and quietism were to interpret the "nothingness" and "emptiness" of Fo's inner doctrine in a mystical and theistic way by suggesting that the ideal of emptying one's heart, mind, and will does not signify the attainment of vacuous torpor but rather true and complete fulfillment by God.

The confluence of the Indo-Iranian and Sino-Japanese streams of information into a pan-Asian monist and quietist philosophy became a *fait accompli* when Bernier himself gave it his stamp of approval. In a "Memorandum about the quietism of the Indies" written shortly before his death, Bernier reports to the many readers of the *Journal des Savants* that he pulled out his old notes from the Indies because "for the last five or six months I heard people talk about nothing but quietism" (Bernier 1688:47). After some critical remarks about the impassivity and detachment of the "*Yogis,* i.e. saints, illuminates, perfect ones" who claim to be "perfectly united with the sovereign Being, the first and general principle of all things," Bernier goes on to describe this first principle according to "the old books" (pp. 47–8). Since Bernier mentioned consulting his own "old notes" and cites "old books" in the context of *fakirs* and *Yogis*, his readers had to assume that this description of Oriental philosophy's "first principle" was based on Bernier's Persian or Indian sources. Bernier wrote:

> Their old books teach that this first Principle of all things is absolutely admirable; that it is something—as they put it— very pure, very limpid, and very subtle; that it is infinite; that it can neither be created nor corrupted; that it is the perfection of all things, sovereignly perfect; and that, as is to be noted, it is in perfect rest and complete inaction—in one word, it rests in an absolutely perfect Quietism. They believe that in its role as the source and origin of all virtue, of all understanding, and of all power—these are again their own words—this [principle] has in itself neither virtue nor reason and power. On the contrary, the proper and sovereign perfection of its essence consists in not doing anything, not understanding anything, and not desiring anything. This is why those who desire to be perfect and to have a good and happy life must, through continual contemplation and victory over themselves do everything possible to become similar to this principle. Having subdued and totally extinguished all human passions, they aim at not being troubled or tormented by anything and to happily enjoy this divine rest or Quietism in the manner of an ecstatic, absorbed in profound contemplation. For them this is the happiest state of life that one could wish for. (Bernier 1688:48-49)

In this manner, Bernier portrayed as the core doctrine of Asian philosophy the very teachings whose translation process we examined in earlier chapters of this book. Orientals share the notion that all is ultimately one, that differences are only apparent, that we perceive only modifications of a single substance, that the first principle is inactive and non-thinking, that quiet meditation renders one similar to this principle, and that union with this principle can be achieved in this life. Shaped as it is by the Buddhism part of *Confucius sinarum philosophus* that, as we saw, is connected to Japan and to Zen, Bernier's description of 1688 stands in a direct line going back one century to Navarrete's catechism (1586).

Whereas Aubert de Versé had noticed a Spinozist trend in some of this, Bernier focused on the similarity to the doctrines of Molinos and other quietists. He ended up throwing Indian Yogis, Chinese bonzes, Siamese monks, and European quietists into a single pot whose labels "irreligion" and "libertine outlook" his readers were—in spite of Bernier's caveat—sure to associate with radicals and Spinozists:

> Incidentally, by this I do not want to say that the Quietism or Molinosism which is causing such a brouhaha is exactly like the Quietism of the Indian Yogis, the Chinese Bonzes, or the Talapois of Siam. I would like to good-heartedly believe that it is a case of excessive devotion and extravagance rather than wickedness. Nevertheless, the great correspondence of these two Quietisms, this abyss of contemplation, this great inaction, this great union of our soul with God, and a hundred other things that are said about it cause me to suspect that all of this great and extraordinary devotion tends to, or cannot but lead to, some kind of irreligion or libertine outlook. One day we will be able to examine this, provided that the true original writings of Molinos come into our hands when his friends conclude that they are worthy of the effort to be read. (pp. 51–52)

Bernier's 1688 essay on quietism thus put the stamp of approval on Le Clerc's merger of the inner teaching of Buddhism with Bernier's "philosophy of most educated Asians." Bernier—the one and only secular European philosopher who had ever lived among brahmins, yogis, and Sufis and had informed himself about "their old books"—confirmed not only the gigantic reach of this philosophy from Turkey to Japan but now also defined its content exactly along the line of the *Confucius* introduction. In fact, "Bernier had written to the Jesuit [Couplet] to express his admiration for the book, and the two met for a meal at the Bibliothèque du roi," and Bernier "was so impressed with Confucius that he decided to start a translation from the Jesuits' Latin into French" (Dew 2009:228).[103] He even repeated Couplet's tale about the presence in China of a sect of "fainéans" (do-nothings), the *secta nihil agentium* that was associated in the *Confucius* introduction with Tamo (Bodhidharma). Using such elements, Bernier proposed a compelling scenario of the spread of this doctrine from India to the Far East:

> Sixty-some years after the coming of Jesus Christ, the idolatry of the Indies passed to China where it still reigns both among the people and among the bonzes, who are the same as the Fakirs and the Yogis of the Indies. This is why Father Couplet notes in his preface to Confucius that this sect in China is called Yu-guei-kiao [Ch. *wuwei jiao*] which means the secta nihil agentium or sect of inaction. One cannot wonder too much, said the Father, about the fact that several of the most eminent men of the empire engage in this folly to the degree of spending several hours at a time without any movement of body and mind and without any use of their senses and their faculties. They are convinced that the more they are plunged in this inaction, the closer they approach perfection since they become similar to the Principle to which they must one day return. It is for this reason that they have a great veneration for a certain Ta-mo [Ch. Damo, Bodhidharma] who spent nine entire years with his face turned to a wall and did nothing at all except contemplating this Principle. (pp. 49–50)

Now the fakirs and yogis of India followed the very same philosophy as Bodhidharma and his "sect of inaction."

103 This meeting took place in June of 1687 (Dew 2009:228).

Finding "this entire doctrine very specious" (p. 50), Bernier expressed his strong disapproval of people who "pass entire hours in rapture and ecstasy" and "pretend seeing the sovereign Being as a very lively and inexplicable light" (p. 48). He accused them of "deep down not believing any of this" (p. 50) and thought that their doctrine of a world-soul and of all-oneness comes close to atheism:

> I know that in the end they all believe, like the Turkish and Persian cabalists, in this great soul of the world of which our souls as well as those of animals and plants form part. If one looks at this closely, it is very near to atheism; because by not recognizing any God except for their great soul that spreads everywhere and animates all beings, they cannot avoid conceiving this soul as something bodily, some sort of flame, or a very subtle light. Attributing parts or particles means fashioning a corporeal God who therefore is divisible, corruptible, etc., and this contradicts the sovereign and absolute perfection of God. (p. 51)

Bernier had amplified the *Confucius* introduction's scope by associating Indian Yogis, Persian Sufis, Muslim fakirs, Chinese bonzes, Siamese talapoins, and Bodhidharma's sect of "do-nothings" with a single doctrine which in fact corresponds to the much-heralded "inner" doctrine of Buddhism that was now conceived as the philosophy of almost all educated people of Asia. There is no doubt that Rodrigues, had he lived as long as the Bodhidharma of legend, would have been pleased by this development.

Toward the end of the seventeenth century one can thus observe the gradual confluence of our two main streams of information: 1. the Sino-Japanese stream whose origin in sixteenth-century Japan and evolution in seventeenth-century China and Vietnam we analyzed; and 2. the Indo-Persian stream that emerged in the second half of the seventeenth century. The overall flow of information can be schematized as follows:

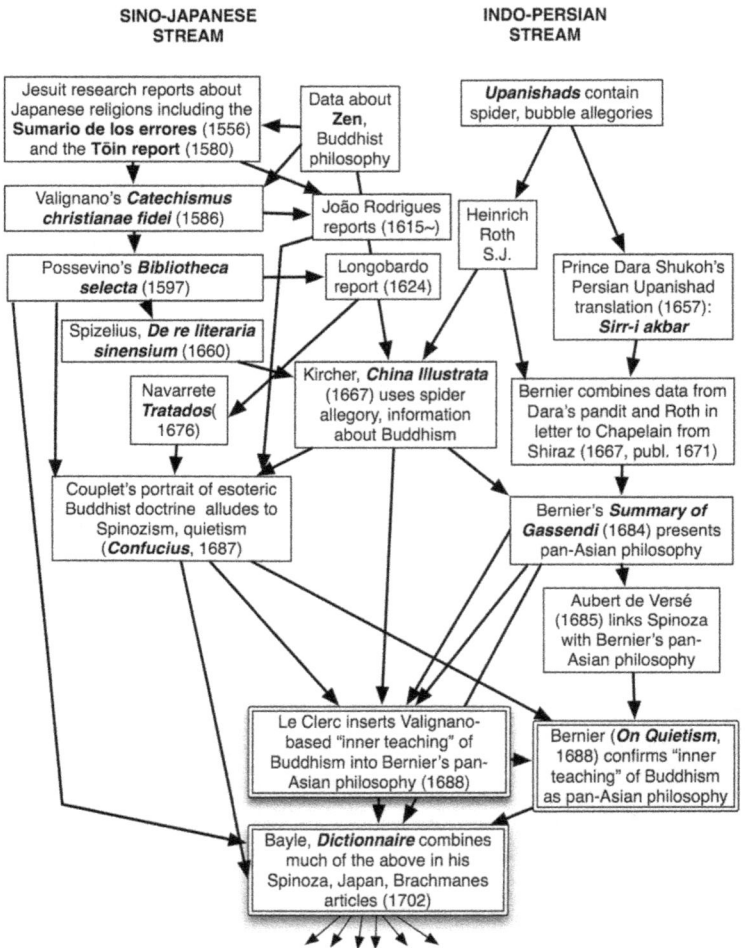

**SINO-JAPANESE STREAM**

**INDO-PERSIAN STREAM**

Jesuit research reports about Japanese religions including the **Sumario de los errores** (1556) and the **Tōin report** (1580)

Data about **Zen**, Buddhist philosophy

**Upanishads** contain spider, bubble allegories

Valignano's **Catechismus christianae fidei** (1586)

João Rodrigues reports (1615~)

Heinrich Roth S.J.

Possevino's **Bibliotheca selecta** (1597)

Longobardo report (1624)

Prince Dara Shukoh's Persian Upanishad translation (1657): **Sirr-i akbar**

Spizelius, **De re literaria sinensium** (1660)

Kircher, **China Illustrata** (1667) uses spider allegory, information about Buddhism

Navarrete **Tratados**( 1676)

Bernier combines data from Dara's pandit and Roth in letter to Chapelain from Shiraz (1667, publ. 1671)

Couplet's portrait of esoteric Buddhist doctrine alludes to Spinozism, quietism (**Confucius**, 1687)

Bernier's **Summary of Gassendi** (1684) presents pan-Asian philosophy

Aubert de Versé (1685) links Spinoza with Bernier's pan-Asian philosophy

Le Clerc inserts Valignano-based "inner teaching" of Buddhism into Bernier's pan-Asian philosophy (1688)

Bernier (**On Quietism**, 1688) confirms "inner teaching" of Buddhism as pan-Asian philosophy

Bayle, **Dictionnaire** combines much of the above in his Spinoza, Japan, Brachmanes articles (1702)

FIG. 21: THE MERGER OF THE SINO-JAPANESE AND INDO-IRANIAN STREAMS (URS APP)

## Chapter Fourteen

## FROM PAGAN TO ORIENTAL PHILOSOPHY

H aving traced what I called the Sino-Japanese and Indo-Persian
streams until their merger toward the end of the seventeenth
century, we will now direct our attention to a third line of information that is mainly associated with Zoroaster and seventeenth-
century visions of the genealogy of philosophy and heresy. With
some notable exceptions (which will be of particular interest for our
inquiry), seventeenth-century histories of philosophy tended to still
be firmly embedded in the biblical framework. The century's first
such history by Otto HEURNIUS (1577–1652), *Barbaricae philosophiae antiquitatum libri duo*, devoted an entire volume to "Barbarian philosophy." Its first book traces the course of philosophy from
Adam and Eve via Seth to Noah and then describes its decline before
it reached, in the year 291 after the deluge, the king of Bactria Zoroaster who was the chief of all magi (Heurnius 1600:7–28). Bactria in northern Afghanistan thus became the distribution hub of
"barbarian philosophy" to "the entire Indies, Ethiopia, and all of the
Orient's philosophers" (p. 28). The second book of Heurnius's work,
though titled "Indicus," contains only two brief paragraphs about
India that trace the "Brachmanni" to Abraham and his wife Ketura
(p. 140). It also mentions some customs and views of contemporary
"Baneanes" and "Bracmanes" such as the cult of cows and the view
that God is a negro (pp. 144–6). But the real focus of Heurnius's
"Indian" book lies on tracing the influence of Zoroaster's doctrine.
It is said to have infected Babylonian, Phoenician, Egyptian, Jewish,
and Samaritan "philosophy" and to form the root of Persian, Afri-

can, and European magic including the practices of the "sect of the druids" in Germany and France (pp. 304–314).

Eighty-five years later, the French Oratorian Louis THOMASSIN (1619–1695) published a history of philosophy that contained far more information about the Orient but was still built on the same old biblical foundation. Having promised to his readers to describe "the birth and progress of philosophy and of all sects of philosophers" (1685:1), Thomassin begins with Adam, the first philosopher:

> One cannot deny that the first of all men was also the first of all philosophers and of all sages, and that this primacy was less a primacy of time than one of perfection and excellence. Having had God as teacher, father, and creator, the first disciple of such an excellent instructor must have been consummate in all sorts of noble knowledge. (Thomassin 1685:16)

In his discussion of Adam's fall, Thomassin introduced an interesting distinction between wisdom and philosophy: having lost perfect wisdom through his sin, the consummate sage Adam turned into a mere philosopher:

> If he [Adam] lost the title of Sage, he did not fail to merit that of Philosopher. However, he took care to maintain possession of as much great and illustrious knowledge as God had provided for him and his descendants. ... The sin [leading to the Fall] was incompatible with the charity and grace of God, but not with the science and knowledge of truths that he [Adam] had obtained. (p. 22)

From such excellent roots in paradise, philosophy spread via Noah and his sons to the Hebrews. But other people were not left out as the human race spread from Mesopotamia toward the Orient (pp. 107-8). Since the Indians "had obtained their doctrine from Noah and from the other Hebrew patriarchs with less intermediaries than the Greeks," Thomassin thought that "the Greek philosophers might have profited from the Indian philosophers" (p. 112). The content of Thomassin's most ancient philosophy is, as we would expect, quite compatible with the Christian faith and contains "the truth of God, the immortality of the soul, providence, virtue and recompense, justice and the just punishment of vices, and the practice of the strongest and most generous virtues" (p. 115).[104] Like his predecessor Heurnius, Thomassin traced the course of philosophy to increasingly pale vestiges in the cults of Persia, Egypt, Greece, Rome, and even to the druid hearths of his homeland.

The English theologian Theophilus GALE (1628–1678), a one-time Senior Dean of Arts at Oxford's Magdalen College and preacher at Winchester Cathedral, also regarded philosophy's beginnings as extremely luminous and pure but had a bleaker view of the fall:

> Philosophie was in its first descent, a generous, Noble thing, a Virgin-beautie, a pure Light, born of the Father of Lights, in whose Light alone we can see light. But, alas! how soon did she lose her original Virginitie, and primitive puritie? how soon was she, of an Angel of Light, transformed into a child of darknesse? Adam no sooner fell, but Philosophie fell with him, and became a common Strumpet, for carnal Reason to commit follie with. And oh! how have the lascivious Wits, of lapsed human nature, ever since gone a Whoring after vain Philosophie? (Gale 1672, vol. 2, beginning of unpaginated preface)

It is to "this bitter Root of *Vain Philosophie*" that Gale traced "all *pestiferous*, and *noxious Heresies*, and *Idolatrie*" of the pagan world and also of Judaism and Christianity. The "vanity of pagan philosophie," to which he devoted an entire volume (Part III of *The Court of the Gentiles*), is based on mixing "human *Figments* and Inventions of their own" with broken traditions that only contain fragments of revealed truth (Gale 1677:3.4). What is valuable and true in philosophy must be rooted in divine revelation, which is why Gale

---

104 It is not surprising that Thomassin became a favorite author of the figurists in the Jesuit China mission who were determined to discover vestiges of Noachic religion in ancient Chinese texts.

traced "the choicest parts" of Pythagoras and Plato to the "Jewish Traditions of God, Angels, and the Human Soul" and thought that the Greek philosophers derived their best "Metaphysic Contemplations" from the Old Testament and "Jewish Mysteries" (Gale 1672:2.15). While Gale, helped by Steuco's *De philosophia perenni*, located numerous nuggets of golden truth in pagan philosophy, he regarded most of it as the dross of human imagination and rationalistic pride. Its "very poisonous pestilential influence on the *Jewish Church*" and its equally pernicious effect on "the *Christian Churches* both *primitive and later*" (Gale 1677:3.120) were of particular concern to him.

> The first great Heresie, which as a Gangrene did overspread and consume much of the beautie, glorie, and vigor of the Primitive Churches, was that of the Gnostics, which had taken a considerable rooting in the Apostles daies. (p. 123)

Gale claimed that "it is generally acknowledged by the Learned" that "the *Gnostic infusions* were but the corrupt off-spring of Pagan Philosophie" (p. 123), and he sprinkled his survey of heresies and perversions with references to "Pythagorising Gnostics" and other "off-spring of Pagan Philosophie." The "cognation betwixt Pagan Philosophie and the Mysteries of the Gospel" by Neoplatonics such as Plotinus and Dionysius Areopagita (pp. 138–140) is particularly harshly criticized and identified as the source of numerous heresies. Not just gnosticism but also "Mystic Theologie," "Monkish Mystic Divinitie," Aristotle-based scholastic philosophy, and numerous features of Catholic "popery" including celibacy, monasticism, "Antichrist's Canon-Law," and the worship of saints are unmasked as direct consequences of pagan philosophy (pp. 152 ff., 210 ff). While ostensibly relying on Jacob Thomasius's research (see Chapter 16), Gale saw such detective work as part of his overall task that consisted in restoring philosophy to its original idea and purity of wisdom. His work would increase, so he hoped, the people's ability to distinguish real from fake philosophy and to clearly understand the difference between the use of genuine philosophy and its abuse.[105]

The search for the "first great Heresie" and the ultimate origin of "pagan" philosophy often involved the figure of Zoroaster. Zoroaster is a typical "figure of memory" in Jan Assmann's sense (1998:11) who probably never existed in the flesh (Kellen 2006) yet played a major role in European visions of the history of philosophy.[106] In earlier chapters of this book we encountered several "incarnations" of this fascinating creature. For João Rodrigues he was identical with Noah's son Ham, the transmitter of the rotten philosophy of the Cainite lineage to the post-diluvian age. Convinced that Zoroaster's teaching was best preserved in China, Rodrigues had informed his superiors that his research on Chinese doctrines would throw light on many Zoroaster-related phenomena including the perversions of Indian and Greek philosophy (see Chapter 8). In Kircher's mind two Zoroasters were at work (see Chapter 9). The first was Noah's son Ham who had purportedly inscribed teachings of antediluvian philosophy on metal and stone plates, smuggled them on his father's ark, and in the aftermath of the deluge mixed such false philosophy with true wisdom. Kircher's second Zoroaster, the king of Bactria and chief of the magi, made northern Afghanistan into a hub from which his abominable doctrine, mixed with grains of truth, infected large swaths of Asia. The composite character of this doctrine helped Kircher explain the presence of vestiges of true wisdom in the giant morass of Asian religions and philosophies, for example an apparent vestige of trinitarian doctrine in form of a three-faced and eight-armed Japanese idol.

---

105 "Hoc autem mihi propositum est, Philosophiam ad suum originarium exemplar primaevamque Ideam reducere, ut genuina Philosophia a simulata ementitaque, ac verus Philosophiae usus ab abusu discriminetur" (*Philosophia generalis*, Dissertatiuncula proeminalis, p. 5; quoted in Malusa 1981:318).

106 For an excellent survey of European views of Zoroaster see volume 1 of Stausberg 1998.

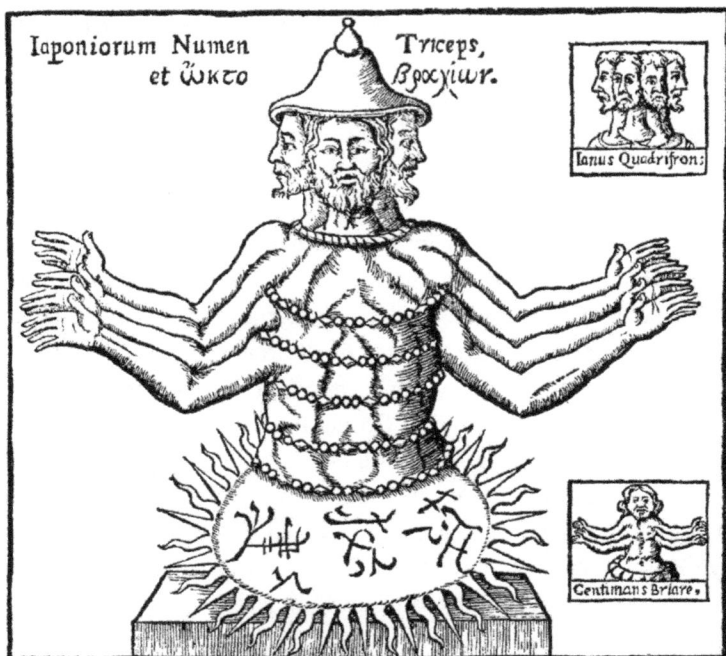

FIG. 22: THREE-FACED AND EIGHT-ARMED JAPANESE DEITY (KIRCHER 1652:1.410)

The manufacture of scenarios involving such figures as Zoroaster required compatible chronologies. In the second half of the seventeenth century traditional Western chronology was undergoing rapid changes because its biblical basis began to crumble under the weight of various kinds of evidence. An important factor was the discovery of Chinese annals that appeared to be both reliable and older than the Old Testament. An example of the impact of this development is the review of *Confucius sinarum philosophus* in the *Philosophical Transactions* (1687, no. 189). This review consisted almost entirely of a discussion about Chinese chronology, a hot-button topic that in 1687 had already produced a mountain of publications.

The *Atlas of China* (1655) and *History of China* (1658) by Martino Martini had presented Chinese chronology as trustworthy in spite of the fact that it went beyond the time frame of the Hebrew Bible. But how could a fully functioning Chinese empire have existed hundreds of years before the deluge? Couplet's chronological table appended to *Confucius sinarum philosophus* (1687) brought this irksome problem once more to the forefront, prompting the English reviewer's comment:

> 'T will be needless to advertise, that this Account places the beginning of the Chinese Empire long before the Deluge, according to the Holy Scriptures; wherefore if this be to be wholly rejected, as fabulous; or if not, how it is to be reconciled with the sacred Chronology, belongs more properly to the Disquisition of the Divines. (Sept.-Oct. 1687, p. 378)

While the Jesuits urged the Vatican to adopt the longer, *Septuaginta*-based chronology in order to gain enough time to let the Chinese empire begin after the deluge, the problem that the English reviewer adroitly dodged was not easily dismissed and gave rise to much speculation. Had the deluge been a local inundation of the Middle East? Had part of China's population survived the flood? Was there a transmission line separate from Noah and his sons? Had Noah himself gone to China after the deluge? Or had he even, as John Webb proposed on page 71 of *The Antiquity of China* (1678), lived in China before the deluge and built his ark with the help of advanced Chinese technology? After all, no country on earth could "better furnish *Noah*, with all manner of conveniences, and every sort of materials proper for the building of such a Machine than *China*"!

The reason why the reviewer of *Confucius Sinarum philosophus* in the *Philosophical Transactions* declined to discuss this problem and decided to let the theologians deal with it was plain enough: it threatened the veracity of the biblical account and consequently of biblical authority. That authority was under increasing attack because of the discovery of hitherto unknown lands and of books that were potentially far older than the Old Testament, for example the Chinese *Yijing* (Book of Changes) that João Rodrigues had associated with Zoroaster=Ham who must have lived long before Moses. Even more threatening were efforts by the likes of La Peyrère, Spinoza, Jean Le Clerc, and Richard Simon to critically examine the Old Testament text itself. Had the Pentateuch really been written by Moses? If other authors had been in play: who were they, and had they also been divinely inspired by God? How could the Old Testament's numerous contradictions and absurdities be accounted for? While authors like Martini, Couplet, and the author of the *Confucius* review in the *Philosophical Transactions* decided to throw disturbing data into the arena and leave it at that, others like La Peyrère and Webb grappled with its implications and attempted to furnish explanations that inevitably ruffled feathers. A third possibility was to ignore such questions and refrain from mentioning the Bible. This was the approach chosen by the man who is sometimes called the father of the history of philosophy, Thomas STANLEY (1625–1678).

The first volume of Stanley's *History of Philosophy*, published in the same year as La Peyrère's *Prae-Adamitae* and Martini's *Novus Atlas Sinensis* (1655), lost not a single word about biblical figures. In his preface Stanley alluded to an Oriental origin of philosophy by stating that the more learned Greeks "acknowledged it derived from the East" and by expressing his opinion that "it is manifest that the Original of the Greek Philosophy is to be derived from Thales, who Travelling into the East, first brought Natural Learning, Geometry, and Astrology thence into Greece" (Stanley 1655, preface to vol. 1). However, the title of the fourth and final volume of Stanley's *History of Philosophy*, *The History of the Chaldaick Philosophy*, showed that what he had in mind was not the biblical East and Adam's paradise-derived philosophy. This book, first published in 1662, begins as follows:

Philosophy is generally acknowledged even by the most Learned of the Grecians themselves, to have had its Original in the East. None of the Eastern Nations, for Antiquity and Learning, stood in Competition with the Chaldeans and Aegyptians. The Aegyptians pretended that the Chaldeans were a Colony of them, and had all their Learning and Institutions from them; but they who are less interested, and unprejudiced Judges of this Controversie, assert that The Magi (who derived their Knowledge from the Chaldeans) were more ancient that the Aegyptians, that Astrological Learning pass'd from the Chaldeans to the Aegyptians, and from them to the Grecians, and, in a word, that the Chaldeans were antiquissimum Doctorum genus, the most ancient of the Teachers (Stanley 1701:1).

A man like Stanley who, unlike Kircher, insisted on the critical use of sources and loathed unfounded speculation, faced insurmountable impediments in his search for this "original" of philosophy. To begin with, the origin of "Chaldaick philosophy" was usually attributed to "Zoroaster." However, while working his way through piles of sources, Stanley noted that there are not just two Zoroasters in play, as Kircher had proposed, but a minimum of six! The first was from Chaldea; the second from Bactria; the third introduced Chaldean sciences to Persia and had been confounded by Kircher with Ham; the fourth was a Pamphilian; the fifth a Proconnesian; and the sixth a Babylonian who "was the chief Person whom Pythagoras had for Master" (pp. 2-3). To account for such a multitude, Stanley explained that "Zoroaster" is not a person's name but rather a generic designation for extraordinary benefactors (p. 3). Thus there could well be many more than six Zoroasters. Stanley regarded the first Zoroaster as the oldest philosopher and "inventor of Arts and Sciences amongst the Chaldeans" (p. 3) but noted with dismay that he could furnish neither a date nor a decent biography of this man:

"Of his Birth, Life, and Death, there is little to be found; and even that uncertain, whether applicable to him, or to the *Persian*" (p. 4). Of the numerous writings of "Zoroaster" that, according to some sources, included as many as two million verses, Stanley regarded the majority as spurious, forged, or recent. Nevertheless, his major source for the portrayal of the world's oldest philosophy was the *Chaldean Oracles*, a collection of fragments that Cumont has called "the Bible of the Neoplatonics" (Majercik 1989:2). A modern editor and translator describes them as follows:

> The Chaldean Oracles are a collection of abstruse, hexameter verses purported to have been 'handed down by the gods' (theoparádota) to a certain Julian the Chaldean and/or his son, Julian the Theurgist, who flourished during the late second century C.E. ... Whatever the mode of transmission, of singular importance is the fact that the Oracles were regarded by the later Neoplatonics—from Porphyry (c. 232–303 C.E.) to Damascius (c. 462–538 C.E.)—as authoritative revelatory literature equal in importance only to Plato's Timaeus. (pp. 1–2)

Today we know that Stanley's account of Chaldean Ur-philosophy is based on Middle Platonic fragments with affinities to both Gnosticism and Hermeticism (p. 3) that may be related to Valentinian gnosis. But the majority of his readers thought they were reading ancient Chaldean oracle verse. Stanley's edition of the Greek text was accompanied by the Latin translation of Francesco PATRIZI (1529–1597) along with Stanley's English rendering of it (Stanley 1701:41–51). This was joined by the commentaries of Gemistos PLETHON (1355–c.1454) and Michael PSELLOS (c. 1017–1096) (pp. 52–62).

Stanley's presentation of Chaldean philosophy begins with Zoroaster's division of all things into three categories: 1. the eternal that has neither beginning nor end; 2. the immortal with beginning but no end; and 3. the mortal with both beginning and end. The first section about "the eternal" discusses God and light:

They conceive there is one Principle of all things, and declare that it is one and good. God (as Pythagoras learnt of the Magi, who term him Oromasdes) in his Body resembles Light, in his Soul truth; That God (according to the Chaldaick opinion) is Light, besides the Testimony of Eusebius, may be inferred from the Oracles of Zoroaster, wherein are frequently mentioned the Light, Beams, and Splendor of the Father. (p. 8)

Next, the "emanation of light or fire from God" to all angels, good daemons, and human souls is explained in descending degrees of perfection down to the rational soul. The lowest of the three realms, "things temporal (or corruptible) and corporeal" (p. 12), is presided over by "Arimanes" and contains seven corporeal worlds, the three last of which consist of matter conceived by the Chaldeans as "a dark substance or rather darkness it self" (p. 13). Based on such theology and physics, Stanley then discusses the famous Chaldean astrology and other arts of divination (pp. 16–20) as well as magic (pp. 20–24). The religion of the Chaldeans is portrayed as "an idolatrous worship of the True God" (p. 24) involving the worship of celestial bodies, various divinities, angels, demons, fire, and other elements (pp. 24–29). Stanley's chapters on the Persians (pp. 29–33) and Sabaeans (pp. 34–39) follow a similar pattern.

Stanley's readers must have been surprised by the Platonic and crypto-Christian flavor of humankind's "oldest philosophy." A single sample from the very beginning of the Oracles must suffice:

Where the Paternal Monad is.
The Monad is enlarged, which generates Two.
For the Dyad sits by him, and glitters with Intellectual Sections.
And to Govern all things, and to Order all things not Ordered,
For in the whole World shineth the Triad, over which the Monad Rules.
This Order is the beginning of all Section.
For the Mind of the Father said, that all things be cut into three.
(p. 48)

Readers with an interest in philosophy were sure to pay far more attention to the first three volumes of Stanley's *History of Philosophy* that are devoted to Greek philosophy. They earned him much praise and the reputation of a pioneer in his field. But the first edition of Stanley's work remained little known on the European continent where readers of English were still scarce. However, the situation dramatically changed when a reprint of Stanley's work in a single volume appeared in the same year as Couplet's *Confucius* (1687). Jean Le Clerc was so taken with Stanley's explanation of Chaldean philosophy that he decided to translate this entire part into Latin. His translation was published in 1690, twelve years after Stanley's death, under a title that the sober Englishman would probably have rejected as hyperbole: *Historia philosophiae orientalis* (History of Oriental philosophy). Le Clerc's renaming was probably a ploy to attract attention to a work whose translation and annotation must have cost him considerable energy and time. But it also raised the temperature in the incubation chamber of the European Republic of Letters where "Oriental philosophy" was coagulating. In his preface, Le Clerc appeared to justify this new title by explaining that the study of "oriental philosophy" is necessary and useful for a better understanding of the history of Judaism and Christianity, and particularly also for the study of the origin of heresies. He also opined that the critical study of ancient oriental sources would significantly contribute to European knowledge about the opinions of ancient oriental peoples (Stanley / Le Clerc 1690, unpaginated preface). Soon after Le Clerc put down his pen, Thomas Burnet—a disciple of the Cambridge Platonists Henry More and Ralph Cudworth—was already following his advice.

# Chapter Fifteen

# PHILOSOPHICAL ARCHAEOLOGY (BURNET)

I n the year 1692 Thomas BURNET (c. 1635–1715) published his *Archaeologiae philosophicae: sive Doctrina antiqua de rerum originibus* (Philosophical archaeologies, that is, the ancient doctrine of the origins of things). It first appeared as an addition to a reprint of *Telluris theoria sacra* (Sacred Theory of the Earth, 1680). Burnet's stunning theory of earth formation was an attempt to twist the arm of the Bible's creation story until it submitted to scientific knowledge.[107] That story's pivotal event, the great deluge, played a central role in Burnet's theory since it completely changed the face of the earth and turned a perfectly smooth spherical paradise into the "fallen" earth as we know it: a planet with seas, mountains, and valleys—"the image or picture of a great Ruine" and "a World lying in its rubbish" (Burnet 1684:193). The deluge divides both Burnet's physical and philosophical archaeologies into two periods, a before and an after. Before the deluge everything was perfect:

> This smooth, perfect surface, over which the air was perennially calm, serene, and free of those disordinate movements that are caused by winds and the existence of mountains, coincides— all of it—with the terrestrial paradise. This world was an inhabited world, for antediluvian humanity lived in it in simplicity, purity, and innocence. (tr. Rossi 1987:34-5)

107 For editions of Burnet's book and additional information see Malusa 1981:359 and Rossi 1987.

FIG. 23: BURNET'S EARTH CREATION AND DESTRUCTION CYCLE (1680).
(clockwise: the formation from chaos, the perfection of paradise, the inundated earth with the Ark, the present world, its end by combustion.)

The task of Burnet's archaeologies was to sift through the debris of our postdiluvian world in order to understand antediluvian perfection. The *Sacred Theory* thus was an attempt to reconstruct the earth's Golden Age by examining the fallout of the deluge, for example the oceans and "rubbish" like mountains. Burnet's *Philosophical Archaeology* of 1692 was an analogous endeavor with the aim of confirming the *Sacred Theory* through the study of another kind of debris, namely, the vestiges of humankind's antediluvian philosophy in the world's religions and philosophies. Dissatisfied with attempts such as Gale's to portray all achievements of philosophy as the result of Hebrew influence, Burnet radically enlarged the field of vision.

> When we abandon these prejudices we must go back farther to search for the origin of barbaric philosophy. Farther than Moses and farther than Abraham: to the Flood and to Noah, the common father of the Jews and the Gentiles. ... Why not believe that from this source, from this original man have descended to posterity, that is to say, to post-diluvian man, those principles of theology and philosophy that can be found among antico-barbarian peoples? (tr. Rossi 1987:39)

This venture required not only a new approach to the history of philosophy (Braun 1973:75-6) but also the critical examination of sources. Just as the archaeologist must be careful not to mistake recent for ancient artifacts, the philosophical archaeologist must apply advanced philological techniques to determine the age and reliability of textual sources. Burnet's investigation of the *Oracula Chaldaica*—the mainstay of Stanley's *Chaldaick Philosophy* (or, as Le Clerc renamed it, of *Philosophia orientalis*)—was devastating: they are only a hodgepodge (*farrago*) of Platonic and Gnostic elements containing no trace of genuine ancient philosophy (Burnet 1692:21-22). The attribution to Zoroaster, too, is criticized. Authors asserting such things are accused of not even knowing which Zoroaster they are referring to (p. 22) and of having "but a few excerpts from Strabo and Diodorus" to rely upon (p. 24). The situation with Persia seemed not much better: both the teachings of Zoroaster and those of the magi who supposedly were his heirs consist of "a few scattered sentences that mostly stem from Platonic authors" (p. 29). After examining extant sources about Arabs, Sabaeans, and Phoenicians in similar fashion, Burnet is forced to conclude that they hardly contribute anything to his objective, namely, to find "remnants of the dogmas of the Noachides which I consider to constitute the roots of Oriental wisdom" (p. 35).

The Bible was not exempt from criticism. In particular, Burnet was concerned about Moses's information policy (pp. 120–2). In his view, Moses was familiar with the truth of the earth's origins and with the most ancient philosophy that was subsequently transmitted by Noah. He thus knew what really happened before and after creation. But due to the limited capacity of his audience he felt forced to dumb down his account, which means that the books of Moses in the Old Testament are severely deficient as a source. Hence Burnet felt obliged to reconstruct the true course of events with the help of both physical evidence and vestiges of Noachic wisdom in various oriental texts, religions, and philosophies. Burnet believed in the transmission of such wisdom in the "real" Jewish Cabala, which is entirely different from the "nominal Cabala" with its childish word plays and letter games (pp. 61–63). According to him, the essence of the "real Cabala" consists in the doctrine of emanation (as expressed in the ten Sephirot) and in the notion of four worlds (pp. 45–49). They explain the rise of multiplicity from the first, infinite One (*En Soph*) through four levels or hypostases. By contrast, the texts of the "nominal" Cabala as well as the majority of theosophical and hermetic texts appeared to him as mere "pseudo-mysticism" (p. 56).

In Burnet's eyes the doctrine of the "real Cabala," by contrast, is an echo of divine revelation and represents a vestige that can give us a genuine idea of antediluvian philosophy. This "antique Cabala" explains "the emergence of all things from the first Cause and their return back into it" (p. 63). It relies on the old tenet "*ex nihilo ni-*

*hil fieri*": nothing can come from nothing. Burnet explains that the emanation doctrine is built on the notion of an "*En soph* that contains everything," that is, a God "who in the state before creation and before the world is simply everything" (p. 63). Hence the true meaning of "creation" is that "God unfolds and evolves by emanations and outflows"—a process that is explained by the metaphors of "vases and flasks" receiving that outflow, or by rays of light (p. 64). According to Burnet this is precisely what "the old wise ones" had taught about origins.

The reader will recall François Bernier's account that uses the same metaphors. Indeed, Burnet hints at this source in a remark printed in the margins: "The same is taught by today's Brachmanes in the Indies" (p. 64). Inspired by Bernier and the spider and flask allegories,[108] Burnet found traces of the doctrines "that God is, in some way, everything" and "has produced the world through emanations or emission of his rays" in the "true" Cabala as well as in some Egyptian, Orphic, Pythagorean, and Platonic sources (p. 65). They are vestiges of what Burnet calls the "doctrina orientalis" (p. 107) whose core teachings he identifies as all-oneness and emanation.

Burnet realized that there was a major problem with all of this: this "doctrina orientalis" neither agrees with the Old Testament nor with Christian doctrine. In fact, its basic tenet that "nothing can come from nothing" (*ex nihilo nihil fieri*) is diametrically opposed to the doctrine of a creation from nothing (*creatio ex nihilo*). Burnet defended his view by stating that he had been unable to find the slightest trace of a creation from nothing in the Old Testament and concluded—like Jacob Thomasius before and Mosheim after him—that it "was first introduced in Christian theology" (p. 63). Burnet's portrayal of the emanation doctrine as the core of Noah's philosophy and of revelation-based antediluvian wisdom was perceived as an at-

---

108 Burnet not only used Bernier's imagery (spider, web, flask, ray of light) but also cited and explained Bernier's spider allegory in his appendix on the doctrine of contemporary Brahmins (see below).

tack on conventional doctrine and appears to have cost him his job (Malusa 1981:358).

In his quest for the "origin of the ancient and barbarian wisdom" (Burnet 1692:105), Greek philosophy played no role at all because it is "chronologically later and derived" from the "Philosophiâ barbaricâ" (p. 108). The Greeks, while "perfecting barbarian mathematics, lost their philosophy" (p. 111). For Burnet the crucial question was "from which source the Egyptians, Ethiopians, Phoenicians, Arabs, Indians, and Orientals had obtained their philosophy and most ancient dogmas" (p. 190). Rejecting that they had developed them independently or adopted them from the Hebrews, he concluded that all such information originated from a single source and that the only man able to furnish it was "the great man and worshiper of the true divinity, Noah" (p. 196).

Though Burnet did not provide transmission lineages from Noah, he pointed out that the teachings of this ancestor of all peoples had survived in the Orient and that they can still be found there today. This is the theme of Burnet's appendix "About today's Brachmans in the Indies and their doctrines." It elicited immediate interest and appeared in English translation the very next year (1693) as part of Charles Blount's *Oracles of Reason*.[109] In this appendix Burnet argues along the line of Kircher that much of Asia had been missionized by Indian Brahmins:

> Under the Name of Indies, we here comprehend, besides the Chineze Empire, and Kingdom of Indostan, or Dominion of the Great Mogul, the Kingdoms of Siam, of the Malabars, of Cochinchina, of Coromandel, and whatever others are known to us in the East, that have in some measure shaken off their Barbarity. Now in each of these are a certain sort of Philosophers or Divines, and in the Kingdoms of Indostan, Siam, and the other adjacent Parts, there are some who seem to

109   Charles Blount, *The Oracles of Reason*, 1693:77-86 (reprint London: Routledge / Thoemmes Press, 1995).

be the Progeny of the ancient Brachmins, being different and distinguished from the rest of the People by their Manner and Way of Living, as well as by a Doctrine and Language wholly peculiar to themselves. (Blount 1693:78)

Burnet's view that the "progeny of the ancient Brachmins" are to this day present not only in North (Mughal) and South India (the Malabar and Coromandel coasts) but also in Thailand and many other regions of Asia is at least partly based on de Marini's mistaken idea of Indian Buddhism on Kircher's idea of a pan-Asian religion founded by Buddha and disseminated by Brahmin missionaries. A large portion of Asia appeared to share a single clergy, doctrine, and sacred language. Having learned from Heinrich Roth's explanations in Kircher's *China Illustrata* that the Brahmins and their scriptures use the ancient language of "Hanscrit" or Sanskrit (p. 79), Burnet regarded this as an explanation for the long-term preservation of Noah's doctrine and as a cause of its protection from degradation through admixture of popular elements. He saw Brahmin doctrine as a kind of *Cabala*, that is, a body of secretly transmitted knowledge. Since this knowledge had survived in so many countries of Asia, Burnet stated that it does not matter "with what Kingdom or Country we begin" (p. 79).

They have a certain Cabala, or Body of Learning, which they receive by Tradition from one to the other. Now this Body of Learning does not treat of each little Point of Nicety in Philosophy, as our modern Philosophers used to do; but like the natural Theology of the Ancients, it treats of God, of the World, of the Beginning and Ending of Things, of the Periods of the World, of the Primitive State of Nature, together with its repeated Renovations. All which Opinions are by some more plainly, by others more obscurely and fabulously delivered; but that they were of old spread amongst these Nations, is plain from several Footsteps of them at this Day remaining. (pp. 78–9)

Burnet was of course particularly interested in ideas about the beginning and ending of things, and here he adduces the explanation
by Bernier which indeed had inspired his conception of the content
of the "real" Cabala and of the "doctrina orientalis:"

> They likewise philosophize after the manner of the Ancients,
> upon the Creation of the Universe, together with its End
> and Destruction; for they explain these things by the Efflux
> or Emanation of all things from God, and by their Reflux
> or Restoration into him again: But this they propound in
> a Cabalistical Mythological Way. For they feign a certain
> immense Spider to be the first Cause of all Things, and that
> she, with the Matter she exhausted out of her own Bowels,
> spun the Web of this whole Universe, and then disposed of it
> with a most wonderful Art; whilst she herself in the mean time
> sitting on the Top of her Work, feels, rules, and governs the
> Motion of each Part. At last, when she has sufficiently pleased
> and diverted herself, in adorning and contemplating her own
> Web, she retracts the Threads she has unfolded, and swallows
> them up again into herself; whereby the whole Nature of
> Things created vanishes into nothing. (p. 80)

Burnet was convinced that if we take off the "fabulous Shell" and
"go to the Kernel," this idea of emanation from and resorption into
One is also present in other ancient sources. Indeed he encourages
his readers to find out more about this in his sources, namely "in
*Henry Lord, F. Bernier*, and other Travellers, who have more diligently enquired into their Literature" (pp. 80-1). Beside the emanation doctrine illustrated with the spider metaphor from Kircher and
Bernier,[110] Burnet drew an additional Noachic tenet confirming his
*Sacred Theory of the Earth* from de la Loubère (1691):

---

110 Both Kircher and Bernier are repeatedly referred to in Burnet's appendix
and the body of his philosophical archaeology. We have seen above that the spider
metaphor is found in Kircher's *China illustrata* as well as Bernier's travelogue and
Gassendi summary.

The Siamese Brachmins not only say, that this Modern Earth must perish, and that by Fire; but even that out of its ashes a new Earth must arise; and without a Sea, that is to say, such a one as St. John the Prophet saw, Apoc. 21.1. and without the yearly Vicissitudes of the Seasons, being blest with a perpetual Spring; such another Earth as we have described in the Fourth Book of our Theory, Cap. 2. (p. 82)

FIG. 24: THAI BUDDHA STATUES IN LA LOUBÈRE 1691 (VOL. 1, P. 418)

For Burnet such Siamese doctrines—Buddhist doctrines described by de la Loubère, a careful reader of *Confucius sinarum philosophus*—represented vestiges of an unbroken tradition going back to Noah and antediluvian transmission. Still, their preservation in the depths of Asia by a "half barbarous" people seemed almost like a miracle:

> Tis really a most wonderful thing that a Nation half barbarous should have retained these Opinions from the very Times of Noah; for they could not have arrived to a Knowledge of these Things any other way than by Tradition; nor could this Tradition flow from any other Spring, than Noah, and the Antediluvian Sages. (p. 82)

Though Burnet deplored the overall degeneration and poor state of the Orient of his day, such nuggets of ancient Oriental philosophy were in his book described in a very positive manner. Whereas Kircher had condemned such teachings as "pests" and "epidemics" and Bernier as irrational rantings and symptoms of "mental illness," Burnet's *Archaeologiae philosophicae* hailed them as the modern world's purest echoes of Noachic wisdom!

Burnet's presentation of the vestiges of Oriental wisdom as part of Noachic wisdom was opposed to Jacob Thomasius's equally influential view that will be explored below. Both authors detected links between Europe's religions and philosophies and a far more ancient Oriental doctrine of emanation (based on the tenet that "nothing can come from nothing"); but they evaluated this doctrine in opposite ways. Whereas Burnet detected in this an echo of the core doctrine of genuine ancient wisdom, the protagonist of our next chapter saw it as the key element in the genealogy of heresy.

## Chapter Sixteen

## ZOROASTER'S LIE (JACOB THOMASIUS)

B attles between exclusivists who believed that the Judeo-Christian tradition has a monopoly of truth and exclusivists who rejected this notion dot Church history from the early centuries and pertained to evaluations both of religions and philosophies. In the sixteenth century, when reformers challenged the legitimacy of the papacy and its "apostolic" pedigree, the struggles were particularly violent and raged even within the Catholic and Protestant factions. In the Catholic camp, inclusivists such as Agostino Steuco who presented many different movements as branches of a single *philosophia perennis* were opposed by exclusivists such as Giovanni Batista CRISPO (1550–1595) and Antonio POSSEVINO (1533–1611) who spearheaded the Jesuit counter-reformation. The circle of late sixteenth-century Jesuit exclusivists also included a friend of both Crispo and Possevino, Alessandro Valignano, whose Japanese catechism plays such a central role in our narrative. Possevino's 1593 reprint of Valignano's catechism in his school reader *Bibliotheca selecta* was a clever move in the battle against inclusivists. He realized that Valignano's catechism could serve as a weapon not only against Japanese atheists but also against European inclusivists, reformists, and other infidels. In Possevino's eyes, the references to Greek philosophy in Valignano's presentation of Japan's "inner" teaching were perfectly in tune with a plan of their common friend and fellow Jesuit Crispo. Convinced that most heresies (including Protestantism) had sprouted on the polluted soil of philosophy, Crispo envisaged a series of books about the hidden dangers of pagan philosophy. His catalogue of philosophers whose works were to be read with much vigilance includes not just usual suspects like Zoroaster, Lucretius, and Xenocrates but also famous philosophers such as Aristotle, Pythagoras, Plato, and the Stoics (Crispo 1594: unpaginated "Philosophorum catalogus"). In total, Crispo listed over eighty names of philosophers whose works must be read with caution, and his list of heresies that are contained in such works features more than 150 entries.

The first volume of Crispo's series (and the only one to be published because of the author's premature death) dealt with Plato and had the title *De Platone caute legendo* (On the need of reading Plato with caution). Crispo advises particular vigilance against Plato's view of the human soul as part of the world soul (p. 59–66) that resulted in such heresies as the Gnostic doctrine of the identity of man's soul with God's substance, and the Manichean doctrine that the soul either forms part of God's substance or "emanates from it as from a source" (p. 67). Such poisons had to be countered by specific antidotes, for example the decree of the Council of Toledo stating that man's soul is *not* part of God's substance but rather exists because it was created by God's will (p. 68). Similarly, the Platonic view of the relationship of soul and body and of the soul's immortality is identified as the source of many heresies that Crispo carefully lists and refutes (pp. 161–210). The chapter on the transmigration of souls is particularly long (pp. 417–489) and focuses both on individuals like Simon Magus and groups like the Gnostics, Manicheans, and Albigensians who are all said to have been victims of Plato's mistaken views.

While Crispo was chasing after heretics with a Platonic profile and prepared his 1594 book for publication, his friend Possevino was preparing Valignano's catechism for publication in his 1593 *Bibliotheca selecta*.[111] Though the heresies presented and criticized by Valignano were of course Japanese, Possevino's readers could be pardoned for believing that Greek philosophy had infected the Far

111 For this textbook by Possevino see the study by Zedelmaier (1992).

East. Like Crispo's Greek philosophers, the Japanese as portrayed by Valignano lack the notion of a creation out of nothing, think that the world is eternal, and ignore the fundamental difference between creator and creatures. Like Parmenides and Melissus they believe that all things are one and that everything forms part of the substance of their first principle. Like the Stoics they hold that our souls form part of a world soul; and like some Neoplatonics and mystics they are convinced that man can realize unity with the first principle in this lifetime (Possevino 1603:462–480).

But exclusivists like Crispo, Possevino, and Valignano were not without competition from inclusivists. In the very year 1593 when Crispo was putting the finishing touches on his Plato-related warnings and Possevino republished Valignano's catechism, Francesco Patrizi's edition of the *Oracula Zoroastris* appeared. Six years later, John Opsopoeus's edition of these *Oracles* together with Georgios Gemistos Plethon's and Michael Psellos's commentaries triggered a wave of interest in ancient theology. In spite of publications such as Casaubon's that as early as 1614 deflated many myths surrounding hermetic texts, this kind of interest continued unabated, as is shown by Kircher's works (1636, 1652–4, 1667) and Stanley's 1662 publication of Zoroaster's *Oracles* along with his English translation of well-known commentaries in the *History of Chaldaick Philosophy*.

It is in this climate and on the backdrop of Cambridge Platonism as well as rising interest in the Orient that Jacob THOMASIUS (1622–1684) published his *Schediasma historicum* in 1665. In seventeenth-century Germany Thomasius was famous as an erudite polymath; but today he is best known as the teacher of Leibniz, father and teacher of Christian Thomasius, and innovative historiographer of philosophy. Though he was a Lutheran, Thomasius followed in the footsteps of the exclusivist hardliner Crispo whose work he esteemed, and like this Catholic predecessor he presented the intermingling of pagan philosophy and Christianity as the source of countless heresies. In tune with Crispo and Valignano, Thomasius regarded the concept of *creatio ex nihilo* as the fundamental doctrine distinguishing heathendom from Christianity. Those who ignore it tend to believe, like Crispo's Greek philosophers, Valignano's Japanese philosophers, and Ricci's Neoconfucians, that "nothing can come from nothing" and that matter is eternal:

> All philosophers (we speak of the heathens) agree that the matter of which the world is made existed beforehand, and that nothing can come from nothing (nihil ex nihilo fiat)" (Thomasius 1665:28).

The heathen philosophers' notion of a *materia prima* that had always existed (possibly alongside God) is diametrically opposed to the Christian doctrine that God created *everything* (including matter) from nothing. Indeed, the principle that "nothing comes from nothing," according to Thomasius, is the first lie (*prôton pseudos*):

> The first lie of the heathens consisted in their conviction that it is impossible to simply create something from nothing. This was one of the reasons [...] why they posited, apart from God, an eternal matter not produced by Him. (p. 12)

Thomasius regarded this "lie" as the ultimate source of the four major traditions of Greek philosophy, of the main Christian heresies, of degenerate mystical theology, and of equally problematic medieval scholasticism. This lie, the mother of all pagan philosophies, also gave birth to the notion that there are two eternal principles, one of which is good and the other evil. That Thomasius associated this dualism with the figure of Zoroaster is of particular importance in our context because this identifies the ultimate oriental source for all these movements.

For Thomasius, the "first lie" led to a number of fundamental errors. The first is a basic and pervasive *dualism*: "That there are two contrary, eternal principles is the capital error and the basis of all pagan impiety" (p. 28). Thomasius held that this dualism was introduced by Zoroaster in form of his teaching that there is a good and an evil divinity (p. 23). Following Apuleios's view that Pythagoras was a disciple of Zoroaster, Thomasius traced the transmission of Zoroastrian dualism to "Plato, Aristotle, and others" in Greece. They all posited a "dark" material principle as the source of evil alongside an eternal, "luminous" God (p. 23). Though the Peripatetics, Stoics, Epicureans, and Platonists embraced different conceptions of the relationship between God and matter, Thomasius saw all of them as offsprings of Zoroastrian dualism and of the "first lie" that posits an eternal, uncreated matter that always existed alongside God.

The second major error was, in Thomasius's view, the conflation of the dual principles of God and matter into the notion of a divine first matter from which all things emanate. As in the philosophy of Strato, this could lead to the opinion that God and matter are identical and thus give rise to materialism and pantheism. Thomasius was convinced that such mistaken notions had not only infected major Greek philosophies but also burrowed their way into Christianity where they resurfaced in the form of heresies. Whereas Gnosticism and Manicheism formed extensions of ancient dualism, Stoicism and Platonism inherited emanation-based notions such as the idea of a world soul from which each human soul emanates and to which it eventually returns. This forms the basis of what Thomasius calls "mystical theology," a heresy that is also rooted in the "first lie" of the heathens:

> The vast majority of such views were based on the condemned hypothesis that our souls do not have their origin in a creation out of nothing but rather in an outflow from God's own essence or substance. (Thomasius 1665:59)

The ancient doctrine of emanation, which found its way into Platonic philosophy and from there into Christian "mystical theology," also forms the basis for the idea that a reunion of the soul with the divine substance is possible. For Thomasius, such platonizing mysticism formed the rotten core of the "enthusiasm" of mystics such as Jacob BOEHME (1575–1624) and of mystical texts such as the

"German Theology" that unfortunately even Luther had admired. Its representatives regard man's soul as an outflow of God and advocate its ascent to and reunion with the divine essence. For Thomasius this was one of the most striking examples of the problems resulting from the insertion of pagan philosophy into Christianity. Thomasius thus was in complete agreement with Crispo and Valignano with regard to the fundamental distinction between a creation out of nothing and emanation: the idea that man's soul—and possibly even the whole universe—had emanated from the eternal divine substance necessarily blurred or even erased the distinction between the creator God and his creatures, thus opening the door for the divinization of man and world.

Thomasius's genealogy of the view that God and world are identical—a view that a few decades after his death received the name of "pantheism"—was one of his most fruitful and influential research topics. The same can be said of his work on the divinization of man associated with "mystical theology" that he also linked to Platonism and the Orient. We have seen that the identification of the first principle with the entire world along with the notion that man's soul is part of God were presented as central doctrines both of Japan's "inner" doctrine as presented by Valignano and of the philosophy ascribed by Bernier to "almost all those who are regarded as learned in Asia." According to Bernier, these Orientals all believe "that they constitute parts of the divine substance and are in some way little Gods" (Bernier 1684:90). The resorption of the world into God, as in the spider allegory, and the reunification of man's soul with the divine were further themes linking Valignano's presentation of Xaca's "inner" doctrine, Bernier's Oriental philosophers, and Thomasius's portrayal of the Neoplatonic and mystical "emanation-and-resorption" doctrine. Though Thomasius probably did not know Valignano's catechism and published his *Schediasma historicum* six years before Bernier's letter to Chapelain appeared in print, it is noteworthy that Valignano, Bernier, and Thomasius were all critical of

Platonic and Neoplatonic doctrines and deplored their corrupting influence on Christianity. Moreover, all three authors disapproved of "mystical" tendencies and saw their root and inherent danger in the erasure of the difference between God and creatures through claims of "emanation" and "unification." However, between the late sixteenth century (when Valignano and Crispo were active) and the prime of Bernier and Thomasius in the latter half of the seventeenth century, an important shift had taken place. For Valignano, the roots of Oriental philosophies still seemed to be firmly lodged in Greece, as his critique of Japanese doctrines shows. But seven decades later Thomasius identified Zoroaster's "first lie" as the source of Greek philosophies and thus moved—much like Rodrigues—the cradle of such philosophy toward Mesopotamia, Persia, and Afghanistan. In 1684, the year of Thomasius's death, Bernier for the first time wrote of a philosophy shared by all the educated people of Asia (Bernier 1684:90), and four years later he confirmed that the "inner teaching" of the Buddha and its Neoconfucian echo (as portrayed by Intorcetta and Couplet in the introduction to *Confucius sinarum philosophus*) represent the content of this philosophy.

Thomasius's contribution to the invention of Oriental philosophy was threefold: first, his research into Greek and Roman philosophy and his genealogies of Christian heresies pointed toward the Orient as ultimate source. Second, these genealogies linked contemporary phenomena in Germany (such as rising pietism and Boehmean mysticism) via elaborate and well-researched lineages of transmission to Greek sources and from there somehow to "Zoroaster" and the Orient. Third, Thomasius's studies—in particular his work on Platonism and Stoicism and their corrosive influence on Christianity—prepared the ground on which men like Bayle, Brucker, and Mosheim would later erect their visions of "Oriental philosophy." When he published his *Schediasma* in 1665 Thomasius was not yet aware of Spinoza, and his genealogies were primarily driven by his will to expose the historical and philosophical background of mid-seventeenth century mystical tendencies that he considered heretical or conducive to heresy. Thomasius traced a direct line from the pietists and mystics of his time back to Scotus Erigena, to the fifth-century Neoplatonic and Christian mystic Dionysios Areopagita, to Alexandrian theology, to Stoic and Platonic teachings about the soul, and ultimately to the "first lie" of his arch-heretic Zoroaster.

Once emanation was accepted instead of creation out of nothing, and once the soul was seen as an outflow of God, the door was open for all kinds of illuminism, quietism, and pantheism. In the detailed heresiology of Thomasius, the above-mentioned transmission line included the twelfth-century heretics Amalric and David of Dinant who had identified God with *materia prima* and taught things that sound rather similar to the teachings of Buddha's "inner" doctrine. Quoting Jean Gerson, Thomasius summarized Amalric's teaching as follows:

> He rejected the resurrection of the flesh as well as paradise and hell. But those who recognize God in themselves find the paradise in themselves. By contrast, those who have mortal sins have hell in themselves, which is not different from a rotten tooth in the mouth. (Thomasius 1665:59)

Two frightening outgrowths of the "first lie" and the emanation doctrine—the pantheist identification of the world with God and the mystical identification of the soul with God—were thus at the top of Thomasius's list of research topics even before he began to read Spinoza in the early 1670s.

After the appearance of Spinoza's *Tractatus theologico-politicus* in 1670 and additional works (including the *Ethics*) in 1679, the similarity to some of Spinoza's teachings gave renewed actuality to Thomasius's essays about the history of heresies.[112] Thomasius saw

---

112 The *Schediasma*, first published in 1665, was reprinted in 1694, and in 1699 a second edition entitled *Origines* appeared. Thomasius's 1676 *Exercitatio de stoica mundi exustione* was reprinted in 1682 in a volume entitled *Dissertationes* that was used by Bayle for his famous article on Spinoza (see next chapter).

the Stoic and Neoplatonic doctrines of the soul and its ascension to
the One as a hotbed for heretics who (exactly like Valignano's Zen
adepts) emphasize the importance of one's own effort and of quiet
meditation for achieving salvation. Thomasius condemned such efforts to achieve a state of sinlessness in this life as a delusion and
traced such "mystical" enthusiasm to Pelagianism and Gnosticism
as well as Stoic philosophy (p. 43 ff.). Thinking that they achieved
salvation, such fanatics and gnostics believe that they can no more
commit sins and are no more bound by the rules of morality (p.
34). Thomasius's condemnation of the mystic enthusiasts' quietism,
moral indifference, and false conception of inner salvation has an almost exact counterpart in Valignano's earlier critique of Zen monks.
Is it possible that Thomasius was familiar with Valignano's catechism
via Possevino's *Bibliotheca selecta* and that he had the chance to read
works by de Marini (1665), Bernier (1672), and Navarrete (1676)?
I do not know. At any rate, Thomasius died in 1684 just before
Couplet's *Confucius* and its reviews disseminated the news of a very
similar teaching reigning in many nations of Asia: a teaching that
Bernier proclaimed to be the philosophy of most educated Asians.
The synthesis of all this and the final push into European consciousness, however, was the work of a thinker and publicist who not only
studied and cited Thomasius's genealogies but also Valignano's catechism, the introduction to *Confucius*, Bernier's writings, and Spinoza: Pierre Bayle.

# Chapter Seventeen

# Ur-Spinozism (Bayle)

The eighteenth-century implementation of "Oriental philosophy" began with a *succès de scandale*: Pierre BAYLE's (1647–1706) *Dictionnaire historique et critique*. This dictionary, of which two editions (11697, 21702) appeared in Bayle's lifetime, exerted "an unprecedented impact right across Europe down to the middle of the eighteenth century" (Israel 2006:87):

> No one else, not even Locke, was a staple of so many libraries or had so wide a general influence, his writings being everywhere acknowledged to be a prime cause of the tide of skepticism, atheism, and materialism sweeping the west of the continent. (p. 87)

In some of the most scandalous and most widely discussed articles of his dictionary, Bayle promoted atheism and monism by rewriting the history of religion and philosophy. His attack on monotheism, which formed part of his strategy of promoting atheism, involved the destruction of the notion of a *consensus gentium* (agreement of all peoples) about the existence of an omnipotent, good creator God. Linked to this was Bayle's argument that atheistic individuals (like Spinoza) and societies (like China) not only do exist but even tend to be more moral than their monotheistic counterparts. In the *Dictionnaire*, Bayle's argument and documentation is for the most part buried in excessively long footnotes to seemingly innocuous articles like "Pauliciens," "Manichéisme," or "Xenophanes" in which he ostensibly attacks heretical notions while in fact presenting and almost openly promoting them.

Bayle's use of Jacob Thomasius's genealogy of heresy is a good example of his general procedure. As we have seen in the previous chapter, Thomasius had identified the idea that "nothing comes out of nothing" as the "first lie" and source of all heresy. He had associated the notion of two eternal substances, God and matter, with the figure of Zoroaster and claimed that this dualism had infected not only the major schools of Greek philosophy including Platonism but also heretical movements such as Gnosticism, Manicheism, and Christian "mystical theology." In his dictionary articles on the "Manichéens" and "Pauliciens," Bayle made extensive use of Thomasius's argument but changed its overall thrust by 180 degrees. Accompanied by the howls of theologians and philosophers, Bayle presented an entirely logical and ostensibly irrefutable argument to the effect that the notions of "nothing comes out of nothing" and of two opposite principles are not the "first lie" but rather the only rationally acceptable and fundamental "first truth." In pages upon pages of intricate argument and counter-argument, Bayle shows that the certified existence of evil in the world renders the notion of a sole, entirely good as well as omnipotent source of everything—a creator God—absolutely untenable. He does so in a unique manner dripping with irony and sarcasm. While accusing the Manicheans of an "entirely absurd and contradictory hypothesis," Bayle in fact shows it to be an optimal way to rationally explain the presence of good and evil in the world.

> Who does not admire—and who does not deplore—the destiny of our reason? Look at the Manichaeans whose totally absurd and contradictory hypothesis explains our experiences a hundred times better than the one advanced by the orthodox, which is based on a supposition so just, so necessary, and so uniquely veritable: that of an infinitely good and omnipotent first principle. (Bayle 1702:2325)

The view that Bayle was a fideist who advocated faith as the only way to overcome bankrupt reason is, as Jonathan Israel (2001, 2006) has conclusively shown, without merit. The problem of theodicy—the origin of evil in the world—occupied Bayle throughout his career, and his increasingly radical attacks on the notion of an "infinitely good and omnipotent first principle" are an unmistakable sign not just of skepticism, as is sometimes claimed, but of his clear and uncompromising rejection of monotheism. What set him apart from ordinary skeptics, radicals, and amateur atheists of his and our time was his philosophical acumen and widely admired ability to present complicated arguments in an entirely lucid as well as entertaining fashion. At least in his time, few readers believed Bayle's assertions—made after pages upon pages of entirely rational argument in a gigantic work highlighting the blindness of faith of all kinds—that one ought to throw reason overboard and rely solely on faith and the Bible:

> They say that [natural revelation via reason] is only good for making known to man his powerlessness and the necessity of a savior and merciful dogma. It had the role of a pedagogue (these are their terms) to lead us to Jesus Christ. Let us say approximately the same thing about reason: it is only good for letting man know about his shadiness, impotence, and the need for another revelation, namely, that of Scripture. (p. 2026)

After calling the Christian doctrine of a creator God "a hypothesis," proving at length how bad a hypothesis this is compared to Zoroastrian / Manichean dualism, and pouring acid over the story of man's Fall under the eye of a purportedly omniscient and omnipotent creator, Bayle closes his discussion with the following, extremely sarcastic observation:

> It is here [in Scripture] that we find the means of invincibly refuting the hypothesis of the two principles and of all objections of Zoroaster. Here we find the unity of God and his infinite perfection, the fall of the first man, and what follows

after that. Let them argue with as much reasoning as they wish that it is impossible that moral evil gets introduced into the world by means of an infinitely good and holy principle: we will reply that this is what indeed happened, and that therefore it is very possible. Nothing is more unreasonable than arguing against facts, as the axiom says: ab actu ad potentiam valet consequentia [the deduction from the actual to the possible is valid]. This is as clear as the proposition that two times two is four. (p. 2026)

The longest article in Bayle's *Dictionnaire* is the one on Spinoza. It begins with the words:

SPINOZA (Benedict of), Jew by birth who later forsook Judaism, and in the end an atheist, was a native of Amsterdam. He was a systematical atheist [athée de système] with (A) an entirely new method. (Bayle 1697:2.1083)

After these two short sentences, Bayle explains to the reader in note A that "Spinoza is the first who boiled down atheism to a system" and goes on to furnish a lengthy genealogy of Spinozism designed to prove that Spinozism is only new in the sense that it is "woven in the manner of geometers" (p. 1083). However, the core of Spinoza's philosophy, namely, the notion "that the entire Universe is a single substance and that God and the world are a single being" (p. 1083), is shown to be an ancient doctrine. This is what Bayle's note A on the genealogy of Spinozism is about. It fills several large pages in small print in the first edition of Bayle's *Dictionnaire* (1697) and was substantially enlarged in the second edition (1702). This genealogy was to play a central role in the eighteenth-century blossom of "Oriental philosophy."

In the first segment of his 1697 genealogy of Spinozism, Bayle leads his readers to Persia where Pietro DELLA VALLE (1586–1652) had discovered two sects of Islam holding such monistic views.

Pietro della Valle mentioned certain Mahommedans that are called Ehl Eltahkik, or men of truth, men of certainty, who believe that everything consists of the four elements that are God, man, and all things. He also speaks of the Zindikites, another Mahommedan sect. [...] They believe that there is neither providence nor resurrection of the dead [...], and one of their opinions is that everything that one sees, all that exists in the world, all of creation, is God. (p. 1083)

The second segment focuses on two figures of medieval Christianity who also played important roles in Thomasius's *Dissertationes* of 1676 that Bayle had studied and cites.

There have been similar heretics among the Christians, for we find at the beginning of the thirteenth century a certain David of Dinant[113] who made no distinction between God and the first matter. [...] David of Dinant knew very well that he did not invent this dogma; did he not learn it from his master? Was he not the disciple of that Amalricus whose cadaver was exhumed and burned in the year 1208—the man who had taught that all things are God and form a single being? Omnia sunt Deus: Deus est omnia. Creator & creatura idem. Idea creant & creantur [All things are God, and God is all things. Creator and creature are the same. Ideas create and are created]. (p. 1083)

The third genealogical way station is Greek antiquity. Here Bayle mentions Alexander Epicureus, another important figure in Thomasius's genealogy of heresy, who had taught that "all is the same [omnia idem esse]" and asserted "that God is matter or not extraneous to matter, that everything is by essence God, and that individual forms are conceived as accidental characteristics without true being" (Thomasius 1676:200). Bayle also repeats Thomasius's doubts about the thought of Strato of Lampsacus (p. 202; Bayle 1697:2.1083).

After the fourth way station, where Bayle discusses the teaching of a world-soul and the Stoics, he leaves the territory covered

---

113 Navarrete also mentioned David of Dinant in his *Tratados* (Navarrete 1676:255), published in the same year as Thomasius's *Dissertationes* (1676).

by Thomasius and strikes out on his own. In his discussion of Gassendi's critique of Fludd in note A, the attentive reader discovers the flask metaphor from Bernier's letter to Chapelain that we discussed in Chapter 12:

> I shall observe, by the way, an absurdity of those who maintain the system of the soul of the world. They say that all the souls, both of men and brutes, are particles of the soul of the world, which are reunited to their whole by the death of the body: and to make us understand it, they compare animals to bottles full of water, floating upon the sea. If those bottles were broken, their water would be re-united to its whole; thus it is with particular souls, say they, when death destroys the organs in which they were shut up. Nay, some say that extacies, dreams, and intense meditations, re-unite a man's soul to the soul of the world, and that this is the reason why people foretell things to come by composing figures of geomancy. (Bayle 1826:3.275)

Without yet mentioning Bernier's name, Bayle even repeats the Frenchman's arguments against this view:

> It is no difficult thing to perceive the falsity of this parallel. The matter of the bottles floating in the sea is an enclosure, which keeps the sea water from touching the water they are full of; but if there were a soul of the world, it would be dispersed through all the parts of the universe, and therefore nothing could prevent the union of the soul to its whole, and death could not produce that re-union. (p. 275)

At this point Bayle finally reveals his source. Bernier's travelogue, he explains, contains evidence for the fact that "Spinozism is but a particular method of explaining a dogma that is very widespread in the Indies [qui a un grand cours dans les Indes]" (Bayle 1697:2.1084). The entire remainder of Bayle's note A consists of a long quotation from Bernier's letter to Chapelain. It lays out "the doctrine that is quite universal among the pagan pandits of the Indies and is current today also in the cabal of the Sufis" (p. 1084). In the first edition of Bayle's *Dictionnaire*, the most remote roots of Spinozism are thus located "in the Indies." Quoting Bernier's letter, Bayle presents the following main elements: (1) Bernier's claim that this is the quasi universal doctrine of the pagan scholars of India and of the Persian intellectuals and Sufis; (2) the emanation of everything from the immutable *Achar*; (3) the spider allegory; (4) the doctrine that all that we see, hear, touch, smell, and taste is only like a dream; (5) the view that "this multiplicity and diversity of things that appear to us are but a single, unique, and identical thing"; (6) the allegory of the water-filled flask and the ocean; (7) the allegory of the light and illuminated objects; (8) Bernier's critique of these allegories; and (9) Bernier's reference to the "beautiful poems of the Goult-chen-raz" that the Sufis cite when explaining their doctrine (pp. 1084–5).

In the first edition of 1697 Bayle thus suggested an Oriental ancestry of Spinozism. Its teachings "that the entire Universe is a single substance and that God and the world are a single being" (p. 1083) are regarded as identical with the Oriental philosophy described by Bernier. According to Bayle, Spinozism is therefore "only a particular method of explaining ... a doctrine that very much prevails in the Indies" (p. 1084). Bayle thus suggested to his readers that Spinoza does not stand alone and is only a "geometric" systematizer of an ancient philosophy which is still dominant in the Orient.

Around 1697 when the *Dictionnaire*'s first edition appeared, a wave of books and pamphlets filled with quarrels about quietism and Chinese rites and terms had begun to swap over Europe. Paris and Bayle's Netherlands were the publication epicenters where scores of attacks and counter-attacks by Jansenists, Dominicans, and Jesuits kept the printing presses busy and attracted Europe-wide attention. Journals such as those edited by Le Clerc and Bayle had begun to discuss such battles and publications with varying degrees of objectivity and detail. China was now in the limelight, and even famous authors such as the philosopher Gottfried LEIBNIZ and the church historian Noël ALEXANDRE joined the fray. Confessional demarcations in this controversy were blurred; for example, the protestant Leibniz took the side of the Jesuits in his *Novissima sinica* of 1697 and his letter to Rémond (1715), whereas the Dominican Alexandre—armed with Navarrete's published and unpublished writings—fought tooth and nail against the Jesuits (1699, 1700).

The quarrel about Chinese rites and terms was a crucial battle in the age-old war between inclusivists and exclusivists. The stakes were extremely high; entire influential orders like the Jesuits and Dominicans manned opposite battle lines, and freethinkers, Jansenists, deists, and atheists entered the fray. The inclusivist camp, which included some early deists, believed with Ricci that ancient Chinese religion was a natural religion whose monotheism was independent of revelation and purely rational: Valignano's "first law" (see Chapter 8). Their opponents—the exclusivists who insisted on the absolute necessity of divine revelation—agreed with Rodrigues, Longobardi, and Navarrete that all Chinese religions were profoundly atheistic. The battle came to a head in 1700 at the illustrious Sorbonne in Paris where the following six opinions were officially condemned:

1. China had knowledge of the true God more than two thousand years before Jesus Christ.

2. China had the honor of sacrificing to God in the most ancient temple in the world.

3. China has honored God in a manner that can serve as an example even to Christians.

4. China has practiced a morality as pure as its religion.

5. China had the faith, humility, the interior and exterior cult, the priesthood, the sacrifices, the saintliness, the miracles, the spirit of God, and the purest charity, which is the characteristic and the perfection of the genuine religion.

6. Of all the nations of the world, China has been the most constantly favored by the graces of God (Pinot 1971:98; Rossi 1987:141).

This was a clear victory for the exclusivist camp; but in an important sense it was a pyrrhic victory because it meant that the world's largest state—one that by most accounts functioned very well and was guided by sound ethical principles—is and has always been thoroughly atheist. This was a topic of supreme interest for Bayle. His interest in China and the issue of religious tolerance led him to study, among many other pertinent publications, Charles Le Gobien's 1698 book about the Chinese emperor's tolerance edict.[114] Possibly already during his studies as a young man at a Jesuit school, Bayle had also become familiar with Valignano's catechism in Possevino's *Bibliotheca selecta*. These two books are among the main sources of additions in the second edition of Bayle's *Dictionnaire* (1702). The ones that primarily concern us here are related to Bayle's newly enlarged genealogy of Spinozism and are found (1) in the revised body of the 1702 Spinoza article; (2) in a supplement to the aforementioned note A that had in 1697 ended with the Indies; (3) in a newly added article on Japan; and (4) in a newly added article on Brahmins.

The beginning of the Spinoza article in the second edition of Bayle's *Dictionnaire* highlights Spinozism's intimate connection with ancient European as well as Oriental philosophy and immediately refers to a specific note in the new Japan article and to Bayle's newly added information regarding the theology of a Chinese sect.

---

114 This book appeared both as a separate book (1698) and as the third volume of Lecomte's *Nouveaux mémoires sur l'état présent de la Chine* (²1697); see Timmermans 1998:578–88 and App 2010:168–9 & 197–201). These were precisely the two works singled out in the Sorbonne condemnation.

| Dictionnaire 1st edition (Bayle 1697:2.1083) | Dictionnaire 2nd edition (Bayle 1702:2767–9) |
|---|---|
| He was a systematical atheist with (A) an entirely new method. | He was a systematical atheist with (A) an entirely new method, even though he shared the core of his doctrine with several other, ancient and modern philosophers from both Europe and the Orient. With regard to the latter one only has to read what I report in note D of the article on Japan along with what I say here below concerning the theology of a sect of the Chinese. |

TABLE 12: ADDITIONS TO THE BEGINNING OF THE SPINOZA ARTICLE IN BAYLE'S DICTIONNAIRE (FIRST AND SECOND EDITION)

Whereas Bayle's initial genealogy of Spinozism in the first edition (1697) had ended with a long excerpt from Bernier's explanations about the philosophy of the Indies and Persia, the second edition of 1702 extended the scope to the entire Orient. Bayle's addition to note A "concerning the theology of a sect of the Chinese" consists of one and a half densely printed pages about the teaching of Fo (Chinese Buddhism). Most of this information is translated from the introduction to *Confucius sinarum philosophus* (1687). Unable to get hold of this book, Bayle used the long excerpts included in Le Clerc's French review article in the *Bibliothèque universelle* and the Latin *Acta eruditorum* (both published in 1688). In the first pages of Bayle's 1702 Spinoza article the seed of Le Clerc's pioneering linkage of Bernier, Couplet, quietism, and Spinozism (see Chapter 13) had already sprouted: Spinoza was now presented as heir and systematizer of an ancient philosophy dominating the entire region between Persia and Japan.

Let us now look at the voluminous information concerning the "theology of a Chinese sect" that Bayle decided to append to his already gigantic note A of the Spinoza article. This is the note that originally ended with Bernier's presentation of Oriental philosophy. In his new supplement whose aim is the expansion of Spinoza's philosophical ancestry toward the Far East, Bayle first explains that the sect in question is *Foe Kiao* (Ch. *fojiao* 佛教, Buddhism) and supplies some information about its founder *Xe Kia* (Ch. *Shejia* 釋迦, Shakyamuni Buddha) including the enlightenment and deathbed confession stories drawn from the reviews of the *Confucius sinarum philosophus* introduction:

> At the age of thirty years, when rising in the morning before daybreak and contemplating the planet Venus, that simple sight gave him at one stroke perfect knowledge of the first principle; so, full of a divine inspiration or rather pride and folly, he began to instruct people, let himself be regarded as a God, and gained as many as 80,000 disciples. ... At seventy-nine years of age, as he felt death approaching, he declared to his disciples that during the forty years of his preaching to the world he had not told them the truth and that he had hitherto concealed it under the veil of metaphors and figures; but that now the time had come to declare it to them. 'There is nothing,' he said, 'to be searched for, and on which one may place one's hopes, other than nothingness and emptiness, which is the first principle of all things.' (Bayle 1702:2769)

Bayle expressed his admiration for the founder's courage by noting that while Europe's freethinkers (*esprits forts*) tend to abandon the fight against religion on their deathbed, Foe (Buddha) "in the same situation began to declare his atheism" (p. 2769). Quoting from the *Bibliothèque universelle* and the *Acta Eruditorum* reviews of *Confucius sinarum philosophus*, Bayle goes on to briefly explain the difference between "inner" and "outer" teachings and presents this "inner doctrine" as one that is withheld from the simple-minded because they cannot understand such subtleties and are in need of "fear of hell and other stories of the kind" (p. 2769):

> [This inner teaching] in their opinion is the solid and true one. It consists in establishing as the principle and end of all things, a certain emptiness and real nothingness [un certain vuide & un néant réel]. They say that our first ancestors sprang from this emptiness and returned into it after death; that all humans are reabsorbed into that principle at death; that we, all the elements, and all creatures form part of that emptiness; and that therefore there is but one and the same substance which only varies in particular beings with regard to shape, qualities, or inner configuration—much like water that always remains essentially water whether it has the form of snow, hail, rain, or ice. (p. 2769)

Bayle was, like Le Clerc before him, struck by the similarity of the Buddha's "true" teaching with Spinoza's doctrine of a single substance and its modifications. He also noted that "these philosopers make supreme perfection consist in the inaction and absolute quietude of this principle." Even though they characterize this principle as "pure, limpid, subtle, and infinite," they "deny that it has heart, virtue, mind, and power" and regard its "lack of action, intelligence, and desire" as essential (p. 2769). The reader will recall the very similar characterization of the first principle in Valignano's catechism. Bayle felt that such descriptions called for a comparison with quietism:

> Let us note in passing that the followers of Foe teach quietism; for they say that all who seek genuine beatitude ought to be so much absorbed in profound meditations as to make no use of their intellect whatsoever; and that they ought through perfect insensibility immerse themselves into the quietude

and inaction of the first principle, which is the true means of resembling it perfectly and to share its happiness. (p. 2769) Ardent followers of this doctrine are said to "approach the nature of a tree trunk or a rock," "remain immobile for several hours," and attain complete absence of any movement of mind or sentiment (p. 2770). Bayle's famous Spinoza article disseminated such information throughout Europe. But he was not content with adopting Le Clerc's idea, documenting it with long quotations from Bernier and *Confucius sinarum philosophus*, and using this for the construction of his oriental genealogy of Spinozism. As a former student of the Jesuits he was aware of additional interesting data, namely, the summary of Japan's "inner doctrine" in Possevino's reprint of Valignano's catechism. Already concerned about the excessive length of his Spinoza article, Bayle decided to present this evidence in a newly added "Japan" article. It contains Bayle's summary of Valignano's discussion of the "outer" and "inner" or true doctrine of Japanese religion and argues that the latter (that is, Zen doctrine as understood by Valignano) forms part of the ancient Oriental genealogy of Spinozism. In the second edition of Bayle's *Dictionnaire* (1702) this genealogy thus pooled all the main streams of information whose origins and trajectories were traced in this book. The first lines of the 1702 Spinoza article now point to note D of the Japan article. This note contains Bayle's summary of the doctrine of Japanese philosophers who "seek inner reality," "reject paradise and hell," and "teach things that are very much connected to the opinion of Spinoza" (p. 1628). Bayle's explanations in note D are wholly based on Valignano's catechism as published in Possevino's *Bibliotheca selecta*. That information in turn relied, as we have seen in Chapters 5 to 7, on particular Jesuit interpretations of data about Zen doctrine provided by native informers. Given this pedigree, it comes as no surprise that the Japanese "ancestors of Spinozism" now use Zen terminology like "Soquxin Soqubut" (*sokushin sokubutsu* 即心即佛; "this very mind is Buddha"). Bayle explains:

They neglect what is exterior and apply themselves exclusively to meditation. They thoroughly reject all discipline consisting of words and are only attached to the exercise they call Soquxin Soqubut, that is, the heart. They confirm that there is only a single principle of all things and that this principle is found everywhere; that the heart of man and the inner nature of other beings does not differ at all from this principle; and that all beings return to this common principle when they are destroyed. They add that it exists from eternity and is unique, limpid and luminous. It can neither grow nor diminish, has no form, does not reason, and lives in idleness and perfect rest. (Bayle 1702:1628, based on Possevino 1603:461 and ultimately Valignano 1586:5r)

Bayle also mentions other facets of this doctrine as presented in Possevino/Valignano, for example the teaching that knowledge is not different from ignorance and that good is not different from evil (p. 1629; Possevino 1603:462)—statements that, as we have seen in Chapter 6, reflect misunderstandings by missionaries of the Buddhist doctrine of nonduality. Bayle then goes on to offer his summary of Valignano's four cardinal points of the "inner doctrine." Unlike the shorter summary in Spizelius (1660:161–2), Bayle's presentation reached a very large pan-European public. It reads:

1. There is only one single principle of all things; and this principle is sovereignly perfect and wise yet does not understand anything and is not at all concerned about the affairs of this world since it remains fully at rest and, like a person strongly focused on something, leaves all other things alone.

2. This principle is in all particular things and communicates its essence to them, so that they form the same thing as it and return to it when they end.

3. The heart of man is not at all different from this common principle of all beings. When men die, their hearts perish and are consumed; but the first principle that in the first place gave

them life still remains in them. As a result there are neither paradise nor hell, and neither recompense nor punishment after this life.

4. Man can in this world elevate himself to the condition and the supreme majesty of the first principle, given that through meditation he can know it perfectly and thus attain the sovereign tranquility that this principle enjoys. Herein lies all the good that man can acquire, and until he has reached it through meditation and through perfect knowledge, he is agitated in perpetual unease, passing from one hell into another, unable to find quietude anywhere. (Bayle 1702: 1629)

While pointing out that this doctrine "contains several things that Spinoza did not teach," Bayle insists that it represents the essence of Spinoza's doctrine: "It is very certain that, like these Japanese priests, he taught that the first principle of all things, and all beings that form the universe, form a single identical substance and that all things are God and God is all things. Therefore God and all existing things are a single and identical being" (p. 1629). Though Bayle did not attempt to invent a transmission scenario for this doctrine, he found the similarity stunning and presented it as a kind of *consensus gentium* (consensus of all peoples) that is diametrically opposed to the universal monotheist consensus propagated by his source Valignano. With his usual measure of sarcasm he noted:

It is cause for wonder that such an extravagant idea that is so full of absurd contradictions could invade the souls of so many people that are so far removed from each other and are so different with regard to temperament, education, customs, and intelligence. (p. 1629)

For Bayle this doctrine was shared not only by Japanese priests and Spinoza but also by Xenophanes, Xenophanes's disciple Parmenides, and Parmenides's disciple Melissus—names that we encountered in Valignano's catechism and Rodrigues's as well as Navarrete's writings.

Bayle's article on Xenophanes, another addition to the *Dictionnaire* in 1702, also presents this doctrine and is once more capped by Bayle's feigned surprise that so many philosophers of antiquity came to the same conclusion:

> They recognize no difference between the principle of which things are composed and the principle that has produced them. They admit only a single being, and they pretend that everything is eternal. ... It is difficult to understand how such a great number of ancient philosophers could believe that there is only one substance in the universe. (p. 3035)

In discussing the monism of Xenophanes, Melissus, and Aristotle, Bayle urges his readers to consult a Jesuit commentary on Aristotle's *Physics* where the logic of this monism is well explained. Bayle probably was familiar with this Coimbra textbook from his days as a student at a Jesuit school. At any rate: his references and remarks clearly show that he intensively studied it while writing his "Japan" and "Xenophanes" articles for the 1702 *Dictionnaire* edition. Here we have the link that goes a long way to explain the similarity between Valignano's vision of the Japanese "all-is-one" doctrine (point two of his summary) and Bayle's view of Greek monism: both Valignano and Bayle had studied philosophy at Jesuit schools and used the same heavily annotated Coimbra edition of Aristotle's *Physics*. Valignano had referred to this work in his critique of the second main point of the inner doctrine and made copious use of its arguments (Valignano 1586:18r–23v):

> This was the error of two ancient philosophers called Parmenides and Melissus, whose ignorance was exposed by Aristotle, who was another pagan philosopher ... They taught that the principle of all things is one and that it forms the very substance and nature of things, so that all things are one and the same thing, and that they have one and the same substance with the first principle. (p. 18r)

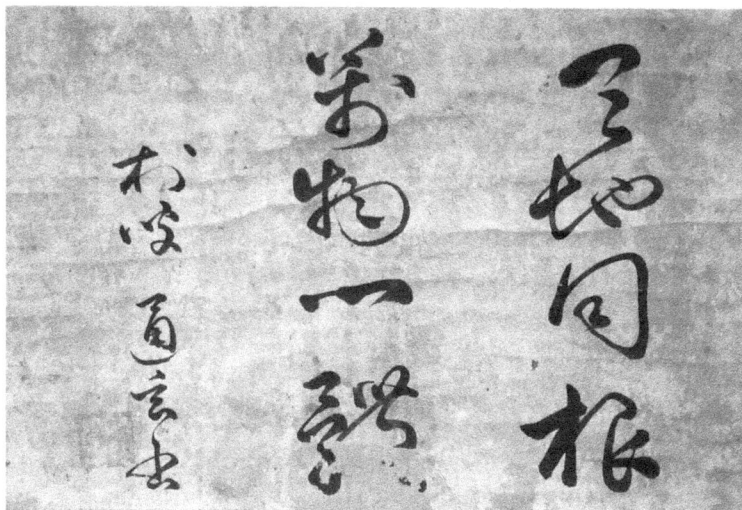

FIG. 25: "Heaven and earth have the same root, the myriad things are one" (Calligraphy by Zen master Tsūgen)

Due to the fortunate preservation of the Evora screen fragments we know that Valignano's Japanese informers had used the phrases "Heaven and earth have the same root, and the myriad things are one" (Jap. *tenchi dōkon, banbutsu ittai* 天地同根、萬物一體) and "the three realms are but One Mind" (Jap. *sangai yui isshin* 三界唯一心), both of which frequently occur in Zen parlance and texts (Valignano 1969:197). Valignano understood this to be the Japanese version of the doctrine of Xenophanes, Parmenides, and Melissus, and he presented and criticized it exactly along the line of the Coimbra edition of Aristotle's *Physics* (Valignano 1586:18r–23v). The very same Coimbra textbook was also used by Matteo Ricci in his Chinese catechism (1604; 1985), by Rodrigues, by Longobardi, by the Jesuit / Dominican / Franciscan missionaries during their detention in Canton, by Navarrete in his *Tratados* (1676), and by Intorcetta / Couplet in *Confucius sinarum philosophus* (1687).

Rather than with a "consensus of peoples," we are thus dealing with an identical pair of spectacles—that is, a common and typically European and Christian way of interpreting monist doctrines. It was constantly in operation from Nunez Barreto's and Valignano's critique of Zen doctrine in the sixteenth century to the flood of publications about "Chinese rites" in Bayle's time and beyond. However, Bayle's use of this Coimbra edition of Aristotle's *Physics* was profoundly subversive and served an altogether different purpose. Unlike all the missionaries who found Aristotle's critique of pre-Socratic monism both sound and applicable to Asian philosophies as they understood them, Bayle in his article on Xenophanes firmly rejects Aristotle's critique of Melissus and calls it extremely weak:

> Take the trouble to consult the Jesuits of Coimbra (paraphrase of the third chapter of the first book of Aristotle's Physics) that presented one of the reasons of Melissus in full strength along with the response of Aristotle. You will see that nothing is more feeble than this response, and that it is not true that Melissus is reasoning badly in this proposition. (Bayle 1702:3034)

In one of his favorite strategic moves, Bayle feigned to attack Xenophanes and Melissus while in reality presenting their argument in such a way that the perceptive reader had to come away convinced that Bayle is in complete agreement with the core argument of these Greeks.

Though Bayle was critical of certain aspects of Spinoza's philosophy, his overall tactic concerning Spinoza was similar to that of his Xenophanes article—which is why Bayle was in his time accused of being a "crypto-Spinozist" in spite of his constant attacks on Spinoza. I think that Bayle's "surprise" about the ancient and modern philosophers' agreement with Spinozism was equally feigned and that his main purpose in erecting an elaborate international genealogy of Spinozism ran diametrically counter to Thomasius's heresiology: Bayle wanted to prove that the consensus of the world's best philosophers consists in accepting that "nothing comes from nothing," that an omnipotent and perfectly good God could not create evil, and that therefore the orthodox notion of a good creator God is absolutely untenable. This was the overall thrust of the articles that were considered most scandalous in his *Dictionnaire*: Manichéens, Pauliciens, Xenophanes, and Spinoza; and Bayle's post-*Dictionnaire* publications continued with increasing vigor exactly along this line.

Presented as an extremely widespread, exotic proto-Spinozism, the "inner teaching" of Japan and of Foe alias Buddha was thus used by Bayle to bolster the worldwide monistic and atheistic portfolio. It is for this reason that he was so interested in the "inner" doctrine on which the Orient's best minds were said to agree. Making use of the full arsenal collected by the Jesuits and Christian philosophers and drawing support from many of the sources described in the chapters of this book, Bayle made a case for the very atheism and monism that Valignano had so harshly criticized. And his strongest ally in this undertaking was the very hero who, instead of recanting on his deathbed like a run-of-the-mill freethinker, had the balls to tell the truth and reveal his atheism. There is no doubt that Bayle—Europe's and perhaps the world's greatest master of irony and specialist of invented stories—would have been utterly delighted to know that not just the final utterance of this man but the core philosophy of the entire Orient was one laborious, glorious invention!

Once it had taken root and begun to bloom on European soil, the beguiling perfume of the flower of imagination called "Oriental philosophy" was to waft through the entire eighteenth century, persistent like musk and clinging like patchouli. It enthralled church historians like Mosheim, historians of philosophy like Brucker, encyclopaedists like Diderot, and even famous orientalists like Joseph de Guignes and Anquetil-Duperron. Hegel's lectures on Asia of the 1820s, French debates about Buddhism's "cult of nothingness" in the 1850s, and countless discussions about the meaning of "nirvana" in the nineteenth and twentieth centuries still exuded its unmistakable, intoxicating scent.

# Bibliography

Aitken, Robert. 1990. *The Gateless Barrier*. San Francisco: Northpoint Press.

Alexandre, Noël. 1699. *Apologie des dominicains missionnaires de la Chine, ou, Réponse au livre du pere Le Tellier jesuite, intitule, Défense des nouveaux chrétiens, et à l'Éclaircissement du P. Le Gobien de la même compagnie, sur les honneurs que les Chinois rendent à Confucius & aux morts.* Cologne: Heritiers de Corneille d'Egmond.

———. 1700. *Conformité des cérémonies chinoises avec l'idolatrie grecque et romaine.* Cologne: Heritiers de Corneille d'Egmond.

Almond, Philip C. 1988. *The British Discovery of Buddhism.* Cambridge: Cambridge University Press.

Anquetil-Duperron, Abraham Hyacinthe. 1801. *Oupnek'hat (id est, secretum tegendum).* 2 vols. Vol. 1. Argentorati: Levrault.

App, Urs. 1994. *Master Yunmen. From the Record of the Chan Master "Gate of the Clouds".* New York / Tokyo / London: Kodansha International.

———. 1995. Wuxinlun 無心論 – The Treatise on No-Mind. *Zenbunka kenkyūjo kiyō* 21:1-68.

———. 1997a. St. Francis Xavier's Discovery of Japanese Buddhism. Part 1: Before the Arrival in Japan, 1547-1549. *Eastern Buddhist* 30 (1):53-78.

———. 1997b. St. Francis Xavier's Discovery of Japanese Buddhism. Part 2: From Kagoshima to Yamaguchi, 1549-1551. *Eastern Buddhist* 30 (2):214-244.

———. 1998. The 'Discovery' of Zen. *Annual Report of the Institute for Zen Studies* 24:1-23.

———. 1998a. St. Francis Xavier's Discovery of Japanese Buddhism. Part 3: From Yamaguchi to India, 1551-1552. *Eastern Buddhist* 31 (1):40-71.

———. 2007. How Amida got into the Upanishads: An Orientalist's Nightmare. In *Essays on East Asian Religion and Culture*, ed. by C. Wittern and L. Shi. Kyoto: Editorial Committee for the Festschrift in Honour of Nishiwaki Tsuneki: 11-33.

———. 2008. The Tibet of Philosophers: Kant, Hegel, and Schopenhauer. In *Images of Tibet in the 19th and 20th Centuries*, ed. by Monica Esposito. Paris: Ecole Française d'Extrême-Orient: 11-70.

———. 2009. William Jones's Ancient Theology. *Sino-Platonic Papers* 191:1-125.

―――. 2010. *The Birth of Orientalism*. Philadelphia: University of Pennsylvania Press.

―――. 2011. *Schopenhauers Kompass*. Rorschach / Kyoto: UniversityMedia.

Aristoteles. 1596. *Commentariorum Collegii Conimbricensis Societatis Iesu, in octo libros Physicorum Aristotelis Stagiritae. ― Qvi nvnc primvm Graeco Aristotelis contextu, Latino è regione respondenti, aucti, ob studiosorum philosophiae vsum in Germania sunt editi*. Vol. 1. Cologne: Heirs of Lazarus Zetzner.

―――. 1616. *Commentariorum Collegii Conimbricensis Societatis Iesu, in octo libros physicorum Aristotelis Stagiritae, Prima Pars*. Cologne: Heirs of Lazarus Zetzner.

Arnauld, Antoine. 1682. *La Morale pratique des Jesuites : divisé en sept parties : où l'on represente leur conduite dans la Chine, dans le Japon, dans l'Amerique, & dans l'Ethyopie : le tout tiré de livres trés-autorisez, ou de pieces trés-authentiques*. Cologne.

Arnold, Gottfried. 1703. *Historie und Beschreibung der mystischen Theologie oder geheimen Gottes Gelehrtheit wie auch derer alten und neuen Mysticorum*. Frankfurt: Thomas Fritsch.

Assmann, Jan. 1998. *Moses the Egyptian. The Memory of Egypt in Western Monotheism*. Cambridge, MA & London: Harvard University Press.

Ast, Friedrich. 1807. *Grundriss einer Geschichte der Philosophie*. Landshut: Joseph Thomann.

Aubert de Versé, Noël. 1685. *L'impie convaincu, ou dissertation contre Spinosa*. Amsterdam: Jean Crelle.

Ballestra-Puech, Sylvie. 2006. *Metamorphoses d'arachné*. Genève: Droz.

Baltrušaitis, Jurgis. 1997. *La quête d'Isis. Essai sur la légende d'un mythe. Introduction à l'Egyptomanie*. Paris: Flammarion.

Barradas, Sebastião. 1599–1611. *Commentaria in concordiam et historiam evangelicam*. Coimbra.

Bayle, Pierre. 1697. *Dictionnaire historique et critique*. 1st ed. in 1 vol. Rotterdam: Reinier Leers.

―――. 1702. *Dictionnaire historique et critique*. 2nd ed. 3 vols. Rotterdam: R. Leers.

―――. 1826. *An Historical and Critical Dictionary, selected and abridged from the great work of Peter Bayle, with a Life of Bayle*. London: Hunt and Clarke.

Beierwaltes, Werner. 1987. *Eriugena redivivus*. Heidelberg: Carl Winter.

Bernard-Maître, Henri. 1941. Hinâyâna indien et Mahâyâna japonais: Comment l'Occident a-t-il découvert le Bouddhisme? *Monumenta Nipponica* 4:284-289.

Bernier, François. 1671. *Suite des mémoires du Sr. Bernier sur l'empire du Grand Mogol.* 2 vols. Paris: Claude Barbin.

———. 1674. *Abrégé de la philosophie de M. Gassendi.* Paris: J. & E. Langlois.

———. 1684. *Abrégé de la philosophie de Gassendi en VII tomes.* Lyon: Anisson, Posuel & Rigaud.

———. 1688. Mémoire sur le Quietisme des Indes. In *Histoire des Ouvrages des Sçavans.* Rotterdam: Reinier Leers: 47-52.

———. 1916. *Travels in the Mogul Empire, A.D. 1656-1668.* London: Oxford University Press.

———. 2005. *Travels in the Mogul Empire, AD 1656-1668.* Translated by A. Constable. Delhi: DK Publishers.

Bertuccioli, Giuliano. 1990. *Travels to Real and Imaginary Lands.* Kyoto: Istituto Italiano di Cultura, Scuola di Studi sull'Asia Orientale.

Blofeld, John. 1958. *The Zen Teaching of Huang Po.* London: The Buddhist Society.

Blount, Charles. 1693. *The Oracles of Reason.* London: s.n.

Bodhidharma (attributed to). 1905-1912. Xuemailun 血脈論 (Bloodstream Treatise). In *Dainihon zokuzōkyō (2-15)*, ed. by T. Nakano. Kyoto: Zōkyō shoin.

Borri, Christopher. 1631. *Relatione della nuova missione delli PP. della Compagnia di Giesu, al Regno della Cocincina.* Roma: Francesco Corbelletti.

Bourdon, Léon. 1993. *La Compagnie de Jésus et le Japon, 1547 – 1570.* Lisboa / Paris: Fondation Calouste Gulbenkian / Centre Culturel Portugais.

Braun, Lucien. 1973. *Histoire de l'histoire de la philosophie.* Paris: Ophrys.

Brockey, Liam Matthew. 2007. *Journey to the East. The Jesuit Mission to China, 1579–1724.* Cambridge, Massachusetts / London: Harvard University Press.

Brucker, Johann Jacob. 1736. *Kurtze Fragen aus der philosophischen Historie, von Christi Geburt biß auf unsere Zeiten.* Ulm: Daniel Bartholomäi und Sohn.

———. 1742-1744. *Historia critica philosophiae.* Leipzig: Christoph Breitkopf.

Burnet, Thomas. 1692. *Archæologiae philosophicae: sive Doctrina antiqua de rerum originibus.* London: R. Norton.

———. 1965. *The Sacred Theory of the Earth.* Translated by B. Willey. London: Centaur.

Busch, Allison. "Hidden in Plain View: Brajbhasha Poets at the Mughal court." *Modern Asian Studies* 44, no. 2 (2010): 267–309.

Camps, Arnulf. 1988. Father Heinrich Roth, S.J. (1620–1668) and the History of his Sanskrit Manuscripts. In *The Sanskrit Grammar and Manuscripts of Father Heinrich Roth S.J.*, ed. by A. Camps and J.-C. Muller. Leiden: Brill: 5–12.

Carré, Patrick. 1985. *Les Entretiens de Houang-po, Maître Tch'an du IXe siècle.* Paris: Les Deux Océans.

Cartas. 1575. *Cartas que los Padres y Hermanos de la Compañia de Iesus, que andan en los Reynos de Iapon escrivieron a los de la misma Compañia.* Alcala.

———. 1598. *Cartas que os Padres e Irmãos da Companhia de Iesus escreuerão dos Reynos de Iapão e China.* Evora: Manoel de Lyra.

Cieslik, Hubert. 1981. Iruman Vicente Tōin. In *Kokugoshi e no michi, vol. 1*. Tokyo: Sanshodo: 357–389.

Cleary, Thomas, and Christopher Cleary. 1977. *The Blue Cliff Record.* Boulder & London: Shambhala.

Colberg, Ehregott Daniel. 1692. *Inquisitio in natales philosophiae.* Greifswald: Daniel Benjamin Starck.

———. 1694. *Sapientia veterum Hebraeorum per universum terrarum orbem dispersa.* Greifswald: Daniel Benjamin Starck.

———. 1710. *Das Platonisch-Hermetisches Christenthum* (sic). Leipzig: J.L. Gleditsch & M.G. Weidmann.

Collani, Claudia von. 1985. *P. Joachim Bouvet S.J. Sein Leben und sein Werk.* Nettetal: Steyler.

Collcutt, Martin. 1981. *Five Mountains. The Rinzai Zen Monastic Institution in Medieval Japan.* Cambridge (Massachusetts): Harvard University Press.

*Confucius sinarum philosophus.* 1687. See under Couplet.

———. 1688. Review of Confucius Sinarum Philosophus. *Philosophical Transactions* 189:376–378.

———. 1688. Review of Confucius Sinarum Philosophus. *Acta Eruditorum*:254–265.

———. 1688. Review by Jean Le Clerc of Confucius Sinarum Philosophus. *Bibliothèque Universelle et Historique* (December):332–390.

Cooper, Michael. 1981. Rodrigues in China. The Letters of João Rodrigues, 1611-1633. In *Kokugoshi e no michi, vol. 2*. Tokyo: Sanshodo: 231–355.

———. 1994. *Rodrigues the Interpreter.* New York / Tokyo: Weatherhill.

Costelloe, Joseph. 1992. *The Letters and Instructions of Francis Xavier.* St. Louis, Missouri: The Institute of Jesuit Sources.

Couplet, Philippe (ed.). *Confucius Sinarum Philosophus: Sive, scientia sinensis latine exposita*. Paris: D. Horthemels, 1687.

Couplet, Philippe and Prospero Intorcetta et al. Manuscript introduction to *Confucius sinarum philosophus*. Bibliothèque nationale, Paris. Ms. Lat. 6277 (for printed version see Couplet).

Crispo, Battista. 1594. *De ethnicis philosophis caute legendis*. Rome: Aloisio Zannetti.

Croze, Mathurin Veyssière de la. 1724. *Histoire du Christianisme des Indes*. The Hague: Vaillant & N. Prevost.

Cummins, J.S. 1993. *A Question of Rites. Friar Domingo Navarrete and the Jesuits in China*. Aldershot: Scolar Press.

Curran, Brian A. 2003. The Renaissance Afterlife of Ancient Egypt (1400–1650). In *The Wisdom of Egypt: Changing Visions through the Ages*, ed. by P. Ucko and T. Champion. London: University College of London Press: 101–131.

Dapper, Olfert. 1670. *Gedenkwaerdig bedryf der Nederlandsche Oost-Indische maetschappye, op de Kuste en in het Keizerrijk van Taising of Sina: Behelzende het tweede gezandschap en het drede gezandschap*. Amsterdam: Jacob Meurs.

DeMartino, Richard. 1983. On Zen Communication. *Communication* 8 (1).

Demiéville, Paul. 1973. Les premiers contacts philosophiques entre la Chine et l'Europe. In *Choix d'études sinologiques (1921-1970)*, ed. by P. Demiéville. Leiden: Brill: 488-517.

Deussen, Paul. 2004. *Sixty Upanishads of the Veda*. Vol. 2. Delhi: Motilal Banarsidass.

Dew, Nicholas. 2009. *Orientalism in Louis XIV's France*. Oxford: Oxford University Press.

Diderot, Denis, and Jean le Rond d'Alembert. 1751. *Encyclopédie ou dictionnaire raisonné des sciences, des arts et des métiers*. Vol. 1. Paris.

DocJ 1. 1990. *Documentos del Japon 1547–1557*. Ed. by J. Ruiz-de-Medina. Vol. 1, *Monumenta missionum Societatis Iesu vol. 52*. Rome: Instituto Histórico de la Compañía de Jesús.

DocJ 2. 1995. *Documentos del Japon 1558–1562*. Ed. by J. Ruiz-de-Medina. Vol. 2, *Monumenta missionum Societatis Iesu vol. 61*. Rome: Instituto Histórico de la Compañía de Jesús.

Doi sensei shōju kinen runbunshū kankōkai. 1981. *Kokugoshi e no michi*. 2 vols. Vol. 2. Tokyo: Sanshodo.

Droit, Roger-Pol. 1997. *Le culte du néant. Les philosophes et le Bouddha*. Paris: Seuil.

Ducoeur, Guillaume. 2001. *Brahmanisme et encratisme à Rome au IIIe siècle ap. J.-C.* Paris: L'Harmattan.

Duteil, Jean-Pierre. 1994. *Le mandat du ciel.* Paris: Éditions Arguments.

Ebisawa, Arimichi. 1963. *Ebora byōbu bunsho no kenkyū.* Tokyo: Natsume.

Ebisawa, Arimichi, and Kiichi Matsuda. 1963. *Porutogaru Ebora shinshutsu byōbu monjo no kenkyū.* Tokyo: Natsume.

Elison, George. 1991. *Deus Destroyed: The Image of Christianity in Early Modern Japan.* Cambridge (Mass.) & London: Harvard University Press.

Faure, Bernard. 1986. Bodhidharma as Textual and Religious Paradigm. *History of Religions* 25 (3):187–198.

———. 1998. *Bouddhismes, philosophies et religions.* Paris: Flammarion.

Filliozat, Jean. 1956. *Les relations extérieures de l'Inde. I: Les échanges de l'Inde et de l'Empire Romain aux premier siècles de l'ère chrétienne. II: La doctrine brahmanique à Rome au IIIe siècle.* Pondichéry: Institut Français d'Indologie.

Fonseca, Pedro da. 1577. *Commentariorvm Petri Fonsecae D. Theologi Societatis Iesv in libros metaphysicorvm Aristotelis Stagiritae Tomus primus.* Rome: Francisco Zanetti.

Fróis, Luís. 1926. *Die Geschichte Japans (1549-1578).* Nach der Handschrift der Ajudabibliothek in Lissabon übersetzt und kommentiert von G. Schurhammer und E. A. Voretzsch. Leipzig: Asia Major.

Gale, Theophilus. 1672. *The Court of the Gentiles: or A Discourse touching the Original of Human Literature, both Philologie and Philosophie, from the Scriptures & Jewish Church.* Part I: Of Philologie. Oxford: Thomas Gilbert.

———. 1672. *The Court of the Gentiles: or A Discourse touching the Original of Human Literature, both Philologie and Philosophie, from the Scriptures & Jewish Church. Part II: Of Philosophie.* Oxford: Thomas Gilbert.

———. 1677. *The Court of the Gentiles, Part III: The Vanity of Pagan Philosophie Demonstrated.* London: A. Maxwell & R. Roberts.

Gernet, Jacques. 1973. La politique de conversion de Matteo Ricci et l'évolution de la vie intellectuelle en Chine aux environs de 1600. *Archives de sciences sociales des religions* 36:71–89.

———. 1979. Sur les différentes versions du premier catéchisme en chinois de 1584. In *Studia Sino-Mongolica, Festschrift für Herbert Franke,* ed. by W. Bauer. Wiesbaden: 406–416.

Godwin, Joscelyn. 2009. *Athanasius Kircher's Theatre of the World.* Rochester, Vermont: Inner Traditions.

Golvers, Noel. 1998. The Development of the Confucius Sinarum Philosophus Reconsidered in the Light of New Material. In *Western Learning and Christianity in China. The Contribution and Impact of Johann Adam Schall von Bell, S.J. (1592–1666)*, ed. by R. Malek. Sankt Augustin: China-Zentrum & Monumenta Serica Institute: 1141–1164.

Gómez, Luis. 1996. *Land of Bliss: The Paradise of the Buddha of Measureless Light: Sanskrit and Chinese Versions of the Sukhavativyuha Sutras*. Honolulu: Hawaii University Press.

Gonoi, Takashi. 2000. A actividade dos cristãos que rodeavam Hideyoshi. Um comentário sobre os manuscritos descobertos nos revestimentos internos do Biombo de Évora. In *Mundo do biombo de Évora*, ed. by G. Itō. Kamakura: Shunju-sha: 75-105.

Gregory, Peter N. 1991. *Tsung-mi and the Sinification of Buddhism*. Princeton: Princeton University Press.

———. 1995. *Inquiry into the Origin of Humanity*. Honolulu: University of Hawai'i Press.

Grosier, Jean-Baptiste Alexandre. 1787. *Description générale de la Chine*. Paris: Moutard.

Haas, Hans. 1909. Tsung-mi's *Yuen-zan-lun*, eine Abhandlung über den Ursprung des Menschen aus dem Kanon des chinesischen Buddhismus. *Archiv für Religionswissenschaft* 12:491–532.

Häfner, Ralph. 1997. Jacob Thomasius und die Geschichte der Häresien. In *Christian Thomasius (1655–1728). Neue Forschungen im Kontext der Frühaufklärung*, ed. by F. Vollhardt. Tübingen: Max Niemeyer: 141–164.

Hauschild, Richard, and Jean-Claude Muller. 1988. Notes on the Content of the Three Manuscripts of Heinrich Roth. In *The Sanskrit Grammar and Manuscripts of Father Heinrich Roth S.J.*, ed. by A. Camps and J.-C. Muller. Leiden: Brill: 13–19.

Hegel, G. W. F. 1991. *Enzyklopädie der philosophischen Wissenschaften*. Ed. by F. Nicolin and O. Pöggeler. Hamburg: Felix Meiner Verlag.

Heurnius, Otto. 1600. *Barbaricae philosophiae antiquitatum libri duo: I Chaldaicus, II Indicus*. Leiden: Christophorus Raphelengius.

Hori, Victor. 2003. *Zen Sand: The Book of capping phrases for Kôan Practice*. Honolulu: University of Hawai'i Press.

Hsia, Po-Chia. *A Jesuit in the Forbidden City*. Oxford / New York: Oxford University Press, 2010.

Huangbo, Xiyun 黃檗希運. 1924–1932. Quanxin fayao 傳心法要 ("Essentials of the Teaching of Transmitting Mind". In *Taishō shinshū daizōkyō vol. 48 (no. 2012B)*, ed. by J. Takakusu and K. Watanabe. Tokyo: Taishō issaikyō kankōkai.

Humbertclaude, Pierre. 1937. La littérature chrétienne au Japon il y a trois cent ans. *Bulletin de la Maison Franco-Japonaise* 8.

———. 1938. Valignani ou Valignano, l'auteur véritable du récit de la première ambassade japonaise en Europe (1582–1590). *Monumenta Nipponica* 1:378–385.

———. 1938. Myôtei mondô. Une apologétique chrétienne japonaise de 1605. *Monumenta Nipponica* 1:515–548.

———. 1941. Notes complémentaires sur la biographie de l'ex-Frère Jésuite Fabian Fucan. *Monumenta Nipponica* 4/2:617–21.

Ide, Katsumi 井出勝美. *Kirishitan shisōshi kenkyū josetsu.* Tokyo: Perikan, 1995.

Inagaki, Hisao. 1994. *The Three Pure Land Sutras.* Kyoto: Nagata Bunshodo.

Intorcetta, Prospero. 1667 & 1669. *Sinarum scientia politico-moralis.* Canton & Goa.

Intorcetta, Prospero et al.. c. 1666–. Manuscript introduction to *Confucius sinarum philosophus.* Bibliothèque nationale, Paris. Ms. Lat. 6277 (for printed version see Couplet).

Intorcetta, Prospero, and Ignacio da Costa. 1662. *Sapientia Sinica exponente P. Ignatio a Costa Lusitano Soc. Ies. à P. Prospero Intorcetta Siculo eiusd. Soc. Orbi proposita* (The Meaning of Chinese Wisdom as explained by Fr. Ignacio da Costa, Portuguese, of the Society of Jesus, and made public by Fr. Prospero Intorcetta, Sicilian, of the same Society). Jianchang: Jesuit society.

Iriya, Yoshitaka 入矢義高. 1969. *Denshin hōyō / Enryōroku* 伝心法要・宛陵録. Tokyo: Chikuma shobō.

Israel, Jonathan I. 2001. *Radical Enlightenment.* Philosophy and the Making of Modernity 1650-1750. Oxford: Oxford University Press.

———. 2006. *Enlightenment Contested.* Philosophy, Modernity, and the Emancipation of Man 1670–1752. Oxford: Oxford University Press.

Itō, Genjirō. 2000. *Mundo do biombo de Évora.* Kamakura: Shunju-sha.

Kaempfer, Engelbert. 1727. *The History of Japan.* Translated by J. G. Scheuchzer. London: Thomas Woodward.

Katō, Bunnō, Yoshiō Tamura, and Kōjirō Miyasaka. 1984. *Threefold Lotus Sutra.* New York / Tokyo: Weatherhill / Kosei.

Kellens, Jean. 2006. *La quatrième naissance de Zarathushtra.* Paris: Seuil.

Ketelaar, James Edward. 1987. *Of Heretics and Martyrs: Buddhism and Persecution in Meiji Japan*. Chicago: University of Chicago Press.

Kircher, Athanasius. 1636. *Prodromus Coptus sive Aegyptiacus*. Roma.

———. 1650. *Obeliscus Pamphilius*.

———. 1652–54. *Oedipus Aegyptiacus, hoc est universalis hieroglyphicae veterum doctrinae temporum iniuria abolitae instauratio*. Roma: Vitalis Mascardi.

———. 1667. *China monumentis, qua sacris qua profanis, nec non variis naturae et artis spectaculis, aliarumque rerum memorabilium argumentis illustrata*. Amsterdam: Jacob Meurs.

———. 1670. *La Chine illustrée de plusieurs monuments tant sacrés que profanes, et de quantité de recherches de la nature & de l'art*. Amsterdam: Jean Jansson.

———. 1675. *Arca Noë*. Amsterdam.

———. 1679. *Turris Babel, sive Archontologia* ... Amsterdam: Jansonia-Waesbergiana.

———. 1987. *China Illustrata with Sacred and Secular Monuments, Various Spectacles of Nature and Art and Other Memorabilia*. Translated by C. v. Tuyl. Bloomington: Indiana University.

Kishino, Hisashi 岸野久. 2001. *Zabieru no dōhansha Anjirō*. Tokyo: Yoshikawa kōbunkan.

Kleeman, Terry. 2008. Sanguan. In *The Encyclopaedia of Taoism*, ed. by F. Pregadio. London & New York: Routledge: 833–834.

Kohn, Livia. 2008. Sanqing. In *The Encyclopaedia of Taoism*, ed. by F. Pregadio. London & New York: Routledge: 840–844.

Kristof, Nicholas D. 2004. God and Sex. *The New York Times* (October 23, 2004).

La Croze, Mathurin Veyssière de. 1724. *Histoire du Christianisme des Indes*. The Hague: Vaillant & N. Prevost.

La Peyrère, Isaac. 1655. *Prae-Adamitae. Sive exercitatio super versibus duodecimo, decimotertio, & decimoquarto, capitis quinti epistolae D. Pauli ad Romanos. Quibus inducuntur primi homines ante Adamum conditi*. Amsterdam: Janssonius.

———. 2004. *I Preadamiti. Praeadamitae (1655)*. Macerata: Quodlibet.

Le Clerc, Jean. 1685. *Sentimens de quelques theologiens de Hollande sur l'histoire critique du Vieux Testament, composée par le P. Richard Simon de l'Oratoire*. Amsterdam: Henri Desbordes.

———. 1688. Confucius Sinarum Philosophus (review). *Bibliothèque Universelle et Historique* (December):332–390.

Le Gobien, Charles. 1698. *Histoire de l'edit de l'empereur de la Chine en faveur de la religion chrétienne; avec un éclaircissement sur les honneurs que les chinois rendent à Confucius et aux morts.* Paris: Anisson.

Lecomte, Louis Daniel. 1696. *Nouveaux mémoires sur l'état présent de la Chine.* Paris: Jean Anisson.

Lehmann-Brauns, Sicco. 2004. *Weisheit in der Weltgeschichte. Philosophiegeschichte zwischen Barock und Aufklärung.* Tübingen: Max Niemeyer Verlag.

Leibniz, G. W. 1697. *Novissima Sinica.* n.p.

⸻. 1977. *Discourse on the Natural Theology of the Chinese.* Translated by H. Rosemont and D. J. Cook. Honolulu.

⸻. 1979. *Das Neueste von China (1697). Novissima Sinica.* Ed. by H. G. Nesselrath. Köln: Deutsche China-Gesellschaft.

⸻. 2002. *Discours sur la théologie naturelle des Chinois.* Ed. by W. Li and H. Poser. Frankfurt am Main: Vittorio Klostermann.

Lenoir, Frédéric. 1999. *La rencontre du Bouddhisme et de l'occident.* Paris: Fayard.

Li, Wenchao, and Hans Poser. 2000. *Das Neueste über China. G.W. Leibnizens Novissima Sinica von 1697.* Stuttgart: Franz Steiner.

Lievens, Bavo. 1987. *The Recorded Sayings of Ma-Tsu.* Translated by J. F. Pas. Lewisten / Queenston: Edwin Mellen Press.

Longobardi, Niccolò, and Antoine de Ste. Marie. 1701. *Traité sur quelques points importans de la mission de la Chine.* Paris: Louis Guerin.

Lord, Henry. 1630. *A Discoverie of the Sect of the Banians.* London: Constable.

Loubère, Simon de la. 1691. *Du Royaume de Siam.* 2 vols. Amsterdam: Abraham Wolfgang.

Lubac, Henri de. 2000. *La rencontre du bouddhisme et de l'occident.* Paris: Cerf.

Lucentini, Paolo. 1987. *L'eresia di Amalrico.* In *Eriugena redivivus,* ed. by W. Beierwaltes. Heidelberg: Carl Winter: 174–191.

Lundbaek, Knud. 1983. The image of Neo-Confucianism in Confucius Sinarum Philosophus. *Journal of the History of Ideas* 44:19–30.

Mahmud, Shabistari. 1880. *The Mystic Rose Garden.* Translated by E. H. Whinfield. London: Trübner.

Majer, Friedrich. 1803. *Allgemeines Mythologisches Lexicon.* Vol. 1. Weimar: Landes-Industrie-Comtoir.

Majercik, Ruth. 1989. *The Chaldean Oracles.* Leiden: Brill.

Malan, S. C. 1882. *The Book of Adam and Eve, also called the Conflict of Adam and Eve with Satan: A Book of the Early Eastern Church.* London: Williams and Norgate.

Malebranche, Nicolas. 1708. *Entretien d'un philosophe chrétien, et d'un philosophe chinois, sur l'existence & la nature de Dieu.* Paris: Michel David.

Malek, Roman. 1998. *Western Learning and Christianity in China. The Contribution and Impact of Johann Adam Schall von Bell, S.J. (1592–1666).* 2 vols. Sankt Augustin: China-Zentrum & Monumenta Serica Institute.

Malusa, Luciano. 1981. Le prime storie generali della filosofia in Inghilterra e nei Paesi Bassi. In *Storia delle storie generali della filosofia. Dalle origini rinascmentali alla "historia philosophica".* Brescia: Edizione La Scuola: 167–402.

Marini, Giovanni Filippo de. 1663. *Delle missioni de padri della Compagnia di Giesu, nella provincia del Giappone, e particolarmente di quella di Tumkino.* Libri cinque. Roma: Nicolò Angelo Tinassi.

———. 1665. *Historia et relatione del Tunchino e del Giappone: con la vera relatione ancora d'altri regni e prouincie di quelle regioni e del loro gouerno politico : con le missioni fatteui dalli padri della Compagnia di Giesù & introduttione della fede christiana.* Venice: Vitale Mascardi.

———. 1666. *Histoire nouvelle et curieuse des royaumes de Tunquin et de Lao. Contenant une description exacte de leur origine, grandeur & estendue, de leurs richesses & de leurs forces; des moeurs & du naturel de leurs habitants; de la fertilite de ces contrees & des rivieres qui les arrosent de tous costez ...* Translated by F.-C. Le Comte. Paris: G. Clouzier.

Martini, Martino. 1655. *Novus Atlas Sinensis.* Amsterdam: Joh. Blaeu.

———. 1658. *Sinicae historiae decas prima.* München: Lucas Straub.

Masuzawa, Tomoko. 2005. *The Invention of World Religions.* Chicago and London: University of Chicago Press.

McRae, John. 2003. *Seeing through Zen. Encounter, Transformation, and Genealogy in Chinese Zen Buddhism.* Berkeley: University of California Press.

Meynard, Thierry. 2011. Chinese Buddhism and the Threat of Atheism in Seventeenth-Century Europe. *Buddhist -Christian Studies* 31:3–23.

Molinos, Miguel. 1688. *Recueuil de diverses pieces concernant le Quietisme et les Quietistes, ou Molinos, ses sentimens et ses disciples.* Translated by J. C. Lacrose. Amsterdam: A. Wolfgang & P. Savouret.

Mosheim, Johann Lorenz. 1743. *Dissertationes ad historiam ecclesiasticam pertinentes.* 2nd ed. Altona & Flensburg: Korte.

———. 1755. *Institutionum historiae ecclesiasticae libri IV.* 4 vols. Helmstadt: Weygand.

Muller, Jean-Claude. 1988. Bibliography on Heinrich Roth, S.J. In *The Sanskrit Grammar and Manuscripts of Father Heinrich Roth S.J.,* ed. by A. Camps and J.-C. Muller. Leiden: Brill: 23.

Mungello, David. 1978. Sinological torque: the influence of cultural preoccupations on seventeenth-century missionary interpretations of Confucianism. *Philosophy East & West* 28:123–141.

———. 1980. Malebranche and Chinese philosophy. *Journal of the History of Ideas* 41:551–578.

———. 1989. *Curious Land: Jesuit Accommodation and the Origins of Sinology.* Honolulu: University of Hawaii Press.

Nanni, Giovanni (Johannes Annius of Viterbo). 1498. *Auctores vetustissimi, vel Opera diversorum auctorum de antiquitatibus loquentium.* Rome: Eucario Silber.

———. 1498. *Co[m]mentaria fratris Ioannis Annii Viterbe[n]sis ordinis p[rae] dicato[rum] Theologiae p[ro]fessoris super opera diuersorum auctorum de Antiquitatibus loquentiu[m] confecta.* Rome: Eucario Silber.

Navarrete, Domingo Fernandez. 1676. *Tratados historicos, politicos, ethicos, y religiosos de la Monarchia de China.* Madrid: Iuan García Infançon.

———. 1704. An account of the empire of China, historical, political, moral and religious. A short description of that empire, and notable examples of its emperors and ministers. Also, an ample relation of many remarkable passages, and things worth observing in other kingdoms, and several voyages. There are added, the decrees of popes, and propositions defined at Rome for the mission of China; and a bull of ... Clement X., in favour of the missioners. Written in Spanish. In *A Collection of Voyages and Travels, some now first Printed from Original Manuscripts,* ed. by J. Churchill. London: Awnsham and John Churchill: 1–424.

Olivelle, Patrick. 1998. *The Early Upaniṣads. Annotated Text and Translation.* New York & Oxford: Oxford University Press.

Paramore, Kiri. 2008. Early Japanese Christian Thought Reexamined. Confucian Ethics, Catholic Authority, and the Issue of Faith in the Scholastic Theories of Habian, Gomez, and Ricci. *Japanese Journal of Religious Studies* 35 (2):231–262.

Pasini, Mirella. 1981. *Thomas Burnet. Una storia del mondo tra ragione, mito e rivelazione.* Firenze.

Pastine, D. 1978. *La nascita dell'Idolatria. L'oriente religioso di Athanasius Kircher.* Firenze: La Nuova Italia.

Pelliot, Paul. 1997. *L'inscription nestorienne de Si-ngan-fou.* Ed. by A. Forte. Paris / Kyoto: Collège de France / Italian School of East Asian Studies.

Pereira, Benito. 1591–99. *Commentariorum et disputationum in genesim.* Rome.

Pignoria, Lorenzo. 1608. *Characteres Aegyptii.* Frankfurt: Matthias Becker.

Pine, Red (Bill Porter). 1987. *The Zen teaching of Bodhidharma*. San Francisco: North Point Press.

Pinkerton, John. 1811. *A General Collection of the Best and Most Interesting Voyages and Travels in all Parts of the World*. Vol. 9. London: Longman, Hurst, Rees, Orme, and Brown.

Pinot, Virgile. 1971. *La Chine et la formation de l'esprit philosophique en France (1640–1740)*. Genève: Slatkine Reprints. Original edition, 1932.

Poceski, Mario [Cheng Chien Bhiksu]. 1992. *Sun-Face Buddha. The Teachings of Ma-tsu and the Hung-chou School of Ch'an*. Berkeley: Asian Humanities Press.

Poceski, Mario. 2007. *Ordinary Mind as the Way: The Hongzhou School and the Growth of Chan Buddhism*. Oxford and New York: Oxford University Press.

Pollock, Sydney. 2001. The death of Sanskrit. *Comparative Studies of Society and History* 43:392–426.

Possevino, Antonio. 1593. *Bibliotheca Selecta Qua Agitur De Ratione Studiorum in Historia, in Disciplinis, in Salutem Omnium Procuranda*. Roma: Typographia Apostolica Vaticana.

———. 1598. *Apparato all' historia di tutte le nationi, e il modo di studiare la geografia*. Venezia.

———. 1603. *Bibliotheca Selecta Qua Agitur De Ratione Studiorum in Historia, in Disciplinis, in Salutem Omnium Procuranda*. Venice: Altobellus Salicatius.

Postel, Guillaume. 1553. *Des merveilles du monde, et principalement des admirables choses des Indes, & du nouveau monde. Histoire extraicte des escriptz tres-dignes de foy, tant de ceulx qui encores sont a present audict pays, comme de ceulx qui encores vivantz peu paravant en sont retournez. Et y est monstré le lieu du Paradis terrestre*. Paris.

Purchas, Samuel. 1613. *Purchas, his Pilgrimage, or Relations of the World and the Religions Observed in All Ages and Places Discovered, from the Creation unto the Present*. London: W. Stansby.

Pye, Michael. 1978. *Skilful Means. A Concept in Mahayana Buddhism*. London: Duckworth.

Reimmann, Friedrich. 1725. *Historia universalis atheismi et atheorum*. Hildesheim: Ludolph Schroeder.

Rhodes, Alexandre de. 1651. *Histoire du royaume de Tunquin*. Lyon: Jean Baptiste Devenet.

Ricci, Matteo. 1615. *De Christiana expeditione apud Sinas suscepta ab societate Jesu ex P. Matthaei Ricci eiusdem societatis commentariis*. Ed. by N. Trigault. Agustae Vindecorum (Augsburg): C. Mangium.

———. 1616. *Histoire de l'expedition chrestienne au royaume de la Chine*. Edited by N. Trigault. Lyon: Horace Cardon.

———. 1942. *Storia dell'introduzione del Cristianesimo in Cina*. Ed. by P. M. d'Elia. Vol. 1, *Fonti Ricciane*. Roma: Libreria dello Stato.

———. 1985. *The True Meaning of the Lord of Heaven*. Ed. by E. J. Malatesta. St. Louis: The Institute of Jesuit Sources.

Rivosecchi, Valerio. 1982. *Esotismo in Roma Barocca. Studi sul Padre Kircher*. Biblioteca di storia dell'arte vol. 12. Roma: Bulzoni.

Rodrigues, João. 1604. *Arte da lingoa de Iapam*. Nagasaki: Collegio de Iapão.

———. 1954. *História da igreja do Japão*. Macao: Notícias de Macau.

———. 1955. *Nihon daibunten*. Ed. by T. Doi. Tokyo: Sanshodo.

———. 1981. Rodriguez in China. The Letters of João Rodriguez (tr. by Michael Cooper). In *Kokugoshi e no michi. Festschrift für Prof. Doi*, ed. by C. Doi. Tokyo: Sanseido: 312-.

———. 2001. *João Rodrigues's Account of Sixteenth-Century Japan*. Ed. by M. Cooper. London: Hakluyt Society.

———. 2002. *Treatise on epistolary style: João Rodriguez on the noble art of writing Japanese letters*. Ed. by L. J. Pieter. Ann Arbor: Center for Japanese Studies, University of Michigan.

Ross, Alexander, and Bernhardus Varenius. 1674. *Alexander Rossen unterschiedliche Gottesdienste in der gantzen Welt: das ist Beschreibung aller bewußten Religionen, Secten und Ketzereyen so in Asia, Africa, America und Europa von Anfang der Welt bis auf diese gegenwärtige Zeit, theils befindlich, theils annoch gebräuchlich*. Heidelberg: Wolffgang Moritz Endters & Johann Andreas Seel. Erben.

Rossi, Paolo. 1987. *The Dark Abyss of Time. The History of the Earth and the History of Nations from Hooke to Vico*. Chicago: University of Chicago Press.

Roth, Heinrich. 1988. *The Sanskrit Grammar and Manuscripts of Father Heinrich Roth S.J.* Ed. by A. Camps and J.-C. Muller. Leiden: Brill.

Ruegg, David Seyfort. 1969. *La théorie du Tathāgatagarbha et du Gotra: Études sur la sotériologie et la gnoséologie du bouddhisme*. Paris: École française d'Extrême-Orient.

Ruiz-de-Medina, Juan (ed.). 1990–5. *Documentos del Japon*. 2 vols. Rome: Instituto Histórico de la Compañia de Jesús. (Referred to in abbreviated form as DocJ 1 and DocJ 2).

Rule, Paul. 1986. *K'ung-tzu or Confucius? The Jesuit interpretation of Confucianism.* Sidney / Boston: Allen & Unwin.

Santinello, Giovanni. 1978. Jakob Thomasius e il medioevo. *Medioevo* 4:173–216.

———. 1981. Jakob Thomasius (1622–1684): Schediasma historicum. In *Storia delle storie generali della filosofia. Dalle origini rinascmentali alla "historia philosophica".* Brescia: Edizione La Scuola: 438–467.

Schmidt-Biggemann, Wilhelm. 1998. *Philosophia perennis. Historische Umrisse abendländischer Spiritualität in Antike, Mittelalter und Früher Neuzeit.* Frankfurt: Suhrkamp.

Schurhammer, Georg. 1923. *Shin-tô, der Weg der Götter in Japan: Der Shintoisnus nach gedruckten und ungedruckten Berichten der japanischen Jesuitenmissionare des 16. und 17. Jahrhunderts.* Bonn & Leipzig: Kurt Schroeder.

———. 1928. *Das kirchliche Sprachproblem in der japanischen Jesuitenmission des 16. und 17. Jahrhunderts.* Tokyo: Deutsche Gesellschaft für Natur- und Völkerkunde Ostasiens.

———. 1929. *Die Disputationen des P. Cosme de Torres S.J. mit den Buddhisten in Yamaguchi im Jahre 1551.* Tokyo: Mitteilungen der Deutschen Gesellschaft für Natur- und Völkerkunde Ostasiens vol. 24, part A.

———. 1932. *P. Johann Rodrigues Tçuzzu als Geschichtschreiber Japans. Archivum Historicum Societatis Iesu* 1 (1):23–40.

———. 1980. *Francis Xavier: His Life, His Times* (vol. 3: Indonesia and India, 1545-1549). Rome: Jesuit Historical Institute.

———. 1982. *Francis Xavier: His Life, His Times.* Vol. 4: Japan and China, 1549–1552. Rome: Jesuit Historical Institute.

Schütte, Josef Franz. 1951. *Valignanos Missionsgrundsätze für Japan.* 2 vols. Roma: Edizioni di storia e letteratura.

Semedo, Alvarez de. 1642. *Imperio de la China.* Madrid: Juan Sanchez.

———. 1653. *Historica relatione del gran regno della Cina.* Rome: Vitale Mascardi.

Spizelius [Spitzel], Theophil. 1660. *De re literaria Sinensium commentarius.* Antwerp.

Standaert, Nicolas (ed.). 2001. *Handbook of Christianity in China. Volume 1: 635–1800.* Leiden / Boston / Köln: Brill.

Standaert, Nicolas and Adrian Dudink, eds. 2002. *Chinese Christian texts from the Roman Archives of the Society of Jesus.* Vol. 1. Taipei: Ricci Institute.

Stanley, Thomas. 1655–62. *The History of Philosophy: Containing the Lives, Opinions, Actions and Discourses of the Philosophers of every Sect: Illustrated with the Effigies of Divers of Them; The History of the Chal[d]aick Philosophy.* 1st ed. London: Humphrey Moseley & Thomas Dring.

————. 1690. *Thomae Stanleii Historia Philosophiae Orientalis.* Translated by J. Le Clerc. Amsterdam: Viduam Swart.

————. 1701. *The History of Philosophy: Containing the Lives, Opinions, Actions and Discourses of the Philosophers of every Sect: Illustrated with the Effigies of Divers of Them; The History of the Chal[d]aick Philosophy.* 3rd ed. London: W. Battersby.

Stausberg, Michael. 1998. *Faszination Zarathushtra. Zoroaster und die Europäische Religionsgeschichte der Frühen Neuzeit.* 2 vols. Vol. 1. Berlin / New York: Walter de Gruyter.

Stephani, Wilhelm. 1701. *Dissertatio historico-moralis de superstitioso mortuorum apud Chinenses cultu.* Magdeburg: Henckel.

Steuco, Agostino. 1542. *De perenni philosophia.* Basel: Nicolaus Bryling and Sebastian Frank.

Stolzenberg, Daniel. 2004. *Egyptian Oedipus. Antiquarianism, Oriental Studies and Occult Philosophy in the Work of Athanasius Kircher.* Palo Alto: Stanford University Ph. D. dissertation.

Strodtmann, Johann Christoph. 1754. *Des Neuen Gelehrten Europa fünfter Theil.* Wolfenbüttel: Johann Christoph Meißner.

Tacchi Venturi, Pietro (ed.). 1911-13. *Opere storiche del P. Matteo Ricci.* 2 vols. Macerata: F. Giorgetti.

*Taishō shinshū daizōkyō,* ed. by J. Takakusu and K. Watanabe. Tokyo: Taishō issaikyō kankōkai.

Thomasius, Jakob. 1665. *Schediasma Historicum, Quo, Occasione Definitionis vetustae, qua Philosophia dicitur Gnōsis Tōn Ontōn, varia discutiuntur Ad Historiam tum Philosophicam, tum Ecclesiasticam pertinentia. Inprimis autem inquiritur in ultimas Origines Philosophiae Gentilis, & quatuor in ea Sectarum apud Graecos praecipuarum; Haereseos item Simonis Magi, Gnosticorum, Massalianorum & Pelagianorum; Denique Theologiae Mysticae pariter ac Scholasticae.* Leipzig: Fuhrmann.

————. 1676. *Exercitatio de stoica mundi exustione.* Leipzig: Christian Michaelis.

————. 1699. *Origines historiae philosophicae et ecclesiasticae.* Leipzig.

————. 1776. *Dissertationes ad Stoicae Philosophiae & caeteram Philosophicam Historiam facientes Argumenti Varii quibus praemittitur de Exustione Mundi Stoica Exercitatio.* Leipzig: Lanckisch.

Thomassin, Louis d'Eynac. 1685. *La Méthode d'étudier et d'enseigner chrétiennement & solidement la philosophie.* Paris: François Muguet.

Timmermans, Claire. 2002. *Entre Chine et Europe: taoïsme et bouddhisme chinois dans les publications jésuites de l'époque moderne (XVIe-XVIIIe siècles).* Lille: Atelier national de reproduction des thèses.

Torres, Cosme de, Juan Fernández, and Balthasar Gago. 1556. *Sumario dos erros em que os gentios de Japão vivem (It.:Sumario degli errori; Sp.: Sumario dos erros)*. Roma: Biblioteca Nazionale, Fondo Gesuitico 1384 no. 7.

Trigault, Nicholas. 1617. *De christiana expeditione apud Sinas suscepta ab Societate Iesu*. Cologne: Bernard Walter.

Ucko, Peter, and Timothy Champion. 2003. *The Wisdom of Egypt: Changing Visions through the Ages*. London: University College of London Press.

Valignano, Alessandro. 1586. *Catechismus christianae fidei*. Lisbon: Antonius Riberius.

———. 1899. *Monumenta Xaveriana*. Madrid: Augustinus Avrial.

———. 1969. *Nihon no catechizumo*. Ed. by T. Ieiri. Tenri: Tenri toshokan.

Varenius, Bernhardus. 1649. *Descriptio Regni Japoniae*. Amsterdam: Ludwig Elzevir.

———. 1649. *Tractatus in quo agitur: De Iaponiorum religione. De Christianae religionis introductione in ea loca. De ejusdem exstirpatione. Adjuncta est de diversa diversarum gentium totius telluris religione brevis informatio*. Amsterdam: Elzevir.

———. 1673. *Descriptio Regni Japoniæ et Siam: item, de Japoniorum religione et Siamensium, de diversis omnium gentium religionibus: quibus, praemissa dissertatione de variis rerum publicarum generibus, adduntur quaedam de priscorum afrorum fide excerpta ex Leone Africano*. Cambridge: Hayes.

———. 1674. *Bernhardi Varenii Kurtzer Bericht von mancherley Religionen der Völcker. In Alexander Rossen unterschiedliche Gottesdienste in der gantzen Welt : das ist Beschreibung aller bewußten Religionen, Secten und Ketzereyen so in Asia, Africa, America und Europa von Anfang der Welt bis auf diese gegenwärtige Zeit, theils besindlich, theils annoch gebräuchlich*. Heidelberg: Wolffgang Moritz Endters & Johann Andreas Seel. Erben: 941-1040.

Walker, D. P. 1972. *The Ancient Theology: Studies in Christian Platonism from the Fifteenth to the Eighteenth Century*. London: Duckworth.

Watson, Burton. 1993. *The Lotus Sutra*. New York: Columbia University Press.

Webb, John. 1669. *The Antiquity of China or an historical Essay endeavoring a probability that the Language of the Empire is the primitive Language spoken through the whole world before the Confusion of Babel*. London: Nath. Brook.

Yampolsky, Philip B. 1967. *The Platform Sutra of the Sixth Patriarch*. New York: Columbia University Press.

Yanagida, Seizan 柳田聖山. 2000. *Shoki zenshū shisho no kenkyū*. Vol. 6, Yanagida Seizan shū. Kyoto: Hōzōkan.

————. 2001. *Zenbunken no kenkyū* (jō). Vol. 2, Yanagida Seizan shū. Kyoto: Hōzōkan.

Zedelmaier, Helmut. 1992. *Bibliotheca universalis und Bibliotheca selecta*. Cologne: Böhlau Verlag.

Zimmel, Bruno, and Arnulf Camps. 1988. A List of the Letters, Reports and Manuscripts written by Father Heinrich Roth. In *The Sanskrit Grammar and Manuscripts of Father Heinrich Roth S.J.*, ed. by A. Camps and J.-C. Muller. Leiden: Brill: 20–22.

Zongmi, Guifeng 圭峰宗密. 1924–1932. Yuanrenlun 原人論. In *Taishō shinshū daizōkyō* vol. 45 (no. 1846), ed. by J. Takakusu and K. Watanabe. Tokyo: Taishō issaikyō kankōkai.

# Index

## A

# C

# O

# V

# W

# X